F L A S H 4 M A G I C

By David J. Emberton and J. Scott Hamlin

Contributions by Scott Balay, Branden Hall, Larry Larsen, Daniel Mcskelly, and Chrissy Rey

New Riders

201 West 103rd Street, Indianapolis, Indiana 46290

Flash 4 Magic

Publisher
David Dwyer

Executive Editor
Steve Weiss

Development Editor
Barb Terry

Managing Editor
Jennifer Eberhardt

Copy Editor
Malinda McCain

Technical Reviewers
Amy Beth Jackson
Emily Kim

Media Development Specialist
Todd Pfeffer

Interior Design
Steve Gifford

Cover Design
Aren Howell

Production
Kim Scott (kim@bumpy.com)
Amy Parker

Proofreaders
Debra Neel
Kristina Knoop
Nancy Sixsmith

Indexers
Brad Herriman
Cheryl Lenser
Lisa Stumpf

I UTILITIES

1	Preloader	2
2	Password Keypad	12
3	Lava Lamp	24
4	Randomizer	34
5	Stopwatch	48
6	Drag-and-Drop Interface	60
7	JukeBox	70
8	Calculator	82
9	Map Explorer	92
10	Online Book Search	112
11	Product Catalog	124
12	E-commerce	142
13	24-Hour Internet Quote Clock	154
14	Poll	162
15	Guestbook	180

II GAMES

16	Quiz Game	196
17	Memory Game	220
18	Wack-a-Mole Game	232
19	Pong Game	244
20	Hangman Game	260
21	Dodge Game	274

APPENDICES

A	Standalone Applications for Flash	292
B	Flash Resources	300
C	ActionScript	304
D	A Look at the Executables for the Flash 4 Magic CD	314
	Index	319

About the Authors

David Emberton

www.flashzone.com, www.shockfusion.com

David Emberton is a Web developer, writer, and columnist. He's also the editor of FlashZone.com and the producer of FlashChallenge.com and ShockFusion.com.

J. Scott Hamlin

www.nav-works.com, www.toylab.com, www.eyeland.com

J. Scott Hamlin is the director of Eyeland Studio, a Web entertainment company and content provider for clients such as Sun Microsystems, Nabisco, and MTV Europe.

Chrissy Rey

www.flashlite.net

Chrissy Rey is an instructor and developer at Fig Leaf Software in Washington, DC. She teaches Flash, Dreamweaver, Fireworks, and Generator. Chrissy is also a freelance writer, editor, and developer.

Scott Balay

www.infinitefish.com, www.nav-works.com

Scott Balay is co-founder of NavWorks and spends most of his time creating new interfaces for that, as well as other client work.

Branden Hall

www.flashlite.net

Branden is a multimedia developer/instructor for Fig Leaf Software, developing, and teaching various Macromedia products, including Flash and Generator 2. Branden is also pursuing a Bachelors degree in Computer Science at the University of Maryland.

Larry Larsen

www.greenjem.com

Larry Larsen is a designer/producer for The Poynter Institute. Larry produced the majority of the Flash interfaces from the FlashPacks from NavWorks (www.nav-works.com) and he teaches and consults on advanced Flash applications.

Daniel Mcskelly

www.wteam.co.uk

Longtime contributor and assistant editor at www.flashzone.com, Daniel Mcskelly works chiefly as a Web designer for The Webteam (www.wteam.co.uk) and spends his free time moaning to David Emberton about getting more sleep.

DEDICATION

We'd like to dedicate this book to everyone we ever caught smiling. You made our day every time.

ACKNOWLEDGMENTS

J. Scott Hamlin

I can't thank anyone before thanking the source. It is only by the grace of God that I came to be capable of writing and illustrating/animating this book. If you find any portion of it worthwhile or inspirational, He should be given the credit—not me.

Thanks also to the great team at New Riders, particularly Barbara Terry. Barb put in a remarkable amount of extra attention into this book. If this is a good or even (hopefully) a great book—trust me, Barbara Terry deserves a lot of the credit. I'd also like to thank Todd Pfeffer, Jennifer Eberhardt, and Steve Weiss for their help and support.

It was also an honor to work with my co-author David Emberton and the contributing authors Scott Balay, Chrissy Rey, Branden Hall, Larry Larsen, and Daniel Mcskelly. I would especially like to thank David for his commitment to excellence and willingness to put in numerous all-nighters to get things done right. Also, a very heartfelt thanks to Chrissy for stepping in as an additional tech and developmental editor, which greatly helped with overall quality and timeliness of the book.

Last but by no means least, I need to express my deepest appreciation for Staci, Aidan, and Audrey—my family. My children's delightful play and enchantingly fresh perspectives are a powerful source of raw inspiration, and I am among the richest of men from having had the opportunity to watch them grow up. Of my wife, Staci, I can only say this: You've heard the phrase, "behind every good man is a good woman," but in my case it's more like "behind this half-decent man is an extraordinary woman."

David Emberton

First of all, I'd like to just thank everyone—that way I won't miss anyone. Secondly, I'd like to thank my ever-so-supportive family and friends for providing such a wonderful working environment (love you guys!). In particular, I'd like to thank Beth, John, Jodie, Peg, Mel, Scott, Marina, Robyn, Natasha, Fee, yak, deem, and all the Fusion crew just for being great people and always being there for me. Finally, extra special thanks to Scott Hamlin. Had it not been for our ICQ conversation last December, this book would not have been possible.

A Note from the Publisher

Granted, a book titled *Flash 4 Magic* should probably have the word "shazaam" in there, too. But then we'd have to hire someone named Gomer to help write it and believe us, there just aren't that many all-star Flash hackers named Gomer (or even Goober) who can also write well…

So you make do. We thank our lucky stars that J. Scott Hamlin, an old friend from earlier technology publishing adventures, was around to partner with us in creating this book. Scott in turn brought on board the astonishing talents of Dave Emberton. And *Flash 4 Magic* pretty much happened from there. Voilá.

What the entire team wanted to do with this book was create an easy-to-use resource for Flash developers of all skill levels. Stepped-out recipes that get you into the particular Flash effect—and the theory behind it—but that also bring you the code. So you can try it, use it, learn from it yourself. Make it your own. And keep moving forward.

We understand that you're probably pretty smart when it comes to hacking on Flash. And that, if you're a working pro or a serious student of web development, you don't have lot of time to get your projects finished so that you can move on to whatever else it is you've got going. Use this book, use the code on the CD, and use your imagination. The web was a pretty interesting place a few years ago, and with the arrival and maturing of Flash, the web has become downright fascinating (in an interactive kinda way) in places. We hope that *Flash 4 Magic* helps things along even more. We don't think there's another resource out there quite like this one. Let us know how it works for you.

How to Contact Us

As the reader of this book, *you* are our most important critic and commentator. We value your opinion and want to know what we're doing right, what we could do better, in what areas you'd like to see us publish, and any other words of wisdom you're willing to pass our way.

As the Executive Editor for the Graphics team at New Riders, I welcome your comments. You can fax, email, or write me directly to let me know what you did or didn't like about this book—as well as what we can do to make our books better.

Please note that I cannot help you with technical problems related to the topic of this book, and that due to the high volume of mail I receive, I might not be able to reply to every message.

When you write, please be sure to include this book's title, ISBN, and author, as well as your name and phone or fax number. I will carefully review your comments and share them with the authors and editors who worked on the book.

For any issues directly related to this or other titles:

Email: steve.weiss@newriders.com

Mail: Steve Weiss
Executive Editor
Professional Graphics & Design Publishing
New Riders Publishing
201 West 103rd Street
Indianapolis, IN 46290 USA

Visit Our Website: www.newriders.com

On our website you'll find information about our other books, the authors we partner with, book updates and file downloads, promotions, discussion boards for online interaction with other users and with technology experts, and a calendar of trade shows and other professional events with which we'll be involved. We hope to see you around.

Email Us from Our Website

Go to www.newriders.com and click on the Contact link if you

- Have comments or questions about this book
- Want to report errors that you have found in this book
- Have a book proposal or are otherwise interested in writing with New Riders
- Would like us to send you one of our author kits
- Are an expert in a computer topic or technology and are interested in being a reviewer or technical editor
- Want to find a distributor for our titles in your area
- Are an educator/instructor who wishes to preview New Riders books for classroom use. (Include your name, school, department, address, phone number, office days/hours, text currently in use, and enrollment in your department in the body/comments area, along with your request for desk/examination copies, or for additional information.

Call Us or Fax Us

You can reach us toll-free at (800) 571-5840 + 9 + 3567. Ask for New Riders. If outside the USA, please call 1-317-581-3500. Ask for New Riders.

If you prefer, you can fax us at 317-581-4663, Attention: New Riders.

Publisher Acknowledgments

A very special and heartfelt thank you to Kim Scott of Bumpy Design in Los Angeles, CA (kim@bumpy.com) for coming in and doing such a great job producing this book. It wasn't easy, and you didn't complain once. We love working with you!

INTRODUCTION

Until recently, Macromedia Flash was probably one of the most under-appreciated Web technologies on the Web. Although Flash was once a low-end interactivity and animation technology for the Web, it's now a much fuller-featured multimedia medium with virtually limitless possibilities. *Flash 4 Magic* is about exploring some of these possibilities.

WHO WE ARE

No one on the writing team of *Flash 4 Magic* is strictly a professional writer. We all work daily with Flash 4 and Web animation. The two main authors of this book are David J. Emberton and J. Scott Hamlin. David is one of the key creative forces behind www.flashzone.com and shockfusion.com. Scott is the author of several books, including *Effective Web Animation* (Addison Wesley Longman), and he is co-founder of Navworks (at nav-works.com) and creator of toylab.com.

Scott and David were joined by several very talented contributors, including Chrissy Rey (www.flashlite.net), Branden Hall (www.flashlite.net), Scott

Balay (infinitefish.com and co-founder of NavWorks), Larry Larsen (green-jem.com), and Daniel Mcskelly (www.mindbomb.net).

WHO YOU ARE

Now that Flash has reached its fourth version, many Flash users have graduated beyond simple animation and basic interactivity. In this book, we assume you are familiar with the basics of Flash. We assume you're ready to take Flash to a new level by leveraging some of the new features in Flash 4—for example, ActionScript, draggable objects, and the capability to access external scripts such as PHP script and JavaScript.

This is why this book doesn't cover the basics of Flash; however, if you're new to Flash, don't be intimidated. This book is designed so that both beginners and advanced users can get a lot out of it. The book is project-based, and we walk you through each project step-by-step, using pre-built artwork. If you flip through the book, you'll see the artwork for each project. And you don't just get to look at this artwork—you get to work with it.

The first few projects in this book are relatively basic. They are designed to help get you acclimated to our step-by-step instructions without requiring you to go through a long, drawn-out project. Carrying out the first few projects will give you an idea of what assumptions we've made in terms of your familiarity with Flash. We encourage you to take the time to do some of the first projects so you will be familiar with the format of this book when you try to tackle more complex ones.

WHAT'S IN THIS BOOK

We've broken this book into three sections: Part I: The Utilities and Part II: The Games, followed by four awesome appendices. In addition, we've included a CD that is worth its weight in gold. It contains the source files for all the projects covered in this book, along with many freebies, demos, and other resources.

Part I: The Utilities

Flash's capabilities have progressed far beyond creating Web interfaces. Now you can use Flash to create any number of useful utilities to augment the content of your Web site or CD project. We tried to choose a variety of utilities that would demonstrate a range of key capabilities in Flash. For example, the Stopwatch utility demonstrates the GetTimer function—a valuable capability for any utility that relies on internal timing.

Although Flash's internal ActionScript substantially increases its capabilities, they become truly limitless when you combine Flash with external scripts such as PHP scripts or JavaScript. *Flash 4 Magic* includes the Poll and Guestbook projects, which demonstrate working with those external PHP scripts. You'll even find a project, the Quote Clock, that involves using JavaScript.

Part II: The Games

All work and no play makes the Web an awfully dull place. Online gaming has become big business, so we decided to help you get in on the action by including a few games in the book. The games featured in *Flash 4 Magic* expand on the concepts covered in Part I, the utilities section of the book. We recommend that even experienced users try a few utilities before moving on to the games; those projects are among the more complex projects featured in this book.

The Appendices

The appendices provide additional resources for taking the concepts you learn in the projects to new levels. Appendix A looks at using inexpensive third-party utilities to turn Flash files into standalone executables or screen-savers (demos of the utilities are on the Flash 4 Magic CD).

Appendix B lists valuable resources on the Web for further learning and additional information on Flash. Appendix C is a handy ActionScript resource full of valuable information on Flash's new internal scripting feature. Finally, Appendix D looks at how the Flash 4 Magic CD was constructed, using Flash and FlashJester's Juggler.

THE CD

The CD that comes with this book is no ordinary book CD. One of the key resources on the CD is the source files for the projects. The CD has two versions of each project in the book—one for doing the project and one fully operational copy you can open and inspect at your leisure. The fully operational copies of the project files include all the assets and ActionScript so you can see exactly how the files work.

In addition, this CD comes with a free copy of FlashBundle 1 from NavWorks (a $24.95 value) and numerous utility and application demos and demos of stock audio collections. Note that the project files included with this book are for learning purposes only. You may not republish any of the project files from this book on the Web or in a CD project without the written permission of the authors of this book.

OUR ASSUMPTIONS AS WE WROTE THE BOOK

You need to know that we had four assumptions when we wrote this book. These assumptions are based on our collective experience in learning and working with software.

If You Want to Learn, You Just Gotta Do It

If you wanted to learn how to play the piano, you probably wouldn't get very far if you only sat in front of the piano staring at those black and white keys. Furthermore, it probably wouldn't help you very much to watch a dozen pianists play, even if you sat down right next to them to watch. Obviously, the way to learn the piano effectively would be to sit down and actually practice with your own hands.

The same thing is true, of course, for learning software applications. One of the best ways to learn Flash is to get in there and make stuff, but it helps to have an idea of how to make things. This book provides detailed and illustrated step-by-step instructions for accomplishing each project. You can take the lessons learned in this book and apply them in any number of ways, but we provide the details you need to go from start to finish with each project.

You Don't Want to Waste Your Time

The projects in this book are focused. You won't have to wade through a lot of cute jokes or introductory material. This book assumes that you have a basic knowledge of Flash; that is, we assume that you can easily learn basic or fundamental tasks in Flash, such as how to center a symbol on a page or how to create a new symbol, if you don't already know them.

You might find it distracting, from time to time, if you have to look something up in the Flash manual or in the Help files. However, we hope you will agree that this is preferable to wasting time and space by writing these basic instructions over and over again throughout the book.

You Don't Want to Use Boring Examples Based on Circles and Squares

Most books that cover programming and scripting use low-quality examples to demonstrate the techniques and principles. It's hard to get excited about any software application when you're learning it by working with circles, squares, or—at best—lame clip art. Each project in this book comes with high-quality graphics and media you can work with directly. In other words, you don't have to look at the graphics and imagine how they work together—you get to actually work with them. Furthermore, each completed application or project is on the CD, which means you can go back into the Flash files to further inspect how they were created or how they work.

You Want Something You Can Use

We tried to devise projects that would not only teach valuable techniques but also give you a useful end product. In other words, each project shows you how to generate a series of useful applications or games. Moreover, as you build each game or application, you will be learning useful techniques that are valuable in and of themselves. For instance, the product catalog shows you how to build various sliders and how to create a Master Library of ActionScript referred to by multiple button symbols using the Call statement. So while you're learning how to generate a useful end product, you're also learning valuable techniques you can apply to any number of other useful end products.

CONVENTIONS USED IN THIS BOOK

Every computer book has its own style of presenting information. In this book, we've used **Bold** type to indicate actual text you must type, as in the following example:

2   Add a keyframe at frame 11 and assign the label name **AdjustView**.

As you flip through the book, you'll notice that we have an interesting layout going on here. Because we know that most of our readers are really into graphics, the project openers are way-cool eye candy. The real meat of projects starts on the next page. Take a look:

In the left column, you'll find step-by-step instructions for completing the project, as well as succinct but extremely valuable explanations. In the corresponding column to the right, you'll find screen captures illustrating these steps and all the ActionScript code the project requires you to enter.

We want to say it one more time: If you get lost at any time in the completion of a project, just refer to the completed project file on the CD and you'll find the answer to your quandary.

JOIN THE REVOLUTION

Unlike most program upgrades, Macromedia Flash 4—Macromedia's third upgrade to the Flash technology—represents a quantum leap in overall features and possibilities, both inside the development environment and for what it can output to the Web. Even most diehard fans of the Flash technology have bemoaned the inevitable frustrations they met while working in past versions of the Flash program. Setting aside the annoyances involved in production, applying Flash to overall Web development has always been limited by Flash's lack of internal scripting capabilities and the capability to effectively communicate with powerful server-side technologies.

All these hindrances have largely evaporated in Macromedia Flash 4. Pinpointing the biggest new development is hard in a version of Flash that substantially supersedes all previous upgrades combined. Probably the most far-reaching improvements are the addition of vastly improved internal scripting with the new "ActionScript" and Flash's new support for draggable objects, editable text fields, and data gathering, complete with e-commerce and the capability to easily pass information to a Web server.

Flash has up to now been known as one of the best Web technologies, but with a notoriously unintuitive development environment. Now Flash the tool is as usable as Flash the technology is powerful. You can afford it, you can create with it, you can animate with it, and you can generate just about anything you can think of with it!

Macromedia Flash is poised to take the Web by storm. Hype over technologies such as DHTML, Push, and—to some extent—Java and Shockwave has boiled down to relatively little real usage on the Web—at least not in mass numbers. However, Flash is inexpensive, it's accessible, and now it's even powerful. With Flash 4, the Flash technology has been upgraded from a Web solution that deserved its almost cult status to a technology that will certainly become as mainstream as the animated GIF.

This book strives to help you take part in this Flash Web revolution. Although we did our best to devise and document top-notch techniques for this book, they will eventually be mere stepping stones to more robust and compelling techniques and implementations of the Flash technology. However, the envelope doesn't move if no one is pushing it, so get going and see what this baby can do.

PART I

UTILITIES

Preloader .2

Password Keypad 12

Lava Lamp 24

Randomizer 34

Stopwatch 48

Drag-and-Drop Interface 60

JukeBox 70

Calculator 82

Map Explorer 92

Online Book Search 112

Product Catalog 124

E-commerce 142

24-Hour Internet Quote Clock 154

Poll .162

Guestbook 180

PRELOADER

"We are the music

makers, and we are the

dreamers of dreams"

—WILLY WONKA

OUTFITTING A FLASH MOVIE TO PLAYBACK SMOOTHLY OVER ANY INTERNET CONNECTION

Preloading in Flash provides for seamless animation playback by loading graphic and audio elements, or symbols, before they are used. Why is preloading important? In Flash, all the elements on a given frame must be loaded before the Flash movie can proceed to the next frame. After a symbol is loaded on one frame, it can be used on subsequent frames without any additional download requirements. If the elements aren't preloaded, however, viewers have to watch them display—piece by piece. This project leverages these characteristics of Flash and demonstrates an efficient approach to preloading elements as well as creating a progress bar.

PROJECT 1:
CHOKE-A-COLA

Scene
  Preload
   Layers
    Progress Bar 1
    Progress Bar 2
    Cover
    Preloaded Elements

GETTING STARTED

In this section, you test the preload.fla movie and set up the Preload scene. If you want your results to match those of the finished project, follow the steps carefully. If you want to customize the project and are familiar with Flash 4, feel free to adapt the instructions to your specifications.

1 From the Flash Web Magic CD, load preload.fla and test it (Control>Test Movie).

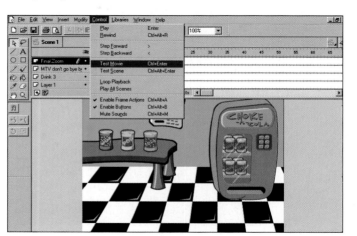

Use the Test Movie option for checking a movie.

2 Close the test and use the Scene Inspector (Window>Inspectors>Scene) to add a new scene, name it **Preload**, and position it before Scene 1.

3 Create four layers, naming them (from top to bottom) **Progress Bar 1**, **Progress Bar 2**, **Cover**, and **Preloaded Elements**; select all four layers and add 30 frames to each.

Set up four layers in the new Preload scene of preload.fla.

SETTING THE STAGE FOR PRELOADING

This animation plays for approximately 30 seconds when uninterrupted and has a fairly large format (469 × 340) with lots of motion and sound. When you export it to an .swf format, the file is around 398KB. A 14.4 or 28.8Kbps modem usually stops and starts such a large animation repeatedly as it downloads over the Internet, substantially reducing its effectiveness. By preloading elements, you ensure that *all* modems play the animation smoothly.

1 Select the Cover layer, make certain that the Preload.fla Library is open, drag an instance of the Intro Screen graphic symbol from the Vector Graphics folder to the Stage, and position it so that it covers the entire Stage.

Drag an instance of the Intro Screen graphic symbol from the Vector Graphics folder.

2 Select the Progress Bar 1 layer, drag the Progress Bar graphic symbol to the Stage, and center the symbol horizontally (below the title text "The Beverage of Choice"), aligning the symbol to the page.

3 Select the Progress Bar 2 layer, drag the Meter Bar graphic symbol, and center it in the hole of the Progress Bar graphic symbol.

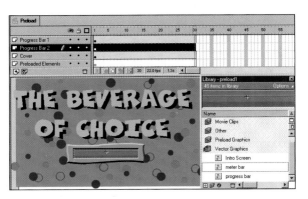

Center the Progress Bar and Meter Bar symbols.

5

4 Hide all the layers except Progress Bar 2, select frame 30 on the Progress Bar 2 layer, and create a keyframe.

5 Select frame 1 of the Progress Bar 2 layer, select the Meter Bar graphic symbol on the Stage, click the Scale modifier, and then click and drag the middle right handle to the left, squishing the Meter Bar graphic symbol until it's only a tiny sliver.

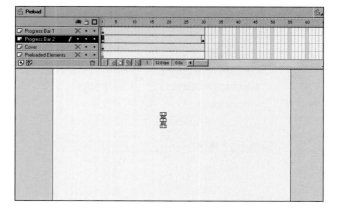

With the other layers hidden, scale the Meter Bar graphic symbol down to a skinny sliver.

6 Show all the layers, select the scaled Meter Bar graphic symbol on frame 1 of the Progress Bar 2 layer, and nudge the symbol to the left until it's just out of sight.

Do not move the Meter Bar graphic symbol up or down. It must stay on the Progress Bar 2 layer for the effect to work properly.

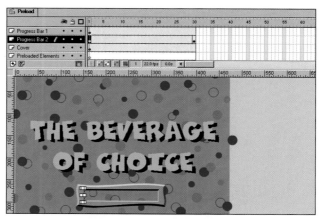

Move the scaled instance of the Meter Bar off to the left.

7 Double-click between frames 1 and 30 of the Progress Bar 2 layer to display the Frame Properties dialog box, click the Tweening tab, click the Tweening down arrow, select Motion, and click OK.

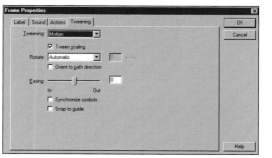

Add a motion tween to the Progress Bar 2 layer.

PRELOADING THE GRAPHIC SYMBOLS AND AUDIO FILES

At this point, you've set up everything the viewer will see during the preload portion of the movie—the intro screen and the progress bar. The next task is to preload the symbols and audio files below the intro screen so that they will remain unseen (and inaudible).

1 Hide all the layers except Preloaded Elements and add keyframes to all the even-numbered frames from 2 through 30.

2 Select frame 2, open the Preload Graphics folder, and drag the first seven graphic symbols to any position on the Stage.

   You start the preloading on frame 2 so that the intro screen and the progress bar load before the pre-loading symbols.

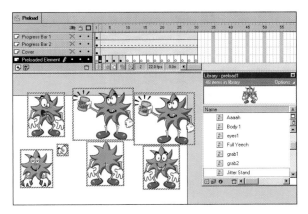

Insert the keyframes and place seven graphic symbols on the second frame of the Preloaded Elements layer.

3 Place the next five graphic symbols on the keyframe at frame 4, the next five graphic symbols on the keyframe at frame 6, and the next five graphic symbols on the keyframe at frame 8 until all the graphic symbols in the Preload Graphics folder are on the Stage.

4 Open the Movie Clips folder and drag the four movie clips to the keyframe at frame 8.

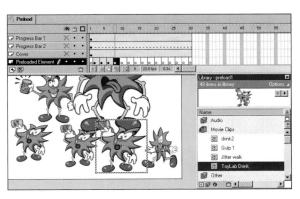

Place the remaining graphic symbols and the four movie clips on the Preloaded Elements layer.

7

5 Open the Audio folder, select frame 10, drag the ah.wav file to the Stage, and turn off the sound while it's preloading (Frame Properties>Sound>Sync>Stop).

6 Place one of the 10 remaining audio files in each of the remaining keyframes on the Preloaded Elements layer. Be sure to use the Stop Sync option with each one.

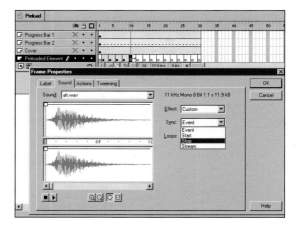

Use the Stop Sync option to turn the sound off for preloading audio files.

EXPORTING THE MOVIE AND CHECKING THE SIZE REPORT

At this point, you have a completed preloading sequence. When the Flash file first loads, the viewer sees the intro screen and the progress bar. The progress bar expands to the right as the graphic symbols and audio files load. After frame 30 loads, the Flash player automatically takes the viewer to the next scene, which contains the actual animation. The animation then plays back smoothly because all the symbols and audio are preloaded.

A size report can come in handy at this point. You use the report to make sure that you've pre-loaded enough symbols, movie clips, and audio files to ensure that your animation will play back smoothly. The Movie Report lists the Frame #, Frame Bytes, Total Bytes, and Page.

1 Choose File>Export Movie, type a filename, select the appropriate directory, and then click Save.

2 In the Export Flash Player dialog box, click the Load Order down arrow, select Top Down, select the Generate Size Report option, and click OK to export the file.

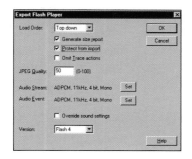

Use the Export Flash Player dialog box to establish the load order and to generate a size report.

The Top Down Load Order option is a bit of added insurance that the intro screen will always load before any preloading symbols. The Protect>From Import option isn't necessary, but it's a handy feature that prevents people from exporting your .swf file into their own Flash document. However, the option isn't a foolproof safeguard against copyright infringement because third-party software is available that provides ways of bypassing this protection.

3 Using a text editor, open the size report text file, which should be in the same directory from which you exported the Flash movie.

4 Compare the Frame # column with the Frame Bytes column for the entire movie (both scenes).

What you should see is that the majority of the bytes for the overall movie are located in the first 30 frames of the movie, confirming that you've successfully preloaded the majority of the elements necessary for the animation to run smoothly. However, you did miss a few.

5 In Flash, go to frame 99 in Scene 1, the frame in which the green character is squinting one eye while sticking his tongue out.

This image was not made into a symbol; consequently, it wasn't preloaded.

6 In the size report text file, find the number under the Frame Bytes column that corresponds to Frame # 129.

Frame 129, which corresponds to frame 99 in Scene 1 because of the 30 frames from the preload layer (30+99=129), should be about 7,474 bytes. The frames before and after it contain preloaded graphic symbols and audio and have only 2 bytes. The difference in size reflects the fact that frame 129 is not preloaded and contains new graphic data . In this example, Frame 129 is nothing to worry about. By the time the Flash player gets to frame 129, the data will already be loaded.

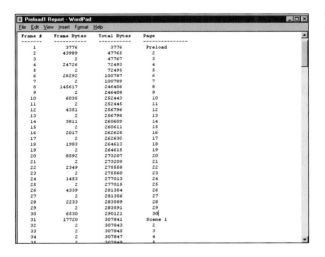

The size report as it appears in WordPad.

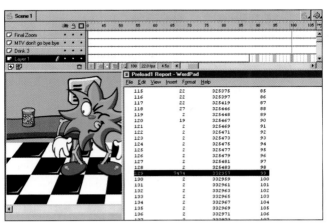

The selected file (line 129) was not made into a graphic symbol, so it is not preloaded.

How It Works

After a symbol has been loaded, Flash can use that symbol again and again without having to download it again. The preloader works by loading a series of symbols behind a title screen for the overall movie so the viewer cannot see that the symbols are being loaded. The majority of the symbols are loaded during the preloading sequence. Any remaining symbols that are not preloaded are given ample time to download while the movie plays, using the assets that have been downloaded.

When a Flash movie plays over the Internet, it can't proceed from one frame to the next until each frame's content has downloaded. Therefore, the progress bar works in concert with this principle. The progress bar is a simple tweened animation. Flash proceeds from frame to frame as each frame's content loads, and the progress bar tracks this progression. The faster the Internet connection (in other words, the faster the movie downloads), the faster the preload sequence will be.

Modifications

Don't think you have to preload everything just the way you did it in this project; you can adapt preloading to your needs. You might want to use one of these modifications:

- You don't have to hide the preloading symbols. An alternative would be to artfully show the preloading symbols as they load. For example, you could have some of the preloading symbols fade in and out in a sort of cinematic fashion.

- To minimize the amount of time your viewers have to wait, consider preloading only some of the symbols for the movie. For instance, you might preload only the symbols used in the first three quarters of the movie. If this portion of the movie is long enough, it can be playing while the rest of the movie loads in the background.

- If you have a sizable amount of preloading to do (anything over half a megabyte), consider providing something to entertain your viewers—perhaps a simple but fun game or animation. It doesn't matter how smoothly your animation plays if the viewer doesn't wait around to see it.

PASSWORD

KEYPAD

"The supreme happiness

in life is the conviction

that we are loved."

—VICTOR HUGO

USING THE IF ACTION TO RESTRICT ACCESS IN FLASH

This project shows how to use Flash 4 variables to create a protected section within a Flash movie. Not only can you add multiple passwords, but you also can direct each password to jump to a different section of the internal movie. The password scheme even traps for the Enter key, enabling a user to press Enter after typing the password instead of clicking a button. Flash 4 also allows tabbing between the interface elements.

Project 2:
PASSWORD

Layers
Password Panel
Door 2
Door 1

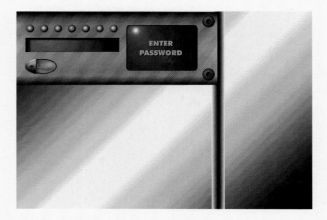

GETTING STARTED

In this first section, you set up a new movie in which to complete this project. If you want your results to match those of the finished project, follow the steps carefully. If you want to customize the project and are familiar with Flash 4, feel free to change the settings to those that meet your needs.

1   Create a new movie, using these settings:

Frame rate:	**20 fps**
Stage dimensions:	**550 × 400**
Background color:	**White**

2   Create three layers, naming them (from top to bottom) **Password Panel**, **Door 2**, and **Door 1**.

3   Open the Password.fla file located on the Flash 4 Magic CD as a Library.

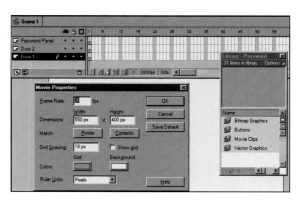

Create three layers and open the Password file as a Library.

HANGING THE DOORS

In this section, you set up the doors for the Door 1 and Door 2 layers. The Door layers should be on top of the layers you are trying to hide or protect. They hide the content of your password-protected section. Later you will animate the doors on the Timeline.

1 In the Door 1 layer, drag an instance of the Leftdoor graphic symbol from the Vector Graphics folder onto the Stage, and use the Object Inspector to position the instance at x: **−6**, y: **−8**.

2 In the Door 2 layer, drag an instance of the Rightdoor graphic symbol from the Vector Graphics folder onto the Stage, and use the Object Inspector to position the instance at x: **384.9**, y: **−8**.

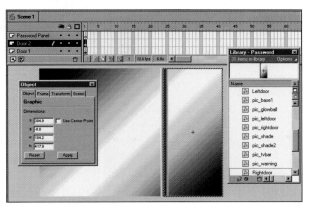

Position the two graphic symbols for the doors on the Stage.

CONSTRUCTING THE PASSWORD PANEL

This section sets up the Password Panel. You work with the Tvbar graphic symbol, the Login Button, TextBackdrop graphic symbol, and the FlashingLights Movie Clip.

1 In the Password Panel layer, drag the Tvbar graphic symbol from the Vector Graphics folder onto the Stage, and use the Object Inspector to position the Tvbar graphic symbol instance at x: **−7.5**, y: **3.5**.

The left edge of the Tvbar should be off the left side of your Stage; the object slides out from the left.

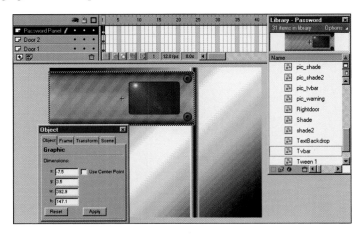

Position the Tvbar graphic symbol on the Stage.

2 In the Password Panel layer, drag an instance of the Login Button from the Buttons directory of the Library, and use the Object Inspector to position the instance at x: **−3.4**, y: **97.3** and resize it to **76.4** wide and **29.7** high.

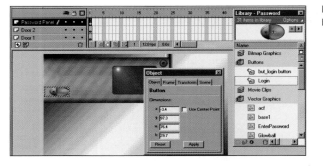

Position and resize the Login Button.

3 Double-click the Login Button to open its Instance Properties dialog box and, on the Actions tab, assign the ActionScript.

With the Key Press action set to **Enter**, the ActionScript associated with the Login Button will be triggered when users either click on the button or press the Enter key on their keyboards.

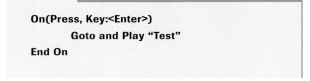

```
On(Press, Key:<Enter>)
        Goto and Play "Test"
End On
```

4 In the Password Panel layer, drag an instance of the TextBackdrop graphic symbol from the Vector Graphics folder onto the Stage, and use the Object Inspector to position the instance at x: **13.4**, y: **56**.

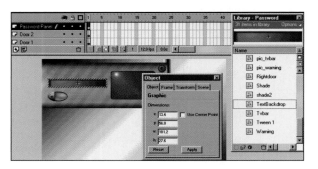

Position the TextBackdrop graphic symbol on the Stage.

5 In the Password Panel layer, drag an instance of the FlashingLights Movie Clip from the Movies folder onto the Stage, and use the Object Inspector to position the instance at x: **14.6**, y: **29.4** and resize it to **176.8** wide by **15.2** high.

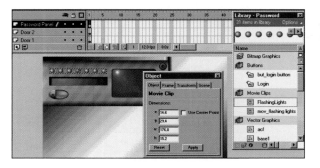

Position and resize the FlashingLights Movie Clip.

ADDING THE PASSWORD PANEL TEXT FIELDS

In this section, you try your hand at setting up text fields. Be sure to include the font out-lines: If you don't, the text will actually render differently, depending on the platform.

1 In the Password Panel layer, select the Text tool, click on the Text Field modifier to turn it on (if it is not already on), and set the following attributes for the text field:

Font: Times New Roman
Font Size: 16 pt
Font Color: Light Gray

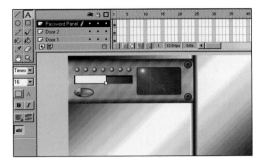

Create the text field for enter-ing the password.

2 In the Password Panel layer, click on the Stage direct-ly over the top left side of the TextBackdrop graphic symbol instance.

3 Choose Modify>Text Field to open the Text Field Properties dialog box and set the following proper-ties:

Variable: **password**
Options: Deselect Draw Border and
            Background
            Select Password
            Select Restrict Text Length
               to 12 Characters
            Select Include All Font Outlines

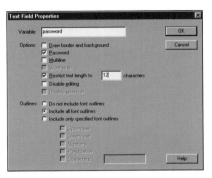

Set the properties in the Text Field Properties dialog box.

4 In the Password Panel layer, select the Text tool, turn off the Text Field modifier, and set the following attributes for the text field:

Font: _sans
Font Size: 12 pt
Font Color: Orange

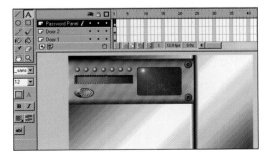

Add a text label to the Login Button to identify the purpose of the button.

5 Click on the Stage, type **LogIn**, and place this text on top of the Login Button instance.

SETTING UP THE PASSWORD PANEL KEYFRAMES

Now it's time to set up the four keyframes for Wait, Bad, Test, and Good for the Password Panel layer, and assign ActionScript to them. You also set up instances of the EnterPassword and IncorrectPassword graphic symbols.

1 Insert a keyframe at frame 10 of the Password Panel layer, double-click the new keyframe to open its Properties dialog box, name the keyframe label **Wait**, and keep the dialog box open.

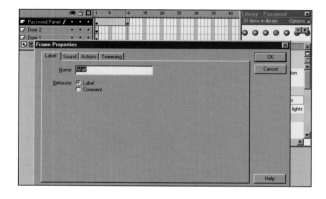

Create the keyframe for Wait.

2 On the Actions tab, assign the ActionScript.

Stop

3 Insert a keyframe at frame 20 of the Password Panel layer, double-click the keyframe to open its Properties dialog box, and name the keyframe label **Bad**.

Create the keyframe for Bad.

4 Insert a keyframe at frame 30 of the Password Panel layer, double-click the keyframe to open its Properties dialog box, and, on the Actions tab, assign the ActionScript.

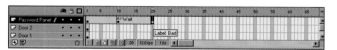

Go to and Stop ("Wait")

When users enter an incorrect password, they see a message on the screen that tells them the password was entered wrong. The ActionScript at frame 30 sends the playhead back to frame 10 to wait for another entry.

18

5 In the Password Panel layer, insert a keyframe at frame 40, double-click the keyframe to open its Properties dialog box, and name the keyframe label **Test**.

This frame is where you will do the testing for the password match.

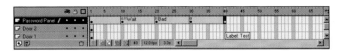

Create the keyframe for Test.

6 In the Password Panel layer, insert a keyframe at frame 50, double-click the keyframe to open its Properties dialog box, and name the keyframe label **Good**.

This frame is where you will send people who enter a correct password.

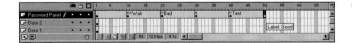

Create the keyframe for Good.

7 Click on frame 80 and press F5 to add enough frames so you can read the label assigned to the keyframe at frame 50.

You will also be adding some animation in frames 50–80 later.

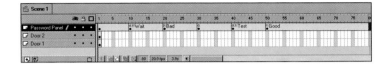

Insert keyframes at frames 50 and 80.

8 In frame 10 of the Password Panel layer, drag an instance of the EnterPassword graphic symbol from the Vector Graphics folder of the Password.fla Library onto the Stage, and use the Object Inspector to position it at x: **234.4**, y: **61.7**.

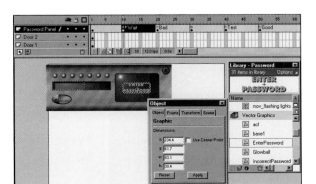

Position the EnterPassword graphic symbol on the Stage.

9 In frame 20 of the Password Panel layer (the keyframe labeled **Bad**), drag an instance of the IncorrectPassword graphic symbol from the Vector Graphics folder of the Password.fla Library onto the Stage, and use the Object Inspector to position it at x: **235.6**, y: **62**.

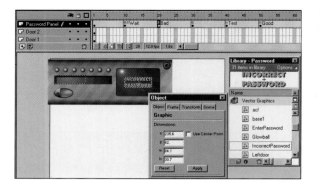

Position the IncorrectPassword graphic symbol on the Stage.

TESTING FOR PASSWORD MATCH

How effective is a password keypad if you don't actually test what the user enters? Not at all. In this section, you set up the ActionScript for testing the password to see whether it matches a predetermined word.

1 Double-click frame 40 of the Password Panel layer to open the Properties dialog box and, on the Actions tab, assign the ActionScript.

The **password** in the first line of the **If** statement refers to the text field named **password**. This **If** statement is essentially saying "if the user enters the word 'Open' in the text field."

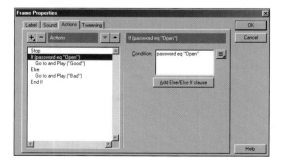

```
Stop
If (password eq "Open")
        Go to and Play ("Good")
Else
        Go to and Play ("Bad")
End If
```

The next lines in the **If** statement provide instructions on what to do when users enter the word **Open** into the Password text field. If "password" equals **Open**, the playhead goes to the frame labeled Good. Otherwise, the playhead goes to the frame labeled Bad. As you can see, this **If** statement is the key ActionScript for your Password application.

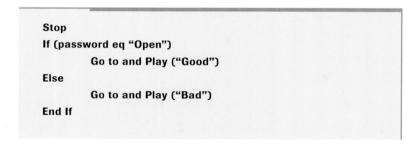

This is the main ActionScript that powers the Password application.

2 Select frame 50 for both the Door 1 and Door 2 layers, and press F6 on your keyboard to insert keyframes.

This is where the Doors and Password Panel open to display the password-protected contents of your Flash movie.

3 Select frame 50 of the Password Panel layer, turn off the visibility of all layers except the Password Panel layer, select all the layers, and group them.

You're grouping these objects so you can tween the Password Panel graphics and text field off of the Stage.

Turn off the visibility of Door 1 and 2 and group all the layers.

4 Turn the visibility of all the layers back on and insert keyframes at frame 80 of the Door 1, Door 2, and Password Panel layers.

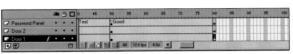

Insert keyframes at frame 80 of the three layers.

5 In the Door 1 layer, select the keyframe at frame 80 and use the Object Inspector to position the Leftdoor graphic instance to x: **–395**, y: **–8**.

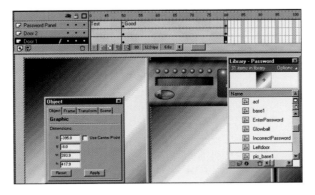

Position the Leftdoor instance at frame 80 of the Door 1 layer.

6 Right-click (PC) or Control+Click (Mac) anywhere between frames 50 and 80 on the Door 1 layer to open the Properties dialog box and select the Create Motion Tween option.

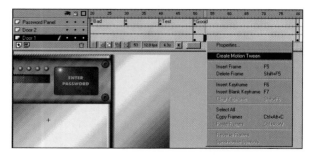

Apply Motion Tweening to frames 50 through 80 of the Door 1 layer.

7 In the Door 2 layer, select the keyframe at frame 80 and use the Object Inspector to position the Rightdoor graphic instance to x: **553**, y: **−8**; right-click (PC) or Control+Click (Mac) anywhere between frames 50 and 80 on the Door 2 layer and select the Create Motion Tween option.

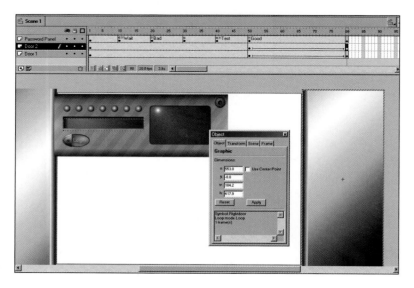

Position the Rightdoor graphic and apply Motion Tweening to the Door 2 layer.

8 In the Password Panel layer, double-click frame 80 to open its Properties dialog box and, on the Actions tab, assign the ActionScript.

Stop

9 Use the Object Inspector to position the *grouped* Password Panel graphics to x: **−398**, y: **3.5**; open the Properties dialog box; and select the Create Motion Tween option.

10 Insert a new layer in your Flash movie, name it **Props**, and place it below the Door 1 layer.

Insert the new Props layer.

11 In the Props layer, insert a keyframe at frame 10, turn off the visibility of all layers except the Props layer, drag an instance of the acf graphic symbol from the Vector Graphics folder onto the Stage, and then center the instance.

Notice that you add your password-protected content to a keyframe under the frame labeled Wait. This means that while users are entering their passwords, your content can be preloading behind the doors.

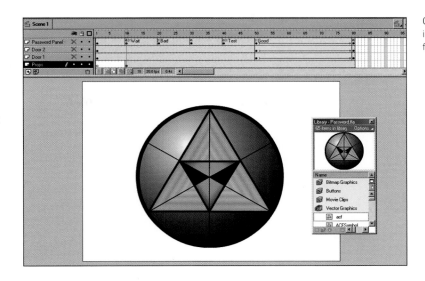

Center the acf graphic symbol instance on the Stage in frame 10 of the Props layer.

HOW IT WORKS

The vault-like password project consists of four sections:

- A waiting keyframe where the movie sits while a user enters a password
- A test keyframe that checks the password for validity
- A bad password area
- A good password area

The ActionScript in the keyframe labeled Test checks the text field when the user clicks on the Login button. If the contents of the text field are the same as the password specified in the **If** statement, the user gains access to the password-protected portion of the Flash movie. If the text field contains text that's not the same as the text specified in the **If** statements, the text field briefly displays "Incorrect Password" and, after a moment, the viewer is given another opportunity to enter the password correctly.

MODIFICATIONS

You probably will want to modify this project to meet specific password criteria. For example, you might want to make the following changes:

- Send each password to a unique or customized section of your Flash movie.
- Send "cancelled" users to a shame screen.
- Add an animated mini-movie to the TV screen on the tvbar.
- Inside the password-protected area, use Flash 4's form elements to make an email contact form that can be used only by authorized users who can't see the email address to which the form posts. Use the action **mailto:user@address.com** to post the form.
- Start the movie with the Password Panel sliding out. To do so, see the source file on the Flash 4 Magic CD.

23

LAVA LAMP

"Creative minds have

always been known to

survive any kind

of bad training."

—ANNA FREUD

USING MOTION TWEENS TO CREATE ORGANIC ANIMATION

Although Flash is perfect for advanced interactivity, applications, and games, its primary strength still lies in good old animation. The Lava Lamp project draws on Flash's capability to shape tween, or take two different keyframes and estimate what should be displayed on the frames in between. Seventies kitsch meets the 21st century!

PROJECT 3:
LAVA LAMP

Layers
Power Switch
Lamp Mask
Blobs
Background

GETTING STARTED

Setting up a Flash file is probably old hat for you now. If you want your results to match those of the finished project, follow the steps carefully. If you want to customize the project and are familiar with Flash 4, feel free to change the settings to those that meet your needs.

1   Begin with a new Flash Movie, load LavaLamp.fla as a Library, and set up four layers, naming them (from top to bottom) **Power Switch**, **Lamp Mask**, **Blobs**, and **Background**.

2   Set up the Stage, using these settings:

Frame rate:	**24 fps**
Stage dimensions:	**150 × 300**
Background color:	**Black**

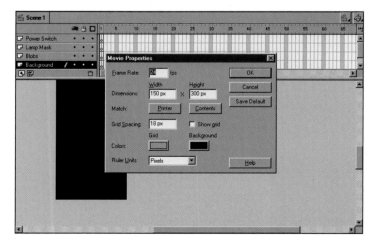

Set up the layers and settings of the new movie.

3 Select the Background layer, drag an instance of Background from the Vector Graphics folder onto the Stage, and center Background horizontally and vertically to the page.

Instance and position the Background symbol on the Stage.

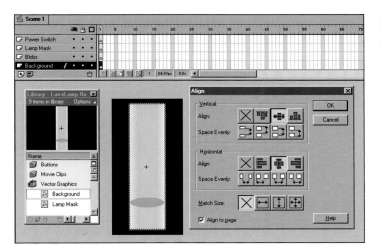

4 Select the Lamp Mask layer, drag an instance of Lamp Mask from the Vector Graphics folder onto the Stage, and center it.

Instance the Lamp Mask symbol and center it on the Stage.

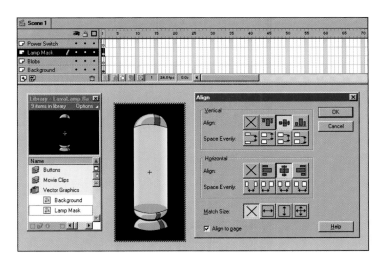

BLOBS GALORE

For variation and interest, three different lava blob animations will play in a random sequence, one after the other. Blob 2 and Blob 3 have been provided as completed examples, so you'll mostly be working with the Blob 1 symbol.

1   Select the Blobs layer, drag an instance of Blob 1 from the LavaLamp.fla Library onto the Stage, double-click the instance, and name it **Blob1**. Repeat the procedure with Blob2 and Blob 3, naming them **Blob2** and **Blob3**, respectively.

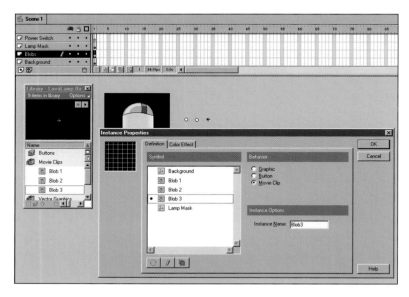

Place three blob animation symbols on the Stage and give them instance names.

2   Use the Object Inspector to position the three blob instances at x: **77**, y: **230**.

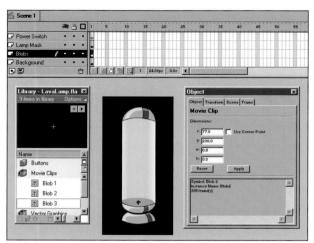

Position Blob 1, Blob 2, and Blob 3, using the Object Inspector.

3 Open your movie's own Library, select Blob 1 from the list of symbols, and choose Edit from the Options menu to edit Blob 1.

4 In the symbol-editing mode, set up two layers, naming them (from top to bottom) **Control Actions** and **Blob 1.**

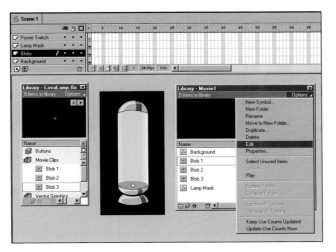

Use the Options menu in the Library to edit your movie's version of Blob 1.

SHAPE TWEENING

Animators use the term "tweening" to describe the process of filling the gaps between keyframes. On a feature film, for instance, the more experienced animators created the main keyframes, and their assistants, or "inbetweeners," judged what would appear onscreen in the remaining frames.

Flash is capable of automatically performing two types of tweens. Motion tweens are used to move an object or group around the Stage and change the object's properties. Shape tweens, on the other hand, work only with ungrouped lines and fills.

Each of your blob symbols contains a series of keyframes with round filled shapes representing pieces of lava. To achieve the look of continuous motion, you need to set the Tweening properties of each keyframe to Shape.

1 Select the Blob 1 layer, double-click keyframe 2 to open the Frame Properties dialog box, select the Tweening tab, and set the Tweening option to Shape.

The Blend type needs to be Distributive rather than Angular, so use the default setting. (Angular blends are more suited to geometric shapes or objects with distinct corners.) Also, your blob shape isn't accelerating or decelerating, so the Easing setting can be 0.

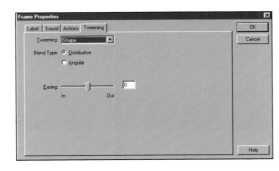

Set the Tweening property of keyframe 2 to Shape.

29

When you click OK, the frames between keyframes 2 and 31 change to a green color with a horizontal arrow, denoting a shape tween.

2   Repeat step 1 for keyframes 31, 61, and 91 through to 271, setting each of the Tweening properties to Shape.

   If you drag the playhead back and forth across the Timeline, you'll see the effect of these new settings. The inbetween frames contain animations now, rather than static images.

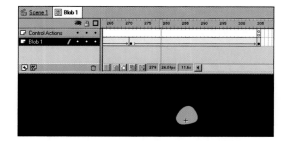

Set the shape tweens, and green shading and a horizontal arrow appear between keyframes on the Timeline.

RANDOM ANIMATIONS

Each time a blob animation finishes, another one must begin for the application to work. You need to add some ActionScript to your blob symbol to activate it.

1   While still editing Blob 1, select the Control Actions layer, double-click keyframe 1 to open the Frame Properties dialog box, and, on the Actions tab, and assign the ActionScript.

Stop

2   Double-click keyframe 2 to access its Frame Properties, select the Label tab, label the keyframe **Play**, and click OK.

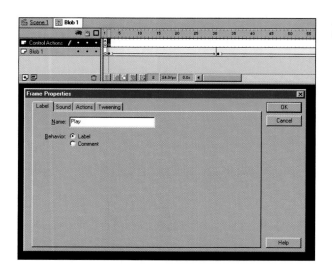

Assign the frame label Play to keyframe 2.

3 Double-click keyframe 305 to open Frame Properties, and, on the Actions tab, assign the ActionScript.

Each blob animation has an instance name: Blob1, Blob2, or Blob3. Each also has a keyframe labeled "Play," so this script dynamically selects the next animation and forces it to play by using a **Tell Target** action.

4 Exit symbol-editing mode and return to Scene 1.

```
Begin Tell Target ("/Blob" & (Random(3) + 1))
    Go to and Play ("Play")
End Tell Target
```

THE POWER SWITCH

Rather than having the Lava Lamp start automatically as soon as the movie begins, the user must first click the Power Switch button to prompt the animation. You set up that button in this section.

1 Select the Power Switch layer and drag an instance of the Power Switch Button symbol from the LavaLamp.fla Library onto the Stage. Use the Object Inspector to position the instance at x: **70.0**, y: **260.0**.

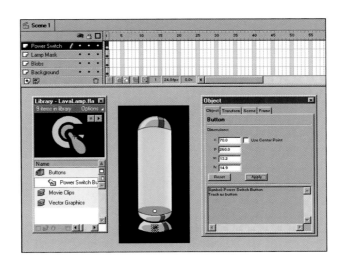

Instance the Power Switch Button and position it, using the Object Inspector.

2 Double-click the Power Switch Button to open its Instance Properties, and, on the Actions tab, assign the ActionScript.

This script is essentially the same as at the end of each blob animation, except that it also includes the **On MouseEvent** action that processes the user's click.

```
On (Release)
    Begin Tell Target ("/Blob" & (Random(3) + 1))
        Go to and Play ("Play")
    End Tell Target
End On
```

HOW IT WORKS

The Flash Lava Lamp uses two main techniques: morphing and randomization. The morphing of the lava blobs is achieved with the help of shape tweening, a mathematical process of filling in the gaps between two keyframes. Each keyframe contains a different shape, and the Flash Player calculates the inbetween shapes, automatically creating an animation, thereby avoiding the need for frame-by-frame drawings.

The second technique employed in this project is randomization. In order to create a more realistic and interesting lamp, a series of different lava animations play in a random sequence. The randomization is created by using the **Random** function and the **Set Variable** and **Tell Target** actions.

MODIFICATIONS

Shape and motion tweening can be used in an endless number of ways, limited only by your imagination. Tweening is especially useful for minimizing the file size of your Flash Player movies; it enables you to use keyframes sparingly and still create continuous movement. The only trade-off is that shape tweening is a mathematical process that can degrade animation performance if the shapes involved are too complex. If you keep the shapes simple, however, as with the Lava Lamp example, the actual frame rates achieved can remain high, even on slower systems.

RANDOMIZER

"Adam and Eve had an ideal

marriage. He didn't have to hear

about all the other men she could have

married, and she didn't have to hear

about the way his mother cooked."

—KIMBERLEY BROYLES

GENERATING RANDOMIZED SEQUENTIAL EVENTS

The Laughinator puts a crazy spin on the idea

of an audio mixer. This project has five sliders

with Randomize and Play buttons and can

deliver a customized series of laughter samples

on demand. The project also includes a number

of useful Flash techniques, including the capa-

bility to "snap" slider controls to predefined

positions and to create a run of events based

on the positions of those same sliders.

PROJECT 4:

LAUGHINATOR

Layers
ActionScript Library
Sliders
Buttons
Background

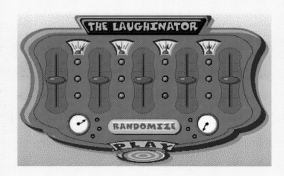

GETTING STARTED

If you want your results to match those of the finished project, follow the steps carefully. If you want to customize the project and are familiar with Flash 4, feel free to
change the settings to those that meet your needs.

1 Begin with a new Flash Movie, open Laughinator.fla
as a Library, and set up the Stage, using these settings:

Frame rate: **24 fps**
Stage dimensions: **362 × 228**
Background color: **White**

2 Set up four layers, naming them (from top to bottom)
ActionScript Library, **Sliders**, **Buttons**, and
Background.

3 Select the Background layer, drag an instance of
the Background graphic symbol from the Vector
Graphics folder in the Laughinator.fla Library
onto the Stage, center the instance, and lock the
Background layer because you won't be dealing
with it again.

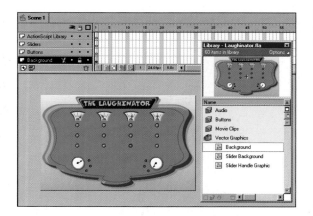

Set up the layers and position
the Background symbol
on the Stage.

GETTING READY FOR SOME SLIPPIN' AND SLIDIN'

The Laughinator's primary interface is a series of five sliding controls. You'll be creating just one
master slider and then duplicating several instances of it.

1 Select the Sliders layer and drag an instance of the
Slider Background graphic symbol from the Vector
Graphics folder onto the Stage.

2 Select your instance of Slider Background, press F8,
and convert the instance to a Movie Clip symbol,
naming it **Slider**.

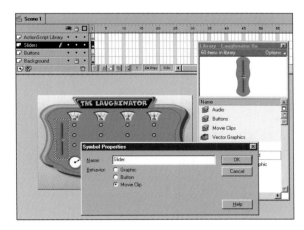

Convert the Slider
Background graphic symbol
into a Movie Clip.

3 Make sure you're in the symbol-editing mode of the
Slider symbol, rename the existing layer **Slider
Background**, and insert an upper layer, naming it
Slider Handle.

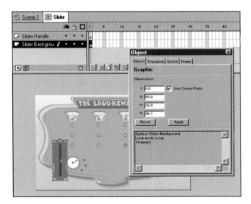

Set up the layers for the
Slider symbol and reposition
the Slider Background symbol.

> **Note:** To enter the symbol-editing mode, right-click
> (Windows) or Control-click (Macintosh) on the instance,
> and choose Edit from the pop-up menu.

4 Select the Slider Background graphic symbol in the
Slider Background layer, open the Object Inspector,
select the Use Center Point option, and reposition
Slider Background at x: **0.0** and y: **50.0**.

Setting these x, y positions is important in order to
avoid dealing with negative numbers when you
manipulate the coordinates of the slider handles later.

5 Select the Slider Handle layer, drag an instance of the Slider Handle Button from the Buttons folder onto the Stage, and use the Object Inspector to position the button at x: **0.0** and y: **50.0**, once again with the Use Center Point option selected.

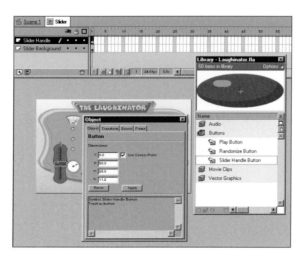

Instance and position the Slider Handle button above the Slider Background.

6 Double-click the Slider Handle Button to open the Instance Properties dialog box, and, on the Actions tab, insert the ActionScript.

This script controls the Slider Handle Movie Clip, (to be created in the next step), based on the mouse events of Slider Handle Button. When the user clicks the Slider Handle button, its parent Movie Clip becomes draggable, following the cursor up and down within its constrained rectangle. When the user releases the mouse button, the script stops the **Drag Movie Clip** statement and also gets the target information of Slider Handle Button's parent symbol (for example, the **_target** information might be "/Slider1/SliderHandle)," which can then be used in a **Tell Target** or **Set Property** action). (By obtaining the target information of a parent symbol this way, you can reuse the same interface element many times but perform operations on each copy individually, provided they all have distinct instance names.)

```
On (Press, Drag Over)
    Start Drag ("", L=0, T=20, R=0, B=80)
End On
On (Release, Release Outside, Drag Out)
    Stop Drag
    Set Variable: "/:CurrentSlider" = GetProperty ("",_target)
    Call ("/Library/:SnapSlider")
End On
```

The SnapSlider function is then called, which "snaps" the slider handle into one of a set of predefined positions. Because of this function, the user can drag the slider freely while the mouse button is held down, but, as soon as the button is released, the slider instantly moves to the nearest snap position.

7 Select the Slider Handle Button symbol, press F8, and convert it to a Movie Clip symbol, naming it **Slider Handle**.

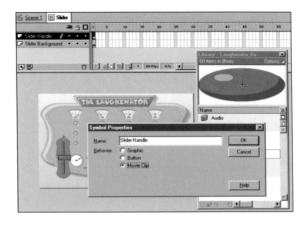

Convert the Slider Handle Button to a Movie Clip symbol.

8 Double-click Slider Handle and name the instance **Slider**.

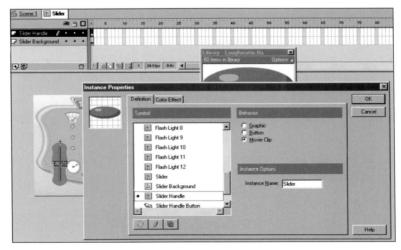

Name the Slider Handle instance.

9 Exit symbol-editing mode and return to Scene 1.

10 Select the Slider symbol in the Sliders layer, duplicate another four instances, place the five sliders in the positions shown in the example at the beginning of the project, and name the instances (from left to right) **Slider1**, **Slider2**, **Slider3**, and so on.

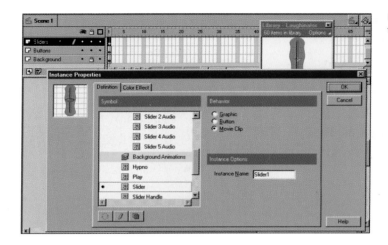

Position and name the five sliders.

BUILDING THE ACTIONSCRIPT LIBRARY

By storing commonly used scripts in a central location, you can simplify the process of creating and debugging the Laughinator. This section is an example of dynamically creating an array of variables in Flash.

1 Ensure that no objects are selected on the Stage, select the ActionScript Library layer, and create a new Movie Clip symbol, naming it **ActionScript Library**.

2 In the symbol-editing mode of the ActionScript Library Movie Clip, name the existing layer **Control Actions** and insert an additional 19 frames to create a total of 20.

3 Insert a blank keyframe on frame 11 and assign the labels **Initialize** to keyframe 1 and **SnapSlider** to keyframe 11.

4 Move the playhead to keyframe 1, double-click the frame, open the Frame Properties dialog box, and, on the Actions tab, insert the ActionScript.

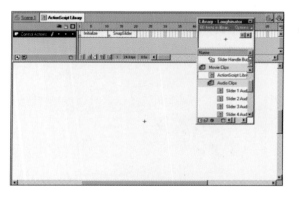

Insert frames and a keyframe and then label the keyframes.

```
Stop
FS Command ("AllowScale", False)
Set Variable: "/:PlayCount" = 0
```

40

The Initialize frame sets the variables to default values. **PlayCount** keeps track of how many samples have been played after the Play button is clicked.

Because the initial position of all five sliders is the vertical center and not actually one of the "snap" positions, each slider default value is set to **2**, just in case the user clicks Play before moving all the sliders into one of the preset positions.

The four positions, representative of a y coordinate, are each set in the last loop. The positions are set in increments of 20 pixels, starting at y: 20, the uppermost level to which the slider handle can be dragged.

5 Move the playhead to frame 11, double-click the SnapSlider keyframe, open the Frame Properties dialog box, and, on the Actions tab, assign the ActionScript.

This script performs the task of "snapping" a slider after the mouse button is released. First of all, it sets a flag variable **Snapped** to **False**. When the nearest snap position is found, the **Snapped** flag is set to **True** and further processing ceases. The actual snapping code recursively checks to see to which of the four snap coordinates the Slider Handle is closest and then moves it to that position.

```
Set Variable: "LoopCount" = 0
Loop While (LoopCount < 5)
    Set Variable: "LoopCount" = LoopCount + 1
    Set Variable: "/Slider" & LoopCount & "/Slider:Snap" = 2
End Loop
Set Variable: "LoopCount" = 0
Loop While (LoopCount < 4)
    Set Variable: "LoopCount" = LoopCount + 1
    Set Variable: "Snap" & LoopCount = 20 + ((LoopCount - 1) * 20)
End Loop
```

```
Set Variable: "Snapped" = False
Set Variable: "LoopCount" = 0
Loop While (LoopCount < 4)
    Set Variable: "LoopCount" = LoopCount + 1
    If (Snapped = False)
        Set Variable: "SliderY" = GetProperty(/:CurrentSlider,_y)
        Set Variable: "Snap" = Eval("Snap" & LoopCount)
        If (Int(SliderY - Snap) < 10)
            Set Property (/:CurrentSlider, Y Position) = Eval("Snap" & LoopCount)
            Set Variable: /:CurrentSlider & "/:Snap" = LoopCount
            Set Variable: "Snapped" = True
        End If
    End If
End Loop
```

6 Exit symbol-editing mode, return to Scene 1, drag an instance of the ActionScript Library from your document's Library, and name the instance **Library**.

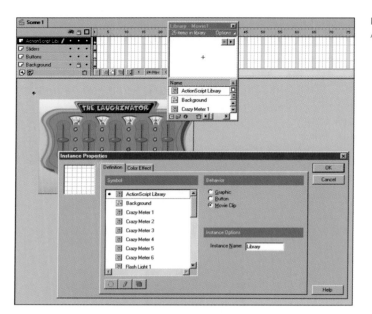

Instance and name the ActionScript Library symbol.

WIRED FOR SOUND

Everything looks fine so far, but you'll need additional buttons and some audio clips to actually make anything happen. The simplest is the Randomize button, so let's start there.

1 Select the Buttons layer and drag an instance of the Randomize Button from the Buttons folder onto the Stage.

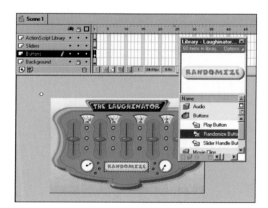

Instance and position the Randomize Button symbol on the Stage.

2 Double-click the Randomize Button and, on the
Actions tab, assign the ActionScript.

This script cycles through each slider, sets its vertical
position to a random number between 20 and 80,
and then calls the **SnapSlider** function. With it, you
can set the positions to an arbitrary number and then
use **SnapSlider** to "clean up" the positioning, just as
if the user had manually dragged each slider.

The Play button is slightly more complicated to put
together, but don't worry. You can do it!

```
On (Release)
    Set Variable: "LoopCount" = 0
    Loop While (LoopCount < 5)
        Set Variable: "LoopCount" = LoopCount + 1
        Set Variable: "CurrentSlider" = "/Slider" & LoopCount & "/Slider"
        Set Property (CurrentSlider, Y Position) = 20 + Random(60)
        Call ("/Library/:SnapSlider")
    End Loop
End On
```

3 Drag an instance of Play Button from the Buttons
folder onto the Stage.

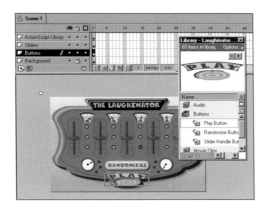

Instance and position the Play
Button symbol on the Stage.

4 Double-click the Play Button instance you created to
open the Instance Properties dialog box, and, on the
Actions tab, assign the ActionScript.

```
On (Release)
    Play
End On
```

5 Select the Play Button instance, press F8, and convert the instance to a Movie Clip symbol, naming it **Play**.

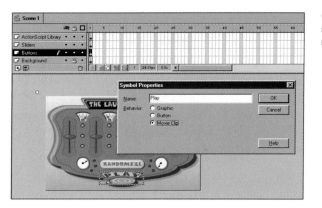

Convert the Play Button symbol to a Movie Clip named Play.

6 Open the Instance Properties dialog box, name the instance **PlayButton**, and, while still in the Instance Properties dialog box, click the Edit Symbol Button to edit Play.

Name the Play instance PlayButton and then enter its symbol-editing mode.

7 Name the existing layer **Play Button** and insert two additional layers, **Control Actions** and **Audio Clips**, above the Play Button layer.

8 Select all the layers and insert 24 frames in each layer, giving each layer a total of 25 frames.

9 Because you want to disable the Play button after it's been clicked and the audio is still playing, select the Play Button layer and create a second keyframe on frame 2.

10 Move the playhead to keyframe 2, double-click the Play Button instance to open the Instance Properties dialog box, and, on the Definitions tab, change the Behavior setting from Button to Graphic.

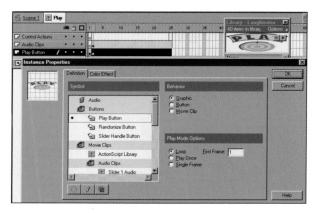

Change the Behavior setting of the Play instance from Movie Clip to Graphic.

11 Select the insert a blank keyframe on frame 2, drag one instance of each symbol from the Movie Clips\Audio Clips folder onto the Stage, and give each instance a name that corresponds with its audio clip name—specifically, **Audio1**, **Audio2**, **Audio3**, **Audio4**, and **Audio5**.

For ease of recognition later, you may choose to position each instance over the actual sliders with which they correspond.

If you take a look inside each of these symbols, you'll see that they simply contain a series of keyframes with one of 20 different sounds attached. These are the laughter sounds that will play when the movie is completed.

12 Select the Control Actions layer, insert blank keyframes in frames 2 and 25, and then assign the label **Stopped** to keyframe 1 and the label **Continue** to keyframe 2.

13 Double-click keyframe 1 to open the Frame Properties dialog box, and, on the Actions tab, assign the ActionScript.

14 Move the playhead to keyframe 2, double-click keyframe 2 to open the Frame Properties dialog box, and, on the Actions tab, assign the ActionScript.

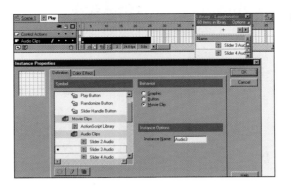

Set up the Audio Clips layer.

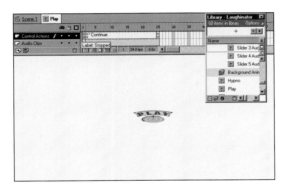

Set up the Control Actions layer.

Stop

Set Variable: "/:PlayCount" = /:PlayCount + 1
Begin Tell Target ("Audio" & /:PlayCount)
    Set Variable: "PrefixText" = "Clip"
    Set Variable: "ClipNumber" = Eval("/Slider" & /:PlayCount &
        "/Slider:Snap") + ((/:PlayCount - 1) * 4)

continues

45

After the user clicks the Play button, this script is executed. It increments the value of **PlayCount** by one and then causes the appropriate sound to play by getting the "snap" value of the current slider and Tell Targetting its corresponding audio clip.

```
        Set Variable: "CurrentClip" = PrefixText & ClipNumber
        Go to and Stop (CurrentClip)
    End Tell Target
    Play
```

15 Double-click keyframe 25 to open the Frame Properties dialog box, and, on the Actions tab, assign the ActionScript.

These statements control the flow of the Play symbol by checking the current value of **PlayCount** and causing the symbol to either continue looping or reset itself.

```
If (/:PlayCount < 5)
    Go to and Play ("Continue")
Else
    Go to and Stop ("Stopped")
    Set Variable: "/:PlayCount" = 0
End If
```

16 Exit symbol-editing mode and return to Scene 1.

In addition to having 1024 laughter combinations on tap, you also now have a cute example of creating sophisticated user interface elements in Flash. The Laughinator takes full advantage of looping and emulated variable arrays, making iterative processing tasks a snap. So laugh it up! Or at least let the Laughinator do it for you.

HOW IT WORKS

The Laughinator works using a combination of techniques. The underlying "content" is a collection of short laughter sounds, and the goal is to play them back in a particular order. The order is stored in a set of variables and is represented and manipulated visually, using a series of sliders.

The sliders use the **Drag Movie Clip** statement that allows a user to move a tab or handle. A collection of ActionScript statements analyzes the position of the handle after it is dropped and automatically moves, or snaps, it into one of a number of predefined positions. Each of these snap positions corresponds to a laughter sound.

In addition to manual placement of the sliders, the project has a randomization option that works by selecting a random number for each slider, corresponding to one of the available snap positions. When a position is selected, the slider handles are moved to it. Finally, playback is achieved by obtaining the snap position and therefore the matching laughter sounds for each slider, and then playing them back in sequence. This is done by means of the **Tell Target** statement.

MODIFICATIONS

You have a number of possibilities for customizing the Laughinator. Because the interface consists mostly of sliders, you can create anything from a more conventional audio mixing board to something completely different, such as an abacus. The most significant part of the Laughinator is its snappable sliders, and these can also be used in any number of applications as a general interface element.

STOPWATCH

"Any simple problem can

be made insoluble

if enough meetings are

held to discuss it."

—MITCHELL'S LAW OF COMMITTEES

USING FLASH'S INTERNAL TIME-TRACKING FEATURES

In this project, you build a stopwatch that takes

advantage of the built-in time-tracking features

of the Flash player, collecting and parsing data

into useful information. The time data is collect-

ed and displayed in a continuous loop, con-

trolled by the user through mouse input. The

stopwatch is a good demonstration of Flash

working in a real-time context because the

timer mechanism remains accurate, regardless

of the speed or capacity of the playback

computer.

PROJECT 5:
STOPWATCH

Layers
Display
Buttons
Background

GETTING STARTED

If you want your results to match those of the finished project, follow the steps carefully. If you want to customize the project and are familiar with Flash 4, feel free to
change the settings to those that meet your needs.

1   Create a new Flash Movie, using these settings:

Frame rate:	**24 fps**
Stage dimensions:	**300 × 155**
Background color:	**White**

2   Set up three layers, naming them (from top to
bottom) **Display**, **Buttons,** and **Background**.

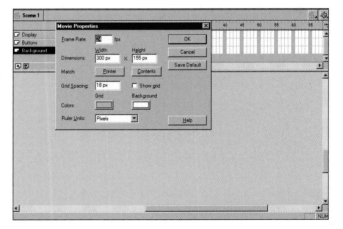

Use the Movie Properties
dialog box to change the
settings of the movie.

3 From the Flash 4 Magic CD, load Stopwatch.fla as a Library, select the Background layer, and drag an instance of the Stopwatch Interface graphic symbol of the StopWatch.fla Library from the Vector Graphics folder onto the Stage.

4 Select the new instance of Stopwatch, center it vertically and horizontally, and align it to the page (Modify>Align).

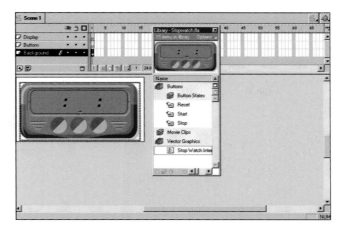

Instance the Stopwatch interface and center and align it to the page.

LAYING OUT THE BUTTONS

The stopwatch has three simple functions: Start, Stop, and Reset. Under the display area of the interface are three spaces, one for each button. You'll place the buttons there now and then assign the appropriate actions in a later section.

1 Select the Buttons layer and open the Buttons folder of the StopWatch.fla Library.

2 Drag one instance of Start, Stop, and Reset onto the Stage and position each instance below the Stopwatch display area.

When you're positioning art in Flash, zoom in as close as possible. After you have one button positioned, you can use the Object Inspector to copy and apply its y-axis to the other buttons. Then you only need to nudge the other buttons into position on their x-axis.

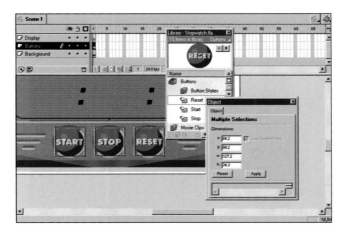

Position the Start, Stop, and Reset buttons below the display.

CREATING THE DISPLAY

This Stopwatch can measure up to 60 minutes at a time, broken down in minutes, seconds, and hundredths of a second (referred to as centiseconds). The digital readouts and logic functions of the movie will all be built into a Movie Clip symbol named Display.

1 Select the Display layer, select the Text tool, and set these attributes:

Font:	Arial
Font size:	48 pt
Style:	Italic
Alignment:	Right

2 Select the Text Field modifier, drag out a text field for minutes and a text field for seconds, type **00** into each field, and resize and reposition them as desired.

3 Change the font size to 36 pt, drag out a text field for centiseconds, type **00** into the field, and resize and reposition it as desired.

4 Select the Minutes text field and set the following attributes in the Text Field Properties dialog box:

Variable:	**Minutes**
Selected Options:	Disable Editing
	Disable Selection
Selected Outlines:	Include only specified font
	outlines
	Numbers

Note: Disabling Editing and Selection prevents the user from manually entering data into the fields but allows you to use text fields as dynamic display elements. The Draw Border and Background option must be deselected to make the text fields transparent.

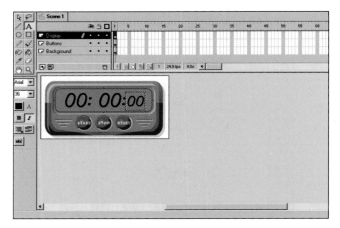

Create the text fields for the minutes, seconds, and centiseconds.

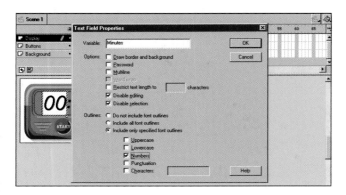

Set the attributes for minutes, seconds, and centiseconds.

5 Select the Seconds text field, type **Seconds** in the Variable field, and set the Text Field Properties attributes listed in step 4.

6 Select the Centiseconds text field, type **Centiseconds** in the Variable field, and set the Text Field Properties attributes listed in step 4.

7 Make certain that the Text Field Properties dialog box is closed, select all three fields, press F8, and create a new Movie Clip symbol, naming it **Display**.

8 Enter the symbol-editing mode for the Display Movie Clip (which should have a Display layer containing your text field); set up two additional layers, naming them **Labels** and **Control Actions**; select all three layers; and insert 50 frames.

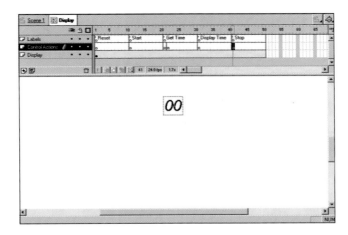

Label the keyframes on the Label layer and insert keyframes on the Control Action layer.

Note: To enter the symbol-editing mode, select the new Display Movie Clip, choose Modify>Instance, and click the Pencil icon on the Definition tab.

9 Select the Labels layer; insert keyframes at frames 11, 21, 31, and 41; and assign these labels:

Frame 1:	**Reset**
Frame 11:	**Start**
Frame 21:	**Get Time**
Frame 31:	**Display Time**
Frame 41:	**Stop**

10 Select the Control Actions layer and insert keyframes at frames 11, 21, 22, 31, and 41.

Adding that extra keyframe at frame 22 is important. No labels are required on this layer. The labels you added to the Label layer can serve as your guide.

53

SETTING UP THE RESET FUNCTION

The first piece of the stopwatch programming is the Reset keyframe (position 1). This is the default position for the Display symbol and is also the frame that will play when users click Reset. It sets the variables **Minutes**, **Seconds**, and **Centiseconds** back to **00** and initializes two other important variables, **Now** and **SavedTime**.

1   Double-click the keyframe on frame 1 on the Control Actions layer to open its Properties dialog box.

Open the Properties dialog box for the keyframe on the Control Actions layer.

2   On the Actions tab, assign the ActionScript.

If you've forgotten how to enter those commands, open the Frame Properties dialog box, select the Actions tab, click the + to display Actions (if necessary), select Set Variable, type **Minutes** in the Variable field and **00** in the Value field, click the button next to the Value field, and select String Literal.

Click String Literal for values that have quotation marks and Expression for values that don't have quotation marks. The difference between a string literal and an expression is this: A *string literal* is used "as is," whereas an *expression* requires evaluation of mathematical or logical operations to determine its value. For example, the string literal "**abc**" is immediately and obviously equal to "**abc**." The expression **"a" & "b" & "c"** is also equal to "**abc**," but only after Flash has evaluated the statement, concatenating the three letters.

> **Set Variable: "Minutes" = "00"**
> **Set Variable: "Seconds" = "00"**
> **Set Variable: "Centiseconds" = "00"**
> **Set Variable: "Now" = 0**
> **Set Variable: "SavedTime" = 0**
> **Stop**

SETTING UP THE START AND STOP FUNCTIONS

The entire **Start** function consists of three parts: **Start**, **Get Time**, and **Display Time**. When the user clicks the Start button, the Display Movie Clip skips to the Start frame, which takes note of the current time, remembers any previously elapsed time, and then proceeds to get the time.

The **Stop** function, consisting of a blank keyframe and a single Stop action, is simpler than the Start function. By parking the playhead at the Stop keyframe, the incrementing of time is paused without resetting any variables.

1 Double-click the keyframe on frame 11 on the Control Actions layer to open its Properties dialog box.

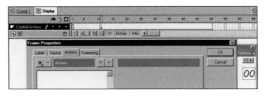

Open the Properties dialog box for the keyframe on frame 11 on the Control Actions layer.

2 On the Actions tab, assign the ActionScript.

GetTimer is the internal Flash Player function that records the number of milliseconds since the movie started. You can use it in expressions just like any other variable.

When you set up **GetTimer** to take note of the number at the point when the **Start** button is clicked and then continuously compare it to the current value, Flash can calculate the period in between. **Get Time** does this comparison by setting the variable Now and evaluating it as the current time minus the start time, plus any leftover time (**SavedTime**) since Reset was last clicked.

> **Set Variable: "StartTime" = GetTimer**
> **Set Variable: "SavedTime" = Now**
> **Go to and Play ("Get Time")**

3 Double-click the keyframe on frame 21 on the Control Actions layer to open its Properties dialog box.

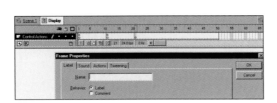

Open the Properties dialog box for the keyframe on frame 21 on the Control Actions layer.

4 On the Actions tab, assign the ActionScript.

> **Set Variable: "Now" = (GetTimer - StartTime) + SavedTime**

5 Double-click the keyframe on frame 21 on the Control Actions layer to open its Properties dialog box.

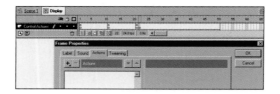

Open the Properties dialog box for the keyframe on frame 22 on the Control Actions layer.

6 On the Actions tab, assign the ActionScript.

The **Go To** statement is on frame 22 instead of frame 21 for a good reason. **Get Time** and **Display Time** pass back and forth between each other in an endless loop, obtaining current time and then displaying it. This looping is achieved with **Go To** statements.

The trouble is that Flash has a built-in bug-protection system to prevent infinite loops that could lock up a user's computer. Flash stops playback of a movie after 20,000 continuous actions have been executed. Without adding the extra frame to break your loop, the magical 20,000 limit would be broken and the movie would stop playback.

Go to and Play ("Display Time")

7 Double-click the keyframe on frame 31 on the Control Actions layer to open its Properties dialog box.

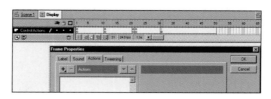

Open the Properties dialog box for the keyframe on frame 31 on the Control Actions layer.

8 On the Actions tab, assign the ActionScript.

The third part of the **Start** function is **Display Time**. **Display Time** takes the number of elapsed milliseconds calculated by **Get Time** and parses it into minutes, seconds, and centiseconds. It makes sure that the three displayed values always have a leading zero if they are single-digit figures, and it resets the timer

```
If (Now > 1000)
    Set Variable: "Minutes" = Int((Substring ( Now, 1, (Length ( Now ) - 3))) / 60)
    Set Variable: "Seconds" = Int((Substring ( Now, 1, (Length ( Now ) - 3))) - (Minutes * 60))
End If
Set Variable: "Centiseconds" = Int(Substring ( Now, (Length ( Now ) - 2), 2 ))
If (Centiseconds < 10)
    Set Variable: "Centiseconds" = "0" & Centiseconds
End If
```

when the 60-minute limit is exceeded. Then a **Go To** statement sends the playhead back to **Get Time** so that the process can start over.

```
If (Seconds < 10)
    Set Variable: "Seconds" = "0" & Seconds
End If
If (Minutes < 10)
    Set Variable: "Minutes" = "0" & Minutes
End If
If (Int(Minutes) > 59)
    Call ("Reset")
End If
Go to and Play ("Get Time")
```

9 Double-click the keyframe on frame 41 on the Control Actions layer to open its Properties dialog box.

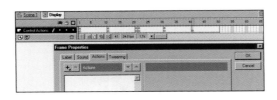

Open the Properties dialog box for the keyframe on frame 41 on the Control Actions layer.

10 On the Actions tab, assign the ActionScript.

Because it's important to retain any previously recorded time, Stop doesn't reset any variables; it just ceases playback. Then when users click Start again, Flash converts the current **Now** value to **SavedTime** so that it can be added during the **Get Time** calculation, enabling the stopwatch to resume counting where it left off.

```
Stop
```

11 Exit the symbol-editing mode and return to the main movie.

WIRING UP THE BUTTONS

In the main Timeline of Scene 1, you need to add the necessary bits and pieces to activate your three buttons.

1 Select the Display layer, select the Display Movie Clip symbol, open the Instance Properties dialog box, and, on the Definition tab, name the instance **Display.**

Naming the instance enables **Tell Target** control of this Movie Clip.

Use the Instance Properties dialog box to name the instance of the Display Movie Clip.

2 Select the Buttons layer, select the Start button, open the Properties dialog box, and, on the Actions tab, assign the ActionScript.

3 Select the ActionScript and copy it (Edit>Copy).

```
On (Release)
    Begin Tell Target ("/Display")
        Go to and Stop ("Start")
    End Tell Target
End On
```

4 With the Buttons layer still selected, select the Stop button, open the Instance Properties dialog box, paste the ActionScript on the Actions tab, and change the **Start** in the **Go to and Stop** statement to **Stop.**

```
On (Release)
    Begin Tell Target ("/Display")
        Go to and Stop ("Stop")
    End Tell Target
End On
```

5 With the Buttons layer still selected, select the Reset button, open the Instance Properties dialog box, paste the ActionScript on the Actions tab, and change the **Start** in the **Go To and Stop** statement to **Reset.**

```
On (Release)
    Begin Tell Target ("/Display")
        Go to and Stop ("Reset")
    End Tell Target
End On
```

How It Works

The Stopwatch works by using the built-in **Get Timer** function to measure time. The Display symbol contains a loop that can continually check the value of **Get Timer** and use the value to calculate the number of minutes, seconds, and centi-seconds measured so far.

When the user clicks the Start button, the ActionScript sets **Display** to start looping. Just like a real stopwatch, previously measured time is added in at this point so that a running total can be kept.

Stop sets the Display symbol's Timeline to halt, breaking the loop and ceasing measurement of time. **Reset** does this also, but goes one step further by clearing any previously measured time so that the stopwatch will start back at zero.

Modifications

The capability to track time in Flash can be used in many other ways beyond making a stopwatch. Check out the following list:

- Make an event occur in a pre-established period of time after another event has occurred.
- Create a time limit for a game.
- Set a screen in a presentation to time out and return to the main screen after a given time has elapsed.

You'll probably run out of time before you find all the valuable uses for this technique.

DRAG-AND-DROP INTERFACE

"Charm is getting the

answer yes without

asking a clear question."

—ALBERT CAMUS

BUILDING A GUI WITH DRAGGABLE AND MINIMIZABLE WINDOWS

Sometimes a simple slide- or page-based Web

site doesn't quite fit the bill. The good news is

that if you want to build a more modular,

window-based interface, you can. In this project,

you create window elements that users can

minimize, restore, and drag around the screen.

PROJECT 6:
FITGIRL

Layers
Control Actions
Channel Bar
Windows
Background

GETTING STARTED

In this section, you set up the new movie. If you want your results to match those of
the finished project, follow the steps carefully. If you want to customize the project and
are familiar with Flash 4, feel free to change the settings to those that meet your needs.

1   Begin with a new Flash Movie, open
WindowToolkit.fla as a Library, and set up the Stage,
using these settings:

Frame rate:	**24 fps**
Stage dimensions:	**550 × 350**
Background color:	**White**

2   Set up four layers, naming them (from top to bottom)
Control Actions, **Channel Bar**, **Windows**, and
Background.

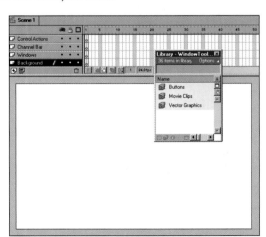

Set up the new movie and
open WindowToolkit.fla as
a Library.

3 Select the Background layer, drag an instance of the Background graphic symbol from the Vector Graphics folder onto the Stage, and center the instance vertically and horizontally, aligning it to the page (Modify>Align).

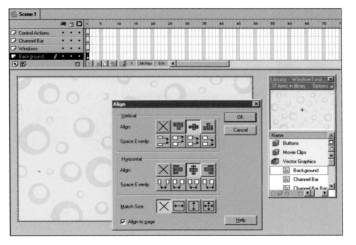

Center the Background symbol on the Stage.

4 Select the Channel Bar layer, drag an instance of the Channel Bar symbol from the Vector Graphics folder onto the Stage, and then use the Align dialog box to position the instance in the lower left corner of the Stage.

In a fully functional site, the buttons in the Channel Bar might be rigged to load movies into the main content window or to pop up a particular menu of options in the Guide window. In this project, you're dealing primarily with the windowed elements. The Channel Bar won't actually be doing anything.

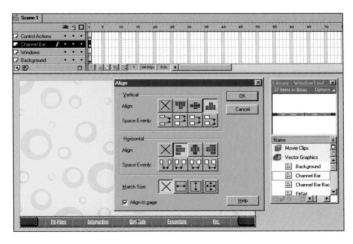

Align the Channel Bar with the bottom left of the Stage.

BUILDING THE GUIDE WINDOW

Single clicks are the only mouse-button combination built into Flash. However, in most computer operating systems, users have the ability to click or double-click. With a little ActionScript magic, you can program Flash to recognize double-clicking. The trick is to set a timer each time a user clicks a button and then calculate the elapsed time between the first and second clicks.

In this project, Flash treats any two clicks within .5 seconds of each other as a double-click. When more than .5 seconds elapse, the click timer is reset, and the cycle begins again. That makes it possible for the user to double-click the title bar of each window and toggle the window open or closed. And, because of the Drag Movie Clip, the user can also drag the title bar to reposition the window.

The three windows used in the FitGirl interface are built almost identically, but you build only the Guide window. The Utilities and Main windows are ready-made symbols in the Movie Clips folder of WindowToolkit.fla. Feel free to refer to them for guidance.

1 Select the Windows layer and create a new empty Movie Clip symbol, naming it **Guide Window**.

You should enter symbol-editing mode automatically.

Create the Guide Window Movie Clip containing five layers with 30 frames each.

2 In the Guide Window, set up five layers, naming them (from top to bottom) **Control Actions**, **Window Handle**, **Window Title**, **FitGirl Graphic**, and **Window Chrome**, select all the layers, and insert 29 additional frames.

3 In the Control Actions layer, select keyframe 1, assign the label **Window Open**, open the Frame Properties dialog box, and, on the Actions tab, assign the ActionScript.

These statements reset the timers and set the variable **Open** to **True**, used to determine which way to toggle (open or closed) when a double-click is recognized.

```
Stop
Set Variable: "FirstClick" = 0
Set Variable: "SecondClick" = 0
Set Variable: "Open" = True
```

Note: To save time, copy this script, paste it, and make minor changes rather than retyping it all for the Window Closed frame.

4 In the Control Actions layer, insert a blank keyframe on frame 16, assign the frame label **Window Closed**, open the Frame Properties dialog box, and, on the Actions tab, insert the ActionScript.

Notice that these are the same as the first set of actions, except **Open** is set to **False**, indicating that the window is currently closed.

```
Stop
Set Variable: "FirstClick" = 0
Set Variable: "SecondClick" = 0
Set Variable: "Open" = False
```

ADDING THE CHROME

The frame around the content of a window is often referred to as "chrome." Don't be confused by the terminology. The chrome in this project is blue, not silver.

1   Select the Window Chrome layer, drag an instance of the Guide Window Chrome (Open) graphic symbol from the Vector Graphics folder onto the Stage, and center the instance horizontally and vertically, aligning it to the page.

2   In the Window Chrome layer, insert a second keyframe (not blank) on frame 16 and drag an instance of the Guide Window Chrome (Closed) graphic symbol in the Vector Graphics folder onto the Stage.

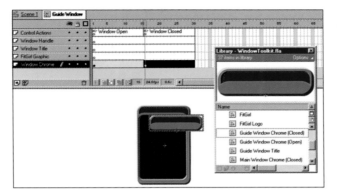

Instance the two Window Guide Chrome graphic symbols.

3   Select both the open and closed chrome instances and use the Align dialog box to position the closed version flush with the top left corner of the open one.

4   Delete the Guide Window Chrome (Open) instance from keyframe 16.

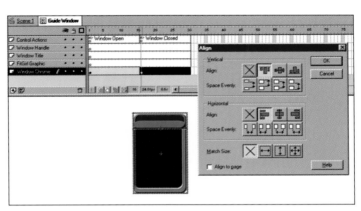

Use the Align dialog box to position the closed instance.

SETTING UP THE WINDOW CONTENTS

The FitGirl Graphic layer contains the window contents. In this case, you're using a static image of FitGirl, the virtual personal trainer, but in a finished version this window might contain a list of menu options or an animated "guide" or agent.

1   Select the FitGirl Graphic layer, move the playhead to frame 1, drag an instance of the FitGirl graphic symbol from the Vector Graphics folder onto the Stage, and center the symbol.

2   Because the window contents shouldn't show after the window is closed, insert a blank keyframe at frame 16.

This blank keyframe will give the illusion that the contents of the window are hidden when you double-click the title bar.

The labels (or titles) make the Guide and Utilities windows in this interface more easily identifiable. Because the titles don't change between open and closed states, they have their own layer with a single keyframe.

3   Select the Window Title layer, drag an instance of the Guide Window Title graphic symbol from the Vector Graphics folder onto the Stage, and position it in the title bar space, centering the instance horizontally.

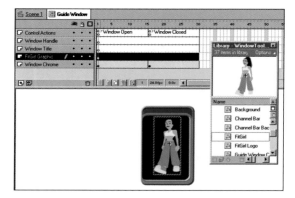

Center the FitGirl symbol in the Guide window.

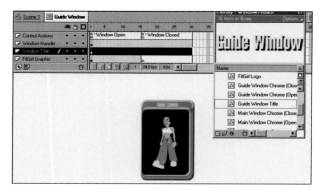

Center the instance of the Guide Window Title graphic in the Guide window.

WORKING WITH INVISIBLE BUTTONS

Invisible buttons are an invaluable tool when you're creating interfaces and interactivity in Flash. They're particularly useful because you can resize and reuse one button over and over rather than constantly converting graphics to buttons and adding bulk to your exported files.

The secret to the invisible button is that the **Up** state (the default state when the mouse isn't over the button) is a blank keyframe. For a completely invisible button such as the one you're going to be using, all the states apart from **Hit** are blank. Hit defines the active area of the button, where the cursor changes to a hand. Defining the Hit area is as simple as drawing a fill or shape inside that particular keyframe.

In this project, the key component to getting Flash to recognize double-clicking is an invisible button that sits on top of the window's title bar. The actions assigned to this button (the Window Handle) calculate the time between clicks, toggle between window open and window closed, and start or stop the dragging of the window (the parent Movie Clip).

1 Select the Window Handle layer, drag an instance of the Window Handle Button from the Buttons folder onto the Stage, and position the instance above the title bar.

 Because the button is invisible, exact positioning isn't necessary, but the closer to the title bar, the better. Also, the Window Handle button is sized specifically for the Guide and Utilities windows, but you can resize it to accommodate your windows.

Position the Window Handle Button over the title bar area.

2 Double-click the Window Handle instance to open the Instance Properties dialog box, and, on the Actions tab, carefully assign the ActionScript.

 This script performs different functions depending on the current mouse event (click, release, drag over, roll out, and so on). Every time the button is clicked—"pressed" is the correct Flash terminology—the script checks to see whether the variable **FirstClick** is greater than **0**. When **FirstClick** is greater than **0**, which denotes that a click has just occurred, the variable **SecondClick** is set to **GetTimer**.

```
On (Press)
    If (FirstClick > 0)
        Set Variable: "SecondClick" = GetTimer
    Else
        Set Variable: "FirstClick" = GetTimer
    End If
    If ((SecondClick > 0)  and (SecondClick - FirstClick < 500))
        If (Open = True)
            Go to and Stop ("Window Closed")
        Else
            Go to and Stop ("Window Open")
        End If
    Else If ((SecondClick > 0) and (SecondClick - FirstClick > 500))
        Set Variable: "FirstClick" = 0
```

continues

Flash then compares **FirstClick** and **SecondClick**. When they are less than half a second apart, the window is either opened or closed, depending on the current value of the **Open** variable.

If the user drags the mouse over or out of the button area, the click timestamps are reset and a **Drag Movie Clip** action is initiated that affects the parent Movie Clip. Conversely, the drag action is stopped whenever the user releases the mouse button, either inside or outside the button area.

```
continued
                Set Variable: "SecondClick" = 0
            End If
        End On
    On (Drag Over, Drag Out)
        Start Drag ("")
        Set Variable: "FirstClick" = 0
        Set Variable: "SecondClick" = 0
    End On
    On (Release, Release Outside)
        Stop Drag
    End On
```

LAYING OUT THE WINDOWS

Now that the Guide window is complete, you can position all three of the finished examples onto your interface.

1   Exit symbol-editing mode and return to Scene 1.

2   Open your movie's own Library and drag an instance of Guide Window onto the left of the Stage. Then, from the Movie Clips folder of WindowToolkit.fla, drag instances of Main Window and Utilities Window onto the Stage.

Position the three draggable windows on the Stage.

How It Works

The Window Interface Toolkit relies mostly on the **On MouseEvent** action. By tracking mouse activity with invisible buttons, it's possible to make the interface "windows" draggable when clicked, and collapsible when double-clicked.

By timing the difference between clicks using the **Set Variable** and **If** statements, you can set Flash to react to double-clicks, in this case changing the content on the screen and toggling between Open and Closed modes. When the user is clicking and dragging the title bar of the windows, Flash makes the window draggable, following the mouse cursor.

Modifications

Apart from collapsing and dragging window-like objects in Flash, you can also add

- Resizing handles
- Close buttons
- Toolbars and scrollbars
- Show/Hide functions
- Customizable color schemes

When you installed Flash 4, the program placed a folder named Sample Pages inside the Flash 4 folder on your hard disk. Inside is a sample named Objects. This excellent "sticky notes" sample—which includes a number of interesting features such as rotation, close buttons, resizing, and saving—is just another example of Flash 4's impressive flexibility.

JUKEBOX

"There are 3 billion

women who don't look

like supermodels and

ONLY 8 WHO DO."

—ANONYMOUS

BUILDING A WORKING JUKEBOX WITH FLASH

The idea of the classic jukebox is simple: click a button, hear a tune. In this project, you build a Flash jukebox that plays a selection of 12 tunes and incorporates some visual and animation effects. This jukebox uses Load Movie to streamline downloading, so it's perfect for use on the Web as well as on your desktop.

PROJECT 7:
JUKEBOX

Layers
  Control Actions
  Flashing Lights
  Track Buttons
  Window
  Arch
  Animation
  Background

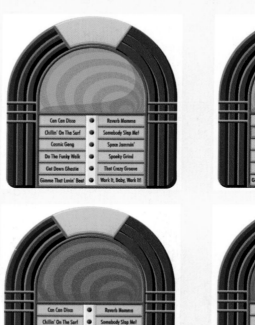

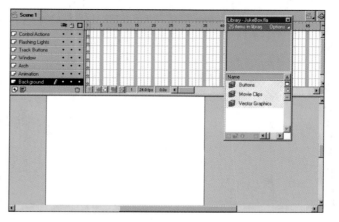

GETTING STARTED

1 Begin with a new Flash Movie, using these settings:

Frame rate:	**24 fps**
Stage dimensions:	**370 × 380**
Background color:	**White**

2 Set up seven layers, naming them (from top to bottom) **Control Actions**, **Flashing Lights**, **Track Buttons**, **Window**, **Arch**, **Animation**, and **Background**.

3 From the Flash 4 Magic CD, load JukeBox.fla as a Library.

Set up the new movie.

LAYING OUT THE ARTWORK

The JukeBox movie uses seven layers, not only for easier construction and editing, but also because you use alpha transparency and layering to create your JukeBox animation effect. To begin, lay out each of the necessary pieces in the corresponding layers, using either the Vector Graphics or Movie Clips folders of the JukeBox.fla Library.

1 Select the Background layer, drag an instance of the Background graphic symbol from the Vector Graphics folder of the JukeBox.fla Library onto the Stage, center the Background symbol horizontally and vertically, and align it to the page.

2 Select the Animation layer and drag an instance of the Animation Movie Clip symbol from the Movie Clips folder of the JukeBox.fla Library off to the left of the Stage.

Animation is a Movie Clip symbol that forms the basis of a random, multicolored visual effect that can be seen through a "glass" window at the top of the jukebox. You'll use it later to build the random effect.

3 Select the Arch layer, drag an instance of the Arch graphic symbol from the Vector Graphics folder of the JukeBox.fla Library onto the Stage, and center it over the Background graphic.

The arch forms the primary artwork for the interface.

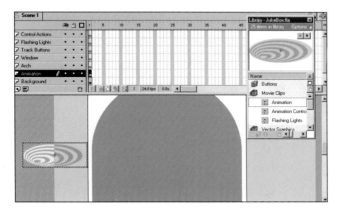

Instance the Background symbol and Animation Movie Clip.

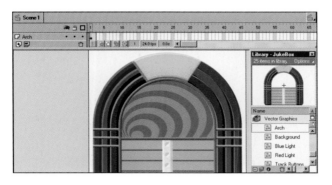

Instance the Arch and Window graphic symbols on their respective layers.

4 Select the Window layer, drag an instance of the opaque Window graphic symbol from the Vector Graphics folder of the JukeBox.fla Library onto the Stage, and position it.

5 Double-click the Window symbol and click the Color Effect tab. From the Color Effect list, select Alpha. Then, in the Alpha setting field, type **30**.

Using the Alpha transparency makes the symbol semitransparent, allowing the random animation to show through from underneath.

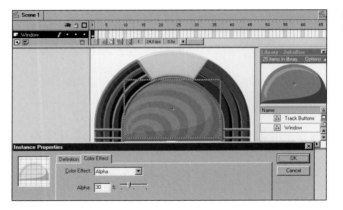

Set up the Window graphic symbol.

6 Select the Track Buttons layer, drag an instance of the Track Buttons graphic symbol from the Vector Graphics folder of the JukeBox.fla Library onto the Stage, and position it in the lower half of the interface.

The track buttons determine which track or tune plays. For ease of setup, we've arranged the buttons in a grid for you. All you need to do is assign the relevant ActionScript commands in the section "Wired for Sound."

As an added touch, we've included a vertical row of lights that blink in sequence while a musical track downloads across the Internet. When the track is loaded, the lights switch off.

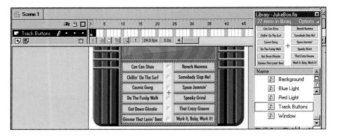

Set up the Track Buttons and Flashing Lights layers.

7 Select the Flashing Lights layer, drag an instance of the Flashing Lights symbol from the Movie Clips folder of the JukeBox.fla Library onto the Stage, and name the instance **flashinglights**.

You assign the Instance Name because Flashing Lights is a Movie Clip symbol controlled by **Tell Target** statements that switch the lights on or off.

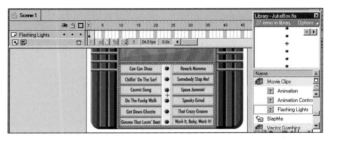

Set up the Flashing Lights graphic symbol.

8 Select the Control Actions layer, double-click the blank keyframe at frame 1, and, on the Actions tab, assign a Stop action.

> Stop

The **Stop** action is necessary because there will eventually be more than one frame in the main scene, and you need to prevent the movie's main Timeline from looping.

WIRED FOR SOUND

The JukeBox is designed to load additional .swf files, containing MP3 audio tracks, as they are required. First, you'll wire up the buttons and loading routine, and then you'll create one of the track movies.

1 Select the first frame of each layer and press F5 to insert a new frame into each layer in Scene 1.

2 Insert a blank keyframe on frame 2 of the Control Actions layer and label the new keyframe **LoadCurrent.**

You'll set up Flash to call this frame each time a visitor clicks a track button.

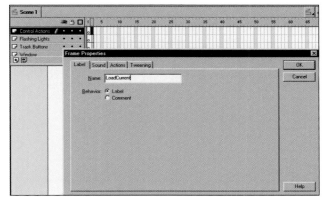

Insert the new frames and label frame 2 of the Control Actions layer.

3 Make certain that LoadCurrent is selected, open the Frames Properties dialog box, and, on the Actions tab, assign the ActionScript.

Each time a user clicks a track button, it sets a variable named **CurrentTrackURL** to contain the URL of the desired track file. After providing the current track URL, the button calls the LoadCurrent frame.

LoadCurrent evaluates **CurrentTrackURL** and then loads the corresponding .swf file into Level 1 of the Flash player. The LoadCurrent script also activates

> **Load Movie (CurrentTrackURL, 1)**
> **Begin Tell Target ("/flashinglights")**
>   **Go to and Play ("On")**
> **End Tell Target**

the Flashing Lights animation, indicating that a file download has begun.

4   Select the Track Buttons layer and open the symbol-editing mode of the Track Buttons instance.

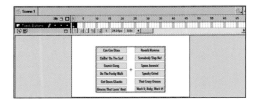

Change the filename for each track.

> **Note:** To enter the symbol-editing mode, right-click (Windows) or Control-click (Macintosh) on the new instance, and choose Edit from the pop-up menu.

Each of the buttons in this symbol has almost exactly the same set of actions. The only thing that changes is the filename of the .swf file containing the corresponding track.

5   Double-click the Can Can Disco button and, on the Actions tab, assign the ActionScript.

6   Select all the ActionScript in the list and copy it so you can reuse it for the other buttons.

7   Double-click each of the remaining track buttons and paste the copied ActionScript onto the Actions tab, replacing the CanCanDisco.swf filename with the correct filename:

```
On (Release)
    Set Variable: "CurrentTrackURL" = "CanCanDisco.swf"
    Call ("LoadCurrent")
End On
```

Chillin' On The Surf	ChillOnTheSurf.swf
Cosmic Gong	CosmicGong.swf
Do The Funky Walk	DoTheFunkyWalk.swf
Get Down Ghostie	GetDownGhostie.swf
Gimme The Lovin' Beat	GimmeTheLovinBeat.swf
Reverb Momma	ReverbMomma.swf
Somebody Slap Me!	SomebodySlapMe.swf
Space Jammin'	SpaceJammin.swf
That Crazy Groove	ThatCrazyGroove.swf
Work It, Baby, Work It!	WorkItBabyWorkIt.swf

Each of the files, with the exception of CanCanDisco.swf, has been provided on your Flash 4 Magic CD. When it comes time to test your jukebox, be sure to copy each of these files from the Flash 4 Magic CD to the same folder as your JukeBox movie.

8   Save the file as **JukeBox.fla**.

DOING THE DISCO

Now that all the buttons and the loading routine are set up, you need to build a music file to load. In this section, you'll be switching temporarily to a new Flash Movie, so be sure to save your jukebox, if you haven't already, before proceeding.

1   Begin with a new Flash Movie, using these settings:

Frame rate:	**24 fps**
Stage dimensions:	**370 × 380**
Background color:	**White**

2   Name the one existing layer **Audio Track**.

3   Select the Audio Track layer and choose File>Import to bring the Can Can Disco audio file into your Library.

For Windows users, this file is cancandisco.wav; for Mac users, it's cancandisco.aiff.

4   In the Frame Properties dialog box, double-click the Sound tab, select the Can Can Disco sound from the list, and type **5** in the Loops field. Keep the Frame Properties dialog box open.

Because this is a short sound, suitable for looping, use 5 in the Loops field.

When the first keyframe (containing the sound) has loaded, you need to set it up to turn off the Flashing Lights animation on the JukeBox movie. You achieve this with a **Tell Target** statement that communicates across Flash player levels.

5   Click the Actions tab and assign the ActionScript.

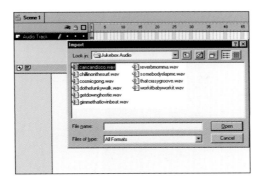

Use the Import dialog box to bring the audio file into the Library.

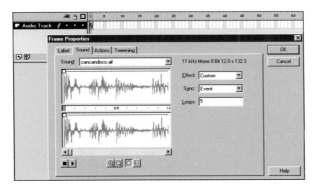

Set up the audio file on the Sound tab.

```
Begin Tell Target ("_level0/flashinglights")
    Go to and Stop ("Off")
End Tell Target
```

6 Save this movie in the same folder as your JukeBox movie, using the filename **CanCanDisco.fla**.

7 Press Ctrl-Enter (Cmd-Return) to test the movie.

Flash automatically exports the movie as the final .swf file required by your JukeBox file.

8 Close CanCanDisco.fla.

If you were creating your own customized jukebox, you'd create as many of these sound files as required by simply repeating the preceding instructions and importing the desired audio files.

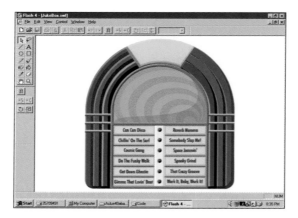

Test the movie.

BUILDING THE RANDOM ANIMATION

In this section, you set up the random animation. Because the Animation symbol contains six frames, each animation state actually contains twelve, allowing for two loops of animation per state. If you find that the animation changes too quickly, you can lengthen each state simply by adding more frames between them, preferably in multiples of six.

1 Return to Scene 1 of the JukeBox movie and select the Animation instance you created earlier on the Animation layer.

2 Open the Object Inspector (Window>Inspectors>Object), type in these new values, and then click Apply.

x: **55**
y: **55**
w: **260**
h: **200**

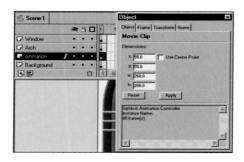

Set up the Animation Controller using the Object Inspector dialog box.

3 Lock all the layers except the Animation layer, make sure that the instance of the Animation symbol is still selected, press F8, and convert the symbol to a Movie Clip, naming it **Animation Controller**.

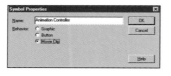

Name the Movie Clip using the Symbol Properties dialog box.

4 In the symbol-editing mode of Animation Controller, name the existing layer **Animation State** and insert a new layer, naming it **Control Actions**.

5 Insert 84 frames in both layers, creating a total of 85 frames.

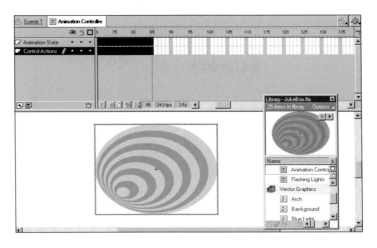

Insert 84 frames in the layers in the Animation Controller Movie Clip.

6 Select keyframe 1 of the Animation State layer and, in the Instance Properties dialog box, use these Color Effects settings:

Color Effect:	Tint
Tint Amount:	50%
Red:	255
Green:	0
Blue:	0

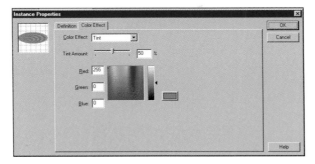

Set the Color Effect using the Instance Properties dialog box.

7 Insert keyframes in the Animation State layer at frames 13, 25, 37, 49, and 61, and use these settings for each:

Keyframe 13:	Tint Amount	50
	R, G, B	0, 255, 0

Keyframe 25:	Tint Amount	50
	R, G, B	0, 0, 255

Keyframe 37:	Tint Amount	50
	R, G, B	255, 0, 0
	Modify>Transform>Flip Horizontal	

Keyframe 49:   Tint Amount   50

               R, G, B   0, 255, 0

               Modify>Transform>Flip Horizontal

Keyframe 61:   Tint Amount   50

               R, G, B   0, 0, 255

               Modify>Transform> Flip Horizontal

8 Select the Control Actions layer of the Animation Controller Movie Clip and insert and label blank keyframes in the following frames:

Frame 1:   **State1**

Frame 13:   **State2**

Frame 25:   **State3**

Frame 37:   **State4**

Frame 49:   **State5**

Frame 61:   **State6**

Frame 73:   **Go Random**

9 Insert a blank keyframe on frame 12 of the Control Actions layer and, on the Actions tab, assign the ActionScript.

10 Copy keyframe 12 and paste it on frames 24, 36, 48, 60, and 72 of the Control Actions layer.

You'll notice that these frames are placed at the end of each state. After each state plays, the frame Go Random is called.

11 In the Actions tab, assign the ActionScript to the Go Random keyframe.

A variable named **NewState** is set to an expression that picks a random number between 1 and 6. Because your frame labels are structured as State1, State2, and so on, all you need to do is tack the value of **NewState** onto the end of the word **State** and go to the resulting frame label. Neat, huh?

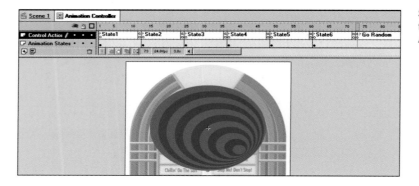

Set up the keyframes and frames in the Control Actions layer.

Call ("Go Random")

Set Variable: "NewState" = Random (6)
Go to and Play ("State" & NewState)

How It Works

The JukeBox makes extensive use of the Load Movie action. The core movie, the JukeBox, itself, is really just a button panel that holds the URLs of a selection of music files. When a button is pressed, the Flash Player movie containing the audio is loaded into an upper level and the music plays. Because the audio files contain only music—no graphics—they appear to be invisible, and the user is unaware of how the effect is being produced. Also, because each of the music files is loaded from an external source, the core movie is small and downloads fast.

Modifications

Believe it or not, your jukebox is now ready to go! This example plays short loops suitable for background music, but it's just as easy to build a personal music collection that plays your favorite pop songs or classic tracks.

■ Use different audio files. To import any audio into Flash, you need to convert it to .wav or .aiff format (depending on whether you're using Windows or MacOS). This holds true for CD music as well, but a variety of quality audio-conversion and extraction programs are available for download on the World Wide Web.

■ Adjust the settings of the MP3 audio. Depending on the context in which you'll be using your jukebox—on the Web or via intranet or local hard disk—you'll probably want to adjust the rendering quality and bit rates of your MP3 audio. To make these adjustments, open the Sound Properties dialog for the sound file in your movie's Library and adjust its compression properties. But be forewarned: Rendering high-quality MP3 audio can take time, so be prepared to take a coffee break while you wait!

CALCULATOR

"Melting an ice cube in

your mouth burns

2.3 calories."

—ANONYMOUS

BUILDING A WORKING CALCULATOR WITH FLASH

Everybody needs a calculator, but the ones that

ship with most computer operating systems are

just plain dull. Now you can whip up a cus-

tomized version that fits with the style and

branding of your Web pages. The Flash

Calculator takes advantage of ActionScript math

functions, variables, and the Call statement to

form a lightweight, functional application.

Layers
Display
Buttons
Background

GETTING STARTED

In this first section, you set up a new movie in which to complete this project. If you want your results to match those of the finished project, follow the steps carefully. If you want to customize the project and are familiar with Flash 4, feel free to change the settings to those that meet your needs.

1 Begin with a new Flash Movie, using these settings:

Frame rate:	**24 fps**
Stage dimensions:	**180 × 200**
Background color:	**White**

2 Create three layers, naming them (from top to bottom) **Display**, **Buttons**, and **Background**.

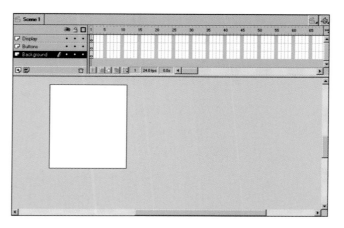

Set up the new movie with its layers.

3 From the Flash 4 Magic CD, load Calculator.fla as a Library, select the Background layer, and drag an instance of the Calculator Interface graphic symbol onto the Stage.

4 Using the Object Inspector, resize the interface to **164.3** wide and **186.6** high and center it horizontally and vertically, aligning it to the page (Modify>Align).

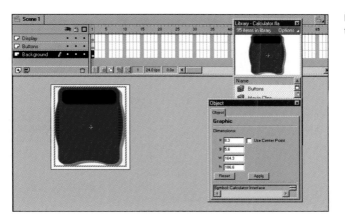

Instance, resize, and align the interface.

Laying Out the Buttons

Rather than going through the specifics of the calculator's buttons individually, we've done all the groundwork for you and provided a pre-wired Keypad symbol in the Buttons folder of Calculator.fla.

Although you'll mainly be dealing with the Display component of the Calculator, the buttons that form the Keypad are quite interesting also. After you've gone through the instructions in this project, take a tour of the various button actions to gain a full appreciation of how the movie is strung together.

1 Select the Buttons layer.

2 Drag an instance of the Keypad graphic symbol from the Buttons folder onto the Stage and position it below the calculator display area.

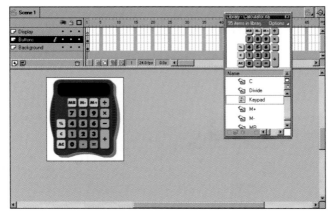

Position the Keypad symbol below the display area on the Calculator interface.

CREATING THE DISPLAY

The core functions of the Calculator will be consolidated into a Movie Clip symbol named Display that controls the digital readout and performs any calculations.

1 Select the Display layer, select the Text tool, and set these attributes:

Font:	_sans
Size:	20 pt
Style:	Italic
Alignment:	Right
Color:	White

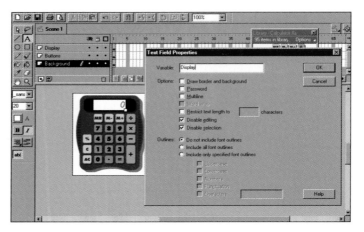

Set up the text field on the Display layer.

2 Select the Text Field modifier, drag a text field roughly 80% of the width of the display area marked out on the interface, type **0** into the field as place-holder text, set the following options in the Text Field Properties dialog box, and click OK.

Variable:	**Display**
Selected Options:	Disable Editing
	Disable Selection
Outlines:	Do not include font outlines

3 Use the Arrow tool to select your text field, press F8, and create a new Movie Clip symbol named **Display**.

4 In the symbol-editing mode of the Display Movie Clip symbol, name the existing layer **Display**, create an additional layer and name it **Control Actions,** select both layers, and insert 34 new frames.

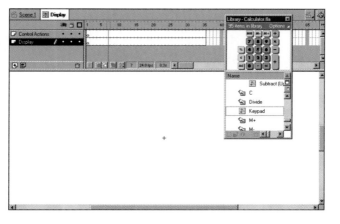

Insert a new Display Movie Clip with two layers, each having 35 frames.

Note: To enter the symbol-editing mode, right-click (Windows) or Control-click (Macintosh) on the instance, and choose Edit from the pop-up menu.

5 Select the Control Actions layer, insert new blank keyframes at positions 11 and 21, and create these labels:

Frame 1: **Initialize**
Frame 11: **Add Digit**
Frame 21: **Perform Operation**

Initialize, as the name suggests, is the frame that instantiates a number of key variables and sets them to their default values.

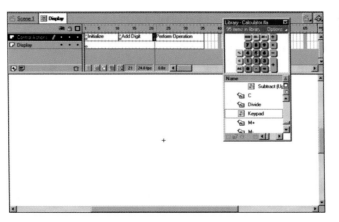

Assign labels to the keyframes.

6 Select the Initialize keyframe on the Control Actions layer, open the Frame Properties dialog box, and, on the Actions tab, assign the ActionScript.

This script resets the Display text field and the stored **Memory** value. It also resets **Decimal** and **Done** to **False**. The **Decimal** variable keeps track of whether a decimal point is already present in the number currently being displayed. **Done** indicates whether the calculator should clear the display and begin adding new digits, or simply append them to the current number.

The next keyframe, Add Digit, is called each time the user clicks a number button, including 0 though 9 and the decimal point. Each of those buttons sets a variable **Digit** to the appropriate value and then uses the **Call** statement to execute the ActionScript on the Add Digit keyframe.

```
Set Variable: "Memory" = "0"
Set Variable: "Display" = "0"
Set Variable: "Decimal" = False
Set Variable: "Done" = False
Set Variable: "Operator" = ""
Stop
```

7 Select the Add Digit keyframe on the Control Actions layer, open the Frame Properties dialog box, and, on the Actions tab, assign the ActionScript.

```
If (Done = True)
    Set Variable: "Done" = False
    Set Variable: "Decimal" = False
    Set Variable: "Display" = "0"
```

continues

You'll notice that if **Done** has been flagged as **True**, the display is reset before the next digit is added. If the Display contains only "0," the **Display** variable is replaced with the current value of **Digit**. If not, **Digit** is simply appended to the end of **Display**, consistent with normal calculator input behavior.

The third and final keyframe, Perform Calculation, does all the calculations that make the movie function correctly.

8 Select the Perform Calculation keyframe on the Control Actions layer, open the Frame Properties dialog box, and, on the Actions tab, assign the ActionScript.

The four main operations are fairly self-evident. Every time someone clicks a button such as Multiply, Flash sets "*" as the variable **Operator**, stores the current Display value as the **Operand**, and then calls **Perform Operation**. **Perform Operation** takes the value of **Operand** and the current **Display** and carries out the appropriate calculation. Flash then resets the **Operator**, **Decimal**, and **Done** variables.

```
continued
    End If
    If (Display eq "0" and not (Display eq "."))
        Set Variable: "Display" = Digit
    Else
        Set Variable: "Display" = Display & Digit
    End If
```

```
If (Operator eq "+")
    Set Variable: "Display" = Operand + Display
End If
If (Operator eq "-")
    Set Variable: "Display" = Operand - Display
End If
If (Operator eq "*")
    Set Variable: "Display" = Operand * Display
End If
If (Operator eq "/")
    Set Variable: "Display" = Operand / Display
End If
Set Variable: "Operator" = ""
Set Variable: "Decimal" = False
Set Variable: "Done" = True
```

WIRING UP THE DISPLAY

In this section, you return to the main Timeline of Scene 1 and define the Display
Movie Clip. Doing so enables you to refer to that Movie Clip in statements.

1   Return to the main Timeline of Scene 1 and select
the Display layer.

2   Select the Display Movie Clip symbol, open the
Instance Properties dialog box, and, on the
Definition tab, type **Display** as the Instance Name.

By assigning a name to a Movie Clip instance, you
make its Timeline a part of the target hierarchy,
enabling **Tell Target** and **Call** statements to that particular instance while it's present on the Stage.

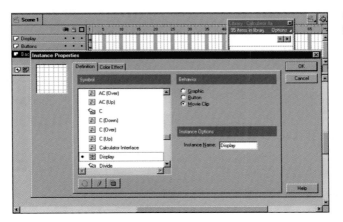

Name the instance so that
you can use it in statements.

HOW IT WORKS

The Calculator is unique because it relies solely on **Set Variable** and **Call** statements to
perform its main functions. There are two primary button types, digits and operators.
The digits, including 0–9 and the decimal point, are rigged for inputting numbers into
the Display. Operators such as add and subtract, on the other hand, are designed to
perform some calculation based on the Display.

To complete the logic of the application, the two "flags," or Boolean variables **Decimal**
and **Done**, are employed to let the movie keep track of what's happening. As mentioned previously, **Decimal** prevents multiple decimal points from being entered in the
Display, and **Done** controls the clearing of the Display after an operation is completed.

Also worthy of note are the MR, M+, and M− functions. The Initialize keyframe
creates a variable named **Memory** that is used to store the current contents of the calculator's memory. MR sets the value of **Display** to that of the **Memory** variable, and
M+ and M− add and subtract the current Display from the number in Memory and
then re-store it with the new value.

Last, C and AC adjust different sets of variables back to their initial state to reset the current **Display** and **Decimal** value, or—in the case of AC (All Clear)—the **Memory** and **Operator** variables also.

MODIFICATIONS

Thanks to the pervasive use of symbols in building the calculator, you'll have an easy time customizing the look and feel of your own version because you only have to substitute graphics. The orientation of the buttons and display can also be easily altered, making it possible to create a standalone version or something more compact that fits into an existing interface.

With some customization and a few additional equations, you also can build special-purpose calculators. Popular examples include currency converters, BMI (Body Mass Index) calculators, and utilities for converting units of measurement. These timesaving gadgets are a big hit with Web surfers and a great way to get people to bookmark your site.

MAP EXPLORER

"Character cannot be developed in

ease and quiet. Only through

experience of trial and suffering can

the soul be strengthened, ambition

inspired, and success achieved."

—HELEN KELLER

GENERATING A ZOOMABLE AND SCROLLABLE MAP

One of the key strengths of Flash is the capability to present information in an interactive, "hands on" manner. In this project, you'll be creating an application designed to display a map with clickable landmarks—a house plan with photographs of room views. To make things interesting, the user can also scroll and zoom the map with a draggable compass interface.

PROJECT 9:
MAP EXPLORER

Layers
ActionScript Library
Compass
Reytex Homes Logo
Pictures
House Plan

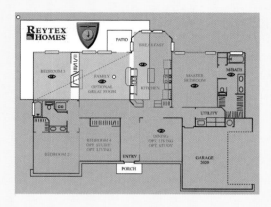

GETTING STARTED

In this section, you set up the Flash movie. If you want your results to match those of the finished project, follow these steps carefully. If you want to customize the project and are familiar with Flash 4, feel free to change the settings to those that meet your needs.

1 Begin with a new Flash Movie, load MapExplorer.fla (on the Flash 4 Magic CD) as a Library, and set up the Stage, using these settings:

Frame rate:	**24 fps**
Stage dimensions:	**550 × 350**
Background color:	**White**

2 Set up five layers, naming them (from top to bottom) **ActionScript Library**, **Compass**, **Reytex Homes Logo**, **Pictures**, and **House Plan**.

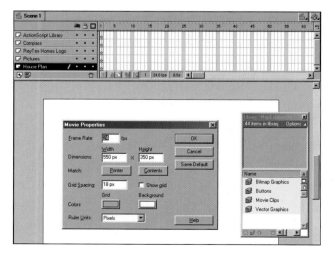

Set up the new Flash movie.

94

3 In the ReyTex Homes Logo layer, drag an instance of the ReyTex Homes graphic symbol in the Bitmap Graphics folder onto the Stage.

4 Select the instance of ReyTex Homes and use the Object Inspector to position the instance at x: **20**, y: **20**.

These coordinates should place the logo neatly in the top left corner.

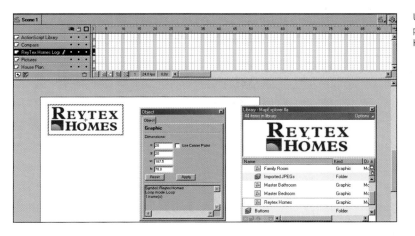

Use the Object Inspector to precisely position the ReyTex Homes logo.

Laying the Foundation

Although the House Plan symbol will mainly be manipulated from the outside for scaling and positioning, it also contains some important internal workings. In the Buttons folder is a subfolder named Dimension Buttons. Each button corresponds to a room in the house plan. The buttons are invisible but have room dimensions drawn into the **Over** state. The user can see the dimensions of a given room as they move the cursor over it. Part of the Map Explorer is a selection of photographs of rooms in the home depicted in the house plan. To trigger the display of a photograph, you place a series of buttons in the appropriate rooms.

1 In the House Plan layer, drag an instance of the House Plan graphic symbol in the Vector Graphics folder onto the Stage, and use the Object Inspector to set the coordinates to x: **45**, y: **45**.

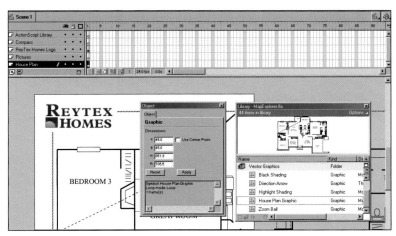

Position the House Plan graphic on the House Plan layer, using the Object Inspector.

95

2 Select the instance of the House Plan graphic, press F8, and convert the instance into a Movie Clip, naming it **Movable House Plan**.

3 In the symbol-editing mode of Movable House Plan, set up a total of three layers, naming them (from top to bottom) **Picture Buttons**, **Dimension Buttons**, and **House Plan Graphic.**

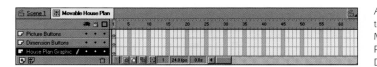

Add two additional layers to the Movable House Plan Movie Clip and name them Picture Buttons and Dimension Buttons.

> **Note:** To enter the symbol-editing mode, right-click (Windows) or Control-click (Macintosh) on the Movable House Plan instance, and choose Edit from the pop-up menu.

4 Select the Dimension Buttons layer, drag one instance of each Dimension Button in the Buttons folder onto the Stage, and position each button above the appropriate room, using these x, y coordinates:

Bedroom 3 Button	**−460, −255**
Bedroom 2 Button	**−460, 98**
Family Room Button	**−268, −254**
Bedroom 4 Button	**−268, 71**
Breakfast and Kitchen Button	**−47, −350**
Dining Room Button	**−10, 30**
Master Bedroom Button	**128, −255**

Because these buttons are self-contained, you don't need to assign any actions to them.

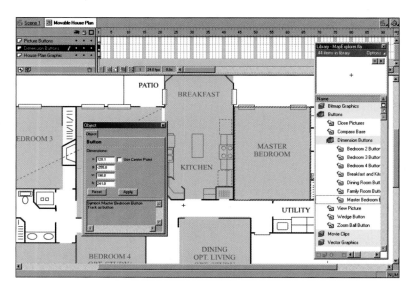

Use the Object Inspector to position the buttons on the Dimension Buttons layer.

5 In the Picture Buttons layer, drag an instance of the View Picture Button in the Buttons folder onto the Stage, open the Properties dialog box, and, on the Actions tab, assign the ActionScript to the instance:

```
On (Release)
    Begin Tell Target ("/Pictures")
        Go to and Stop ("Room Name")
    End Tell Target
End On
```

6 Use the Edit>Duplicate command to create five additional instances of View Picture, and position them.

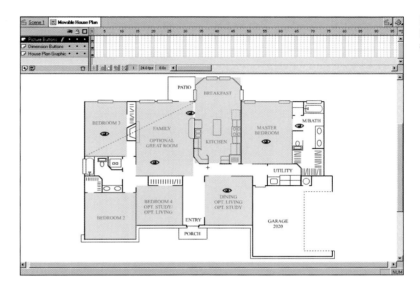

Place instances of the View Picture Button in the rooms, as shown here.

7 Double-click the first instance (in Bedroom 3) of View Picture and edit the **Go to and Stop** action, replacing the label Room Name with **Bedroom**.

```
On (Release)
    Begin Tell Target ("/Pictures")
        Go to and Stop ("Bedroom")
    End Tell Target
End On
```

8 Moving from left to right through the View Picture instances, continue replacing each reference to Room Name in the **Go to and Stop** statement with these labels:

Family Room
Breakfast and Kitchen
Dining Room
Master Bedroom
Master Bathroom

9 Exit the symbol-editing mode, return to the main Timeline, double-click the House Plan instance, and name it **HousePlan**.

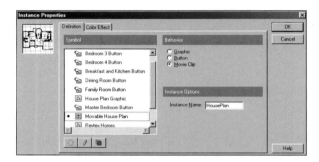

Name the House Plan instance so that you can use it in Actionscript commands.

SETTING UP THE PICTURES MOVIE CLIP

In this section, you create the Pictures Movie Clip symbol and set up its Close Button and Pictures layers. Then, you lay out the keyframes in the Pictures layer.

1 In the Pictures layer, ensure that nothing is selected, and then create a new empty Movie Clip symbol, naming it **Pictures**.

2 In the symbol-editing mode of Pictures, set up two layers, name them (from top to bottom) **Close Button** and **Pictures**, select both layers, and insert an additional 139 frames into both layers for a total of 140.

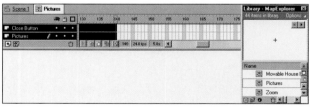

Create two layers named Close Button and Pictures and give each layer 140 frames.

3 In the Pictures layer, insert blank keyframes at frames 21, 41, 61, 81, 101, 121, and 131, making a total of eight blank keyframes on the Pictures layer.

Insert eight blank keyframes.

98

4   Double-click frame 1 to open the Frame Properties dialog box, and, on the Actions tab, assign the ActionScript.

5   Continue adding **Stop** actions in each frame and assign the following frame labels:

Frame 1	**None**
Frame 21	**Master Bedroom**
Frame 41	**Master Bathroom**
Frame 61	**Family Room**
Frame 81	**Dining Room**
Frame 101	**Breakfast and Kitchen**
Frame 121	**Bedroom**

These are the frame labels to which the View Picture buttons each refer.

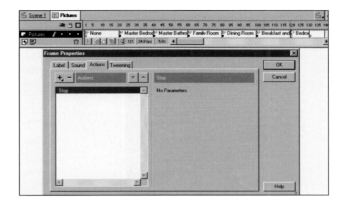

Add **Stop** actions and labels to keyframes on the Pictures layer within the Pictures Movie Clip.

ADDING THE PHOTOGRAPHS

Now that the keyframes are laid out, it's time to insert the actual photographs, which are in the Bitmaps Graphics folder.

1   Move the playhead to each keyframe; drag an instance of its matching graphic from the Bitmaps folder onto the Stage; and then use the Object Inspector to set the x, y, w, and h properties of each graphic to

x: **−144.9**
y: **−97.4**
w: **290**
h: **189**

To save on file size, the photographs share a single Close button that hides the picture display by moving the playhead to the None frame, which is intentionally blank.

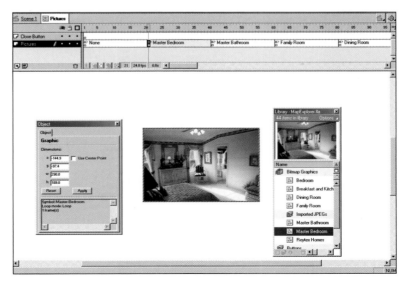

Add the pictures of each room to keyframes with names that correspond to the room names.

2 In the Close Button layer, insert a blank keyframe at frame 21.

3 Drag an instance of the Close Pictures symbol in the Buttons folder onto the Stage and use the Object Inspector to position it at x: **125.1**, y: **–97.4**.

The exact placement of the button isn't important, but for the sake of convention, place it at the top right.

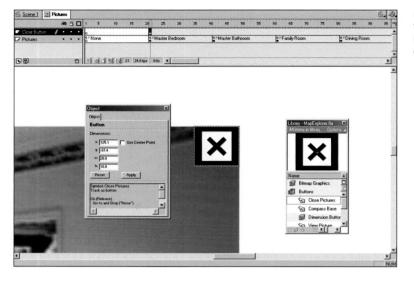

Use the Object Inspector to position the Close Pictures Button on the Close Button layer.

4 Double-click the instance of Close Pictures and, on the Actions tab, assign the ActionScript.

This set of actions sends the Movie Clip back to the blank None frame, effectively hiding the Pictures symbol. Another way to achieve this on/off effect would be to use the **Visibility** property of Movie Clip symbols, but in this situation **Go to Frame Label** works just as effectively.

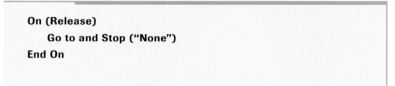

```
On (Release)
    Go to and Stop ("None")
End On
```

5 Exit symbol-editing mode, return to Scene 1, press Control+L (PC) or Command+L (Mac) to open the Library for your version of the MapExplorer Flash movie, drag an instance of the Pictures Movie Clip from your Library onto the Stage, and use the Object Inspector to position the instance at x: **400**, y: **250**.

The Pictures Movie Clip is represented by a small white dot because the first frame of the Pictures Movie Clip is empty.

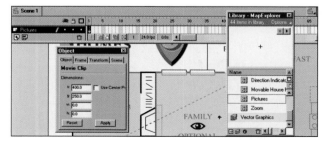

Instance the Pictures Movie Clip.

6 Double-click the instance and name it **Pictures**.

Use the Pictures Movie Clip from the Library that Flash created for your file (not the MapExplorer Library).

SETTING UP THE COMPASS BASE

The third major component of the MapExplorer application is the compass. This nifty gadget enables the user to scroll the house plan in eight different directions, as well as to zoom it from 10% to 190% of its original size.

1 In the Compass layer, drag an instance of the Compass Base Button in the Buttons folder of the Map Explorer Library onto the Stage, and position the instance at x: **240**, y: **10**.

Place the Compass Base Button on the Compass layer.

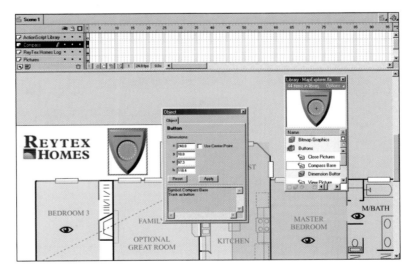

2 Select the Compass Base instance, press F8, and convert the instance to a Movie Clip symbol, naming it **Compass**.

3 In the symbol-editing mode of Compass, set up five layers, naming them (from top to bottom) **Shading**, **Direction Indicator**, **Direction Buttons**, **Zoom Ball**, and **Base**.

Add five layers to the Compass Movie Clip and name them as shown.

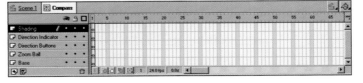

4 Double-click the Compass Base Button to open the Instance Properties dialog box, and, on the Actions tab, assign the ActionScript.

This code makes the entire compass draggable, enabling the user to move it out of the way if it obscures a part of the map they're interested in.

```
On (Press)
    Start Drag ("")
End On
On (Release, Release Outside, Roll Out, Drag Out)
    Stop Drag
End On
```

SETTING UP THE ZOOM BALL

Users of interactive maps have come to expect zoom capability, and you can easily provide it with this project. The hard work is already completed for you. You just need to instance the Zoom Ball Button symbol and assign the ActionScript that makes it function properly.

1 In the Zoom Ball layer, drag an instance of the Zoom Ball Button symbol in the Buttons folder onto the Stage, and position it at x: **−5**, y: **−45**.

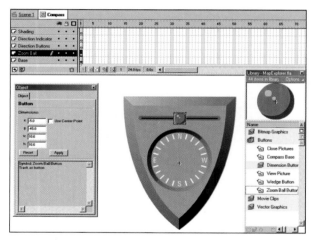

Position the Zoom Ball Button on the Zoom Ball layer.

2 Double-click the Zoom Ball Button on the Stage and, on the Actions tab, assign the ActionScript.

In the next step, you'll be nesting this button inside a Movie Clip. Notice that clicking the button triggers a **Drag Movie Clip** action referring to its parent symbol. The drag rectangle is constrained so that the only

```
On (Press)
    Start Drag ("", L=-30, T=-40, R=30, B=-40)
End On
On (Release, Release Outside, Drag Out)
    Stop Drag
    Set Variable: "/:ZoomFactor" = 100 + (GetProperty( "",_x ) * 3)
```

way the zoom ball can be dragged is horizontally between these two points: a minimum zoom and a maximum zoom.

When the button is released, Flash calculates the zoom factor by determining the current x position of the zoom ball. A variable named **MasterStep** is also set. The scrolling scripts use **MasterStep** to determine how quickly the map is moved. The higher the zoom, the faster the scroll.

```
Set Variable: "/Library/:MasterStep" = Int((/:ZoomFactor /
    100) * 5)
If (/Library/:MasterStep < 1)
  Set Variable: "/Library/:MasterStep" = 1
End If
Call ("/Library/:DoZoom")
End On
```

3 Select the Zoom Ball Button, press F8, and convert it to a Movie Clip symbol, naming it **Zoom**.

Setting Up the Wedge Button

Time to move on to the Wedge Button. With this instance, you get to use the Track as Menu Item option and **Roll Over**, **Drag Over**, **Get Property**, and **Call** statements. Don't worry, though. The process isn't at all complicated because of the prefab work that is already in place.

1 Select the Direction Buttons layer, drag an instance of the Wedge Button in the Buttons folder onto the Stage, and use the Object Inspector to position it at x: **–10.3**, y: **–30.7**.

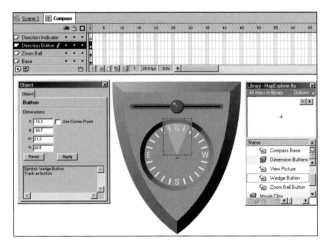

Use the Object Inspector to position an instance of the Wedge Button on the Direction Buttons layer.

2 Double-click the Wedge Button instance, set the Tracking Options to Track as Menu Item on the Definition tab.

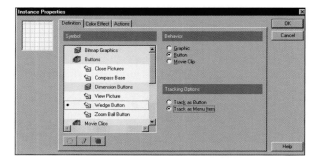

Set the Tracking Options to Track as Menu Item.

3 On the Actions tab, assign the ActionScript.

This button will be nested inside a Movie Clip symbol, which will be given an instance name equaling one of the eight allowed directions. The Wedge Button script takes this instance name and then calls an ActionScript routine from the Library.

Because the direction value is set in the Instance Name of the button's parent Movie Clip symbol, you need only one button. This makes the direction buttons extremely modular and a snap to build.

You'll notice that two different scripts are being called. One is for rollovers and changes only the current position of the direction arrow. The other is for clicks that manipulate the direction arrow and move the house plan.

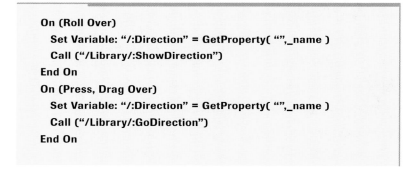

```
On (Roll Over)
    Set Variable: "/:Direction" = GetProperty( "",_name )
    Call ("/Library/:ShowDirection")
End On
On (Press, Drag Over)
    Set Variable: "/:Direction" = GetProperty( "",_name )
    Call ("/Library/:GoDirection")
End On
```

4 Select the Wedge Button you just edited, press F8, and convert it to a Movie Clip symbol, naming it **Direction Button**.

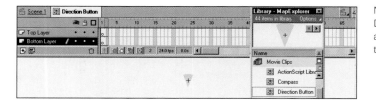

Name two layers in the Direction Button Movie Clip and add an additional frame to each layer.

5 In the symbol-editing mode of the Direction Button Movie Clip, set up two layers, name them (from top to bottom) **Top Layer** and **Bottom Layer**, and insert an extra frame on both layers so that the symbol has two layers with two frames each.

6 Select the Bottom Layer layer, insert a blank keyframe in frame 2 (add a frame and delete the Wedge Button), copy keyframe 1 (making sure that you copy the frame rather than its contents), and paste it onto frame 2 of the Top Layer layer.

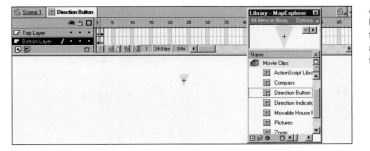

Add a blank keyframe to the Bottom Layer, and copy the first frame of the Bottom Layer and paste it onto the second frame of the Top Layer.

You might be wondering why the crazy keyframes. The symbol arrangement you just created is known as a continuous feedback button. Flash buttons can accept only a single click event and won't detect that the button is being held down, so you create a looping Movie Clip that contains distinct multiple instances of the same button. This looping tricks the Flash Player into generating a continuous stream of mouse events you can use to provide more natural responses.

In this particular instance, holding down the mouse button over any of the direction buttons will cause the house plan to move repeatedly rather than forcing the user to click over and over again. This technique is also applicable to scrollbar buttons and various other uses.

7 Return to the Compass symbol.

MULTIPLYING THE DIRECTION BUTTON

Now you need to lay out the eight direction buttons that should already be on the
Stage. Using Edit>Duplicate will speed up the process. To simplify the rotation of the
button symbols, use the Transform Inspector.

1 In the symbol-editing mode of the Compass, select
the Direction Buttons layer, select the Direction
Button instance, and use Edit>Duplicate to replicate
seven more instances.

2 Rotate each instance of the additional seven
Direction Button symbols until they form a snug cir-
cular arrangement with all the pointed ends facing
inward. Use the Transform Inspector to numerically
rotate each instance as indicated and then use the
Object Inspector to position each instance as indicated. Then double-click each symbol in turn and assign
the correct Instance Names:

Instance Name	Degree of Rotation	X,Y Positions
Up		
UpRight	45	−7.1, −30
Right	90	−1, −13
DownRight	135	−7.8, 9.9
Down	180	−11.1, −9.9
DownLeft	225	−28, −9.9
Left	270	−28.4, 13.1
UpLeft	315	27.3, −30.1

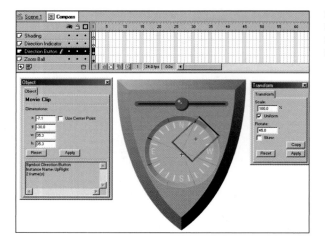

Use the Transform and Object
Inspectors to position each
instance of the Direction
Button Movie Clip.

CREATING THE DIRECTION INDICATOR

In this section, you set up an instance of the Direction Indicator Movie Clip. The Direction Indicator contains a series of labeled keyframes with a red point facing in each of the eight possible directions.

1   Select the Direction Indicator layer, drag an instance of the Direction Indicator Movie Clip from the Movie Clips folder onto the Stage, and position the instance at x: **−6**, y: **−25**.

2   Double-click the Direction Indicator instance and name it **Direction**.

    Naming the instance enables the symbol to be manipulated with **Tell Target** statements to display the current direction.

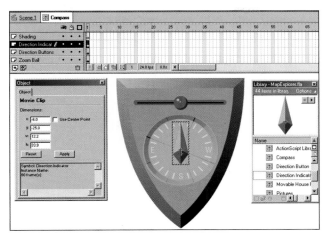

Position the Direction Indicator Movie Clip on the Direction Indicator layer.

FINALIZING THE COMPASS

The final touch is a graphic that gives the appearance of glass atop the compass face. You use the Highlight Shading and Black shading symbols to complete the process.

1   Select the Shading layer, drag an instance of the Highlight Shading symbol in the Vector Graphics folder onto the Stage, and position it at x: **−15**, y: **−18**.

2   Double-click on the Highlight Shading symbol instance and change the Alpha to **50%**.

3   Drag an instance of the Black Shading symbol from the Vector Graphics folder onto the Stage and position the instance at x: **−19.4**, y: **−22.2**.

4   Double-click on the Black Shading symbol instance and change the Alpha to **50%**.

5   Exit symbol-editing mode, return to Scene 1, double-click the Compass symbol, and name the instance **Compass**.

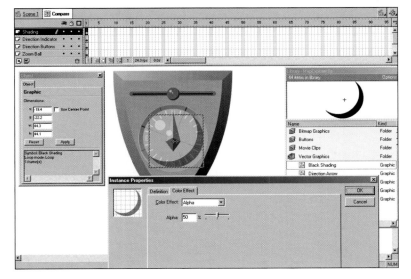

Set up the Highlight Shading and the Black Shading graphic symbols on the Shading layer.

QUIET! WORKING IN THE LIBRARY

The last step in building the Map Explorer is to create the Library of reusable ActionScript routines that zooms and scrolls the house plan. One of the variables set by the Initialize keyframe is **MasterStep**. **MasterStep** acts as a throttle, controlling how quickly the house plan can be scrolled vertically and horizontally. This value is used in the other scripts when calculating new position data, so increasing or decreasing the value of **MasterStep** has a cascading effect, causing the scrolling to be faster or slower.

1 Select the ActionScript Library layer, ensure that nothing on the Stage is selected, and create a new empty Movie Clip symbol, naming it **ActionScript Library**.

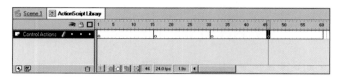

Name the Control Actions layer in the ActionScript Library Movie and set up its frames and keyframes.

2 In the symbol–editing mode of the ActionScript Library, name the existing layer **Control Actions**, insert an additional 59 frames (making a total of 60), and insert keyframes at frames 16, 31, and 46.

3 Double-click keyframe 1, label it **Initialize**, and assign the ActionScript.

```
Stop
Set Variable: "MasterStep" = 5
```

4 Double-click keyframe 16, label it **GoDirection**, and, on the Actions tab, assign the ActionScript.

This and the following scripts draw on global variables set by buttons on the compass. When you set out scripts in this way, debugging is much easier because all the actions are located in a central location rather than dispersed throughout various layers and symbols.

```
Begin Tell Target ("/Compass/Direction")
    Go to and Stop (/:Direction)
End Tell Target
If (/:Direction eq "Up")
    Set Variable: "Xstep" = 0
    Set Variable: "Ystep" = 0 + MasterStep
Else If (/:Direction eq "UpRight")
    Set Variable: "Xstep" = 0 - MasterStep
    Set Variable: "Ystep" = 0 + MasterStep
Else If (/:Direction eq "Right")
    Set Variable: "Xstep" = 0 - MasterStep
    Set Variable: "Ystep" = 0
```

```
Else If (/:Direction eq "DownRight")
    Set Variable: "Xstep" = 0 - MasterStep
    Set Variable: "Ystep" = 0 - MasterStep
Else If (/:Direction eq "Down")
    Set Variable: "Xstep" = 0
    Set Variable: "Ystep" = 0 - MasterStep
Else If (/:Direction eq "DownLeft")
    Set Variable: "Xstep" = 0 + MasterStep
    Set Variable: "Ystep" = 0 - MasterStep
Else If (/:Direction eq "Left")
    Set Variable: "Xstep" = 0 + MasterStep
    Set Variable: "Ystep" = 0
Else If (/:Direction eq "UpLeft")
    Set Variable: "Xstep" = 0 + MasterStep
    Set Variable: "Ystep" = 0 + MasterStep
End If
Set Property ("/HousePlan", X Position) = GetProperty( "/HousePlan",_x ) + Xstep
Set Property ("/HousePlan", Y Position) = GetProperty( "/HousePlan",_y ) + Ystep
```

5 Double-click keyframe 31, label it **ShowDirection**, and assign the ActionScript.

```
Begin Tell Target ("/Compass/Direction")
    Go to and Stop (/:Direction)
End Tell Target
```

6 Double-click keyframe 46, label it **DoZoom**, and assign the ActionScript.

7 Exit symbol-editing mode to return to the main Timeline.

```
Set Property ("/HousePlan", X Scale) = /:ZoomFactor
Set Property ("/HousePlan", Y Scale) = /:ZoomFactor
```

8 Select the ActionScript Library layer, drag an instance of ActionScript Library from your movie's Library and place it anywhere on the Stage, double-click the small white dot (indicating a symbol with an empty first keyframe), and name the instance **Library**.

You now have a completely functional interactive house plan. Apart from the concept and structure of the Map Explorer itself, you've also learned a number of useful techniques in this project. Continuous feedback buttons, draggable sliders, reusable button symbols, and an ActionScript Library are all invaluable tools for creating Flash applications, games, and interfaces.

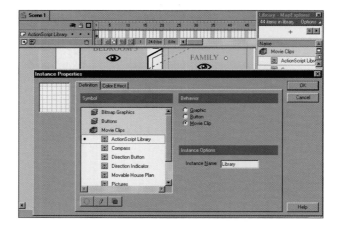

Name the ActionScript Library Movie Clip instance.

HOW IT WORKS

The Map Explorer project revolves around the capability to set particular properties of a Movie Clip symbol instance. In this case, you're setting the scale and position properties, but you could also set rotation, opacity, and visibility.

The "compass" device has two main inputs, the zoom ball and the direction indicator. Both enable the user to alter the scale or position properties of the house plan image. When the user clicks the direction buttons or zoom ball, a script is run that takes the current position of the house plan and adjusts it accordingly.

MODIFICATIONS

Now that you have a working house plan, experiment with different subjects:

- Geographical maps
- Portfolios
- A Web site menu
- A simple game

Have fun and remember—the major limitation in using Flash is your imagination.

ONLINE BOOK SEARCH

"A great many people think

they are thinking when

they are merely rearranging

their prejudices."

—WILLIAM JAMES

BUILDING A SEARCH ENGINE WITH FLASH

You can create an interface to point readers to

specific URLs. This project creates an interface

to help promote your favorite books on a par-

ticular subject or by a certain author.

BOOK FINDER

Layers
Top Picks
Search Box
Buttons
Background

GETTING STARTED

If you want your results to match those of the finished project, follow the steps carefully. If you want to customize the project and are familiar with Flash 4, feel free to
change the settings to those that meet your needs. Remember, too, that the finished
file is on the Flash 4 Magic CD. Refer to it if you need to.

1   Begin with a new Flash movie, using these settings:

Frame rate:	**24 fps**
Stage dimensions:	**210 × 350**
Background color:	**White**

2   Create four layers, naming them (from top to
    bottom) **Top Picks, Search Box, Buttons**,
    and **Background**.

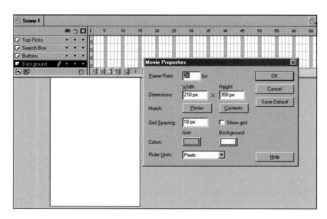

Set up the new movie file.

3 From the Flash 4 Magic CD, load BookFinder.fla as a Library and then select the Background layer.

4 In the BookFinder.fla Library, locate the Book Finder Interface graphic symbol in the Vector Graphics folder, drag an instance onto the Stage, and center it vertically and horizontally to the Stage.

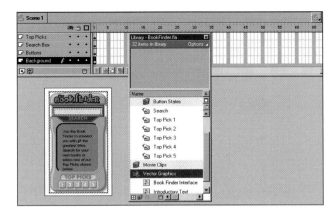

Instance the Book Finder Interface graphic symbol and align it on the Stage.

CREATE THE SEARCH INTERFACE

The Book Finder works by interfacing with existing server-side scripts. It demonstrates the process of taking a standard HTML form and turning it into something more attractive and easy to use. There are, however, some caveats in leveraging existing CGI systems. To operate, this movie passes variables to the server in a way similar to clicking the Submit button on an HTML form.

The problem arises when the variable names used by the server contain characters not allowed in Flash variable names. For example, hyphens are illegal characters in Flash variable names. You can test the validity of your variable names by entering them in the Name field of the Text Field Properties dialog box and clicking OK. Flash tests the variable name before assigning it and warns you of any errors.

1 Select the Search Box layer, select the Text tool, and set these text attributes:

Font: _sans
Font Size: 12pt
Text Color: black

2 Click the Text Field button and draw out an editable text field in the space provided on the interface graphic.

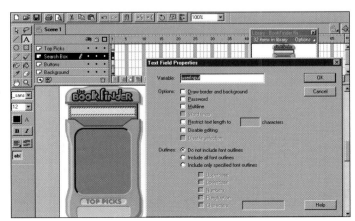

Create the text field and set its properties.

3 Open the Text Field Properties dialog box and set
the following options for the text field:

Variable:	**userInput**
Options:	Deselect Draw border and background
Outlines:	Select Do not include outlines

Remember that the variable names must be those
allowed in Flash variable names.

4 Select the Buttons layer and then select the Search
Button in the Button States folder in the Library.

5 Drag an instance of the Search Button onto the
Stage, positioning the button just below the Search
text field.

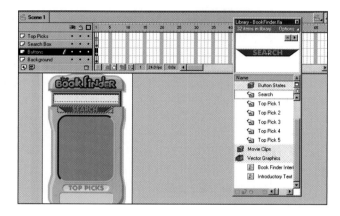

Position the Search Button
below the text.

6 With only the Search Button selected, select Instance
from the Modify menu to open the Instance
Properties dialog box, and on the Actions tab, assign
the ActionScript.

The variable **Choice** in the **Set Variable** action is
part of the Barnes and Noble quick-search script.
Before passing your search string to the server script,
set **Choice** to **K** to denote that you are searching
for keywords.

```
On (Release)
    Set Variable: "choice" = "K"
    Get URL ("http://www.barnesandnoble.com/include/rdnav/q_search_redirect.asp", vars=POST)
End On
```

CREATING THE TOP PICKS MOVIE CLIP

The Book Finder includes a Top Picks Movie Clip. This Movie Clip will contain six "slides," including some initial text and then images of the five Top Picks book covers. Similar to presets on a car radio, the Top Picks are buttons that link directly to pages at the Barnes and Noble Web site. From there, visitors can read more about the book and perhaps buy a copy.

1   Ensure that no objects are selected, and create a new empty Movie Clip symbol named Top Picks.

    After you have created the Top Picks Movie Clip symbol, Flash switches to symbol-editing view.

2   In the symbol-editing view of Top Picks, create three layers, naming them (from top to bottom) **Book Buttons**, **Control Actions**, and **Text/Images**.

3   Select all the layers and insert 59 blank frames.

    You'll be using frame labels to distinguish each of six "slide" sections, so be sure to leave some space for these.

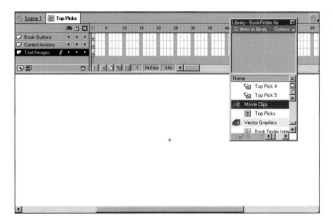

Create a new Top Picks Movie Clip that has three new layers.

ADDING THE BOOK COVER IMAGES

In this section, you set up the introductory text and place the book cover images on the Stage. The images are in the Bitmap Graphics folder.

1   Select the Text/Images layer, drag an instance of the Introductory Text graphic symbol in the Vector Graphics folder onto the Stage, and center the instance over the reference point crosshairs.

2   In the Text/Images layer, insert blank keyframes at the following frames on the Timeline: 2, 11, 21, 31, 41, and 51.

    These numbers are arbitrary, but they allow for the frame labels to fit in legibly.

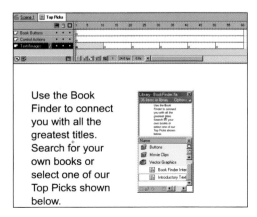

Instance the Introductory Text graphic symbol and insert keyframes.

3 In the Text/Images layer, drag an instance of each book's cover image from the Bitmap Images folder onto the Stage, starting at keyframe 11 (one cover on frame 11, another on frame 21, and so on). Insert the book cover images in the following order:

Effective Web Animation
Computer Graphics Industry Reference
Inside Photoshop 5
Designing Web Graphics 3
Digital Character Animation 2

Don't be too concerned with exact placement; you will position them correctly later.

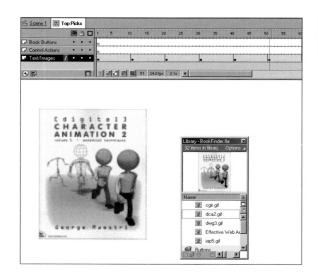

Instance the book cover images in the Text/Images layer.

ADDING ACTIONS TO THE TOP PICKS MOVIE CLIP

The purpose of the Top Picks Movie Clip symbol is not to run as a continuous animation, but rather to be like a stack of index cards that are reshuffled as the user clicks on the preset buttons. You'll be assigning frame labels and **Stop** actions in the Control Actions layer so that the "slides" will show only when requested.

1 Select the Control Actions layer and insert blank keyframes at frames 11, 21, 31, 41, and 51.

2 On each of the six blank keyframes on this layer, open the Frame Properties dialog box, assign a **Stop** action to each keyframe, and then assign the following labels:

Keyframe 1:	**Intro**
Keyframe 11:	**Top Pick 1**
Keyframe 21:	**Top Pick 2**
Keyframe 31:	**Top Pick 3**
Keyframe 41:	**Top Pick 4**
Keyframe 51:	**Top Pick 5**

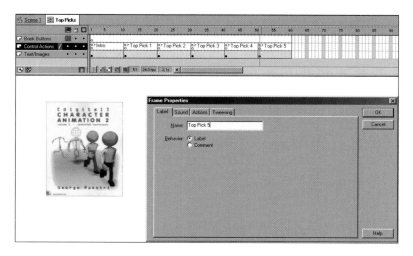

Add **Stop** actions and labels to all the keyframes on the Control Actions layer.

ADDING THE BUTTONS

Now that the book covers are set up, you need to add buttons the user can click for more information. To save on file size, use a single button and assign different actions in each keyframe.

1 Select the Book Buttons layer and add a blank keyframe at frame 11.

Don't add the others just yet—you'll be setting up one button and then duplicating it.

2 Drag an instance of the Book Button symbol in the Buttons folder onto the Stage, roughly centered over the book cover image on the Stage.

The Book Button symbol is an invisible button.

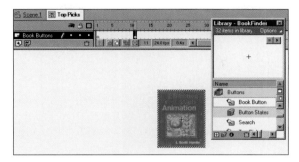

Instance the invisible Book Button symbol and center it over the book cover image.

3 Select the Book Button instance you just created, open the Instance Properties dialog box, and, on the Actions tab, assign the ActionScript.

Notice the **isbn=** part at the end? This is where you will insert the ISBN numbers for each of the five Top Pick books. The script described in the URL uses the number supplied to display the correct book information. Leave the ISBN blank for now; you will duplicate this keyframe and then add the numbers afterward.

```
On (Release)
    Get URL ("http://shop.barnesandnoble.com/booksearch
        /isbnInquiry.asp?isbn=")
End On
```

4 Close the Instance Properties dialog box, select the keyframe containing the Book Button you edited in step 3, copy the frame, and then paste a copy at keyframes 21, 31, 41, and 51.

Copy frame 11 and paste it at the four other keyframes.

5 Edit the Instance Properties of all five buttons, adding the following ISBNs to the URL, following **isbn=**.

Keyframe 11 Effective Web Animation	**0201606003**
Keyframe 21 CG101: Computer Graphics Industry Reference	**073570046X**
Keyframe 31 Inside Photoshop 5	**1562058843**
Keyframe 41 Designing Web Graphics 3	**15620679491**
Keyframe 51 Digital Character Animation 2	**1562069300**

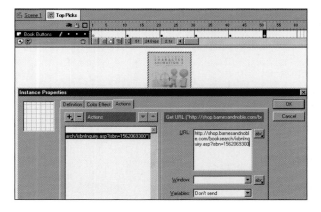

Change the ISBNs in the ActionScript.

6 To make sure that all buttons, book covers, and text are centered and positioned neatly, click the Edit Multiple Frame button and then drag the Start Onion Skin and End Onion Skin markers until all 60 frames are selected.

You will apply this operation to all of the layers within the Top Picks Movie Clip symbol Timeline.

7 Use the Select All command to select all objects; align them vertically, horizontally, and to the page; and then click the Edit Multiple Frame button once again to turn that feature off.

8 Exit symbol editing-mode and return to Scene 1.

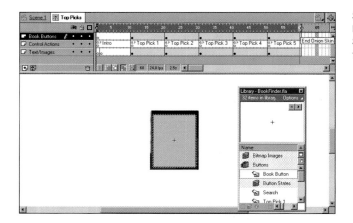

Select the Edit Multiple Frame button and drag the Onion Skin markers on the Timeline to encompass the frames.

INSTANCING THE TOP PICKS MOVIE CLIP

In this section, be sure to work with your own movie's Library, not the Bookfinder.fla Library. You use your new Top Picks Movie Clip to create an instance.

1 Open your own movie's Library, select the Top Picks layer, drag an instance of the Top Picks Movie Clip symbol you just created onto the Stage, and position it so that the Introductory Text is centered evenly in the large blue window on the interface.

To be able to assign **Tell Target** actions to the Top Picks Movie Clip symbol, you need to give the instance a name—that is your next step.

2 Select the Top Picks Movie Clip symbol on the Stage and name the instance **Top Picks** in the Instance Properties dialog box.

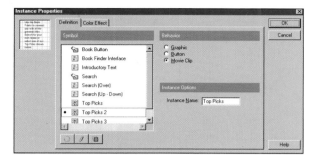

Instance the Top Picks and assign it an Instance Name.

CREATING THE ROW OF PRESET BUTTONS

The Top Picks are all set up and wired for **Tell Target** control. Now the only remaining task is to create the row of preset buttons. You might want to zoom in on the instances so you can see their positions better. Don't forget that you can use the Object Inspector to set the y-axis of one button and then use that same axis setting for all of the others.

1 Select the Buttons layer, drag an instance of each of the five Top Pick buttons in the Buttons folder onto the Stage, and position them in a row.

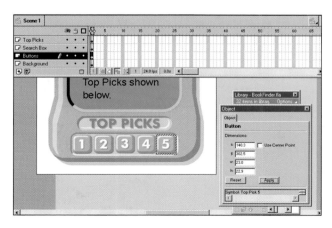

Use the Object Inspector for aligning multiple objects on the screen.

2 Select the Top Pick 1 button and, on the Actions tab, assign the ActionScript.

Note that in the **Go to and Stop** action, Top Pick 1 is a label name and not a frame number.

3 Repeat step 2 for each Top Pick button, substituting the correct number for the corresponding Top Pick button.

```
On (Release)
    Begin Tell Target ("/Top Picks")
        Go to and Stop ("Top Pick 1")
    End Tell Target
End On
```

FINISHING TOUCHES

To save download time, each of the book cover bitmaps is set to export in JPEG format at the compression level set in the document's publish settings. Depending on the book covers used and level of optimization required, you can use the Library Properties dialog box to individually set and test the format and compression settings of each image.

To edit the properties of an individual bitmap object, double-click its icon in the Library, or select it and choose Properties from the Library's Options menu. In the Properties dialog box, you can choose the appropriate compression method. For photographics, either JPEG or PNG will perform well, whereas GIF/PNG format is best suited to line art or images containing continuous block color.

In the example file, the JPEG compression level for the movie is 75% to cut down on file size while retaining moderate image quality.

Use the Library Properties dialog box to preview the effects of the default JPEG compression on your bitmap images.

How It Works

This application has two distinct parts: the Book Search and the Top Picks. Book Search works by taking some user input (the search text) and then passing it and other variables to a server-side script. The server sends back a Web page of results in return.

Top Picks uses a Movie Clip symbol to act as a slideshow controlled by an array of buttons that correspond to the various slides. When a user clicks one of the Top Pick buttons, a book cover appears with an invisible button on top. When the user clicks the book cover, a server-side script is called and a resultant Web page displayed in the browser.

Modifications

The Book Finder application is a great way to link to books on sites such as Barnes and Noble or Amazon.com, but plenty of other excellent e-commerce affiliate programs are on the Web for which you could use a variation of the BookFinder. The Search and Top Picks features can easily be used to reference a variety of products, including software, electronics, and health products.

By using a Flash interface as opposed to traditional HTML, you can place an attractive, compact "store" on each page of your Web site. That way, users never have to change locations to view your selection of products.

PRODUCT CATALOG

"He who dies with

the most toys, is,

nonetheless, still dead."

—ANONYMOUS

BUILDING A SCALABLE APPLICATION FOR PRODUCT DEMONSTRATIONS

One of the most popular uses of multimedia on the Web is for product demonstrations prior to sale. By taking advantage of Flash's modular downloading and scripting features, you can create a scalable, robust Product Catalog application. The Product Catalog incorporates a wide range of techniques, including scrolling text fields and reusable interface elements.

PROJECT 11:
PRODUCT CATALOG

Layers
ActionScript Library
View Port
Text
Scrollbars
Buttons
Background

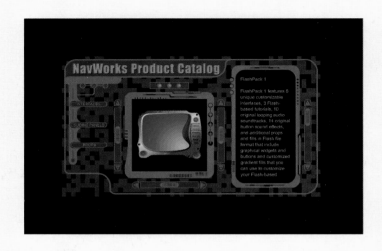

GETTING STARTED

If you want your results to match those of the finished project, follow the steps carefully. If you want to customize the project and are familiar with Flash 4, feel free to change the settings to those that meet your needs.

1 Copy all the .swf files from the
ProductCatalog\ProductFiles folder into the folder on your hard disk in which you'll be working.

Flash loads these .swf files into the catalog; they are essential for testing purposes.

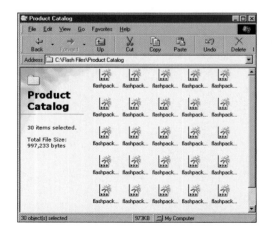

Copy all the .swf files from the ProductCatalog\ProductFiles folder into a folder on your hard disk.

2 Begin with a new Flash Movie, using these settings:

Frame rate:	**24 fps**
Stage dimensions:	**550 × 310**
Background color:	**Black**

3 Set up six layers, naming them (from top to bottom) **ActionScript Library**, **View Port**, **Text**, **Scrollbars**, **Buttons**, and **Background**.

4 From the Flash 4 Magic CD, load ProductCatalog.fla as a Library.

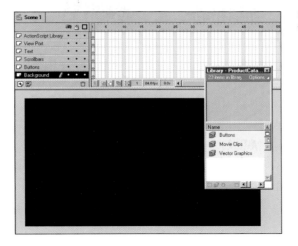

Load the ProductCatalog.fla file as a Library.

5 Select the Background layer, drag an instance of the Background graphic symbol from the Vector Graphics folder onto the Stage, center the instance on the Stage. If you want, you can lock the Background layer. You won't be dealing with it again in this project.

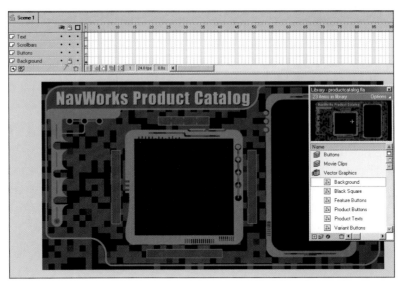

Center the Background graphic symbol on the Background layer.

LAYING OUT THE PRODUCT BUTTONS

While Product Buttons is a graphic symbol, it is in fact a group of three buttons. Each of the three buttons represents a product that visitors can view when they click the appropriate button in the catalog.

1   Select the Buttons layer and drag an instance of the Product Buttons symbol in the Vector Graphics folder onto the Stage.

2   Select your instance of Product Buttons and use the Object Inspector to set the coordinates to x: **41.8**, y: **61.1**.

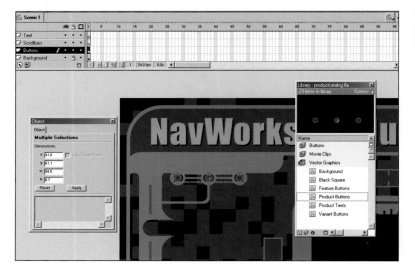

Use the Object Inspector to position the Product Buttons instance.

3   Enter the symbol-editing mode for the Product Buttons graphic symbol instance, select the far left button (FlashPack 1 Button), double-click to open its Instance Properties dialog box, and, on the Actions tab, assign the ActionScript.

> **Note:** To enter the symbol-editing mode, right-click (Windows) or Control-click (Macintosh) on the instance, and choose Edit from the pop-up menu.

The script sets the current product to FlashPack 1, loads the corresponding product text into the text area, and scrolls it to the top. The **.scroll** property of the text field named Text enables your text scroller, but more on that later. The script also sets the x-position of the text scroll handle to **0**. This is

```
On (Release)
    Set Variable: "Product" = "flashpack1"
    Set Variable: "Text" = FlashPack1Text
    Set Variable: "Text.scroll" = 1
    Set Property ("/TextScroll/ScrollHandle", X Position) = 0
    Call ("/Library/:LoadView")
End On
```

necessary because the product text might have changed and therefore is scrolled to the top for convenience. Finally, the button calls the **LoadView** function, which loads the current product's picture into the main viewer.

4   Double-click the FlashPack 2 Button to open the Instance Properties dialog box and, on the Actions tab, assign the ActionScript.

```
On (Release)
    Set Variable: "Product" = "flashpack2"
    Set Variable: "Text" = FlashPack2Text
    Set Variable: "Text.scroll" = 1
    Set Property ("/TextScroll/ScrollHandle", X Position) = 0
    Call ("/Library/:LoadView")
End On
```

5   Double-click the FlashPack 3 Button symbol to open the Properties dialog box and, on the Actions tab, assign the ActionScript.

You'll notice that each script is identical except for the **Product** and **Text** values.

6   Exit symbol-editing mode and return to Scene 1.

```
On (Release)
    Set Variable: "Product" = "flashpack3"
    Set Variable: "Text" = FlashPack3Text
    Set Variable: "Text.scroll" = 1
    Set Property ("/TextScroll/ScrollHandle", X Position) = 0
    Call ("/Library/:LoadView")
End On
```

SETTING UP THE FEATURE BUTTONS

Each product has three different features: interfaces, sliding panels, and props. In turn, each feature has three variations to give the user a good idea of what each product includes.

As with the Product Buttons graphic symbol, the Feature Buttons graphic symbol contains nested buttons to make positioning the buttons easier. This time around, you set the value of the currently selected Feature and then call the **LoadView** function to display the appropriate image.

1 Select the Buttons layer, drag an instance of the Feature Buttons graphic symbol from the Vector Graphics folder onto the Stage, and use the Object Inspector to position the instance at x: **20.0**, y: **100.0**.

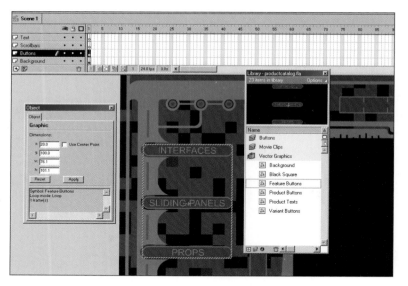

Use the Object Inspector to position the Feature Buttons graphic symbol.

2 Open the Instance Properties dialog box of the Interfaces Button and, on the Actions tab, assign the ActionScript.

```
On (Release)
    Set Variable: "Feature" = "interface"
    Call ("/Library/:LoadView")
End On
```

3 Open the Instance Properties dialog box of the Sliding Panels Button symbol, and, on the Actions tab, assign the ActionScript.

```
On (Release)
    Set Variable: "Feature" = "slidingpanel"
    Call ("/Library/:LoadView")
End On
```

4 Open the Instance Properties dialog boy of the Sliding Props Button symbol, and, on the Actions tab, assign the ActionScript.

5 Exit symbol–editing mode and return to Scene 1.

```
On (Release)
    Set Variable: "Feature" = "props"
    Call ("/Library/:LoadView")
End On
```

SETTING UP THE VARIANT BUTTONS

The final set of buttons controls the current feature variation, or Variant.

1 On the Buttons layer, drag an instance of the Variant Buttons symbol from the Vector Graphics folder onto the Stage, and use the Object Inspector to position the symbol instance at x: **203.4**, y: **60.1**.

This time each button sets the value of **Variant** to either **1**, **2**, or **3** and then calls **LoadView** again to refresh the currently displayed picture.

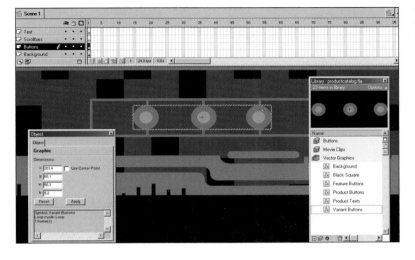

Use the Object Inspector to position the Variant Buttons symbol.

2 Open the Instance Properties dialog box of the Left Button symbol, and, on the Actions tab, assign the ActionScript.

```
On (Release)
    Set Variable: "Variant" = "1"
    Call ("/Library/:LoadView")
End On
```

3 Open the Instance Properties dialog box of the Middle Button symbol, and, on the Actions tab, assign the ActionScript.

```
On (Release)
    Set Variable: "Variant" = "2"
    Call ("/Library/:LoadView")
End On
```

4 Open the Instance Properties dialog box of the Right Button symbol, and, on the Actions tab, assign the ActionScript.

5 Exit symbol-editing mode and return to Scene 1.

```
On (Release)
    Set Variable: "Variant" = "3"
    Call ("/Library/:LoadView")
End On
```

SETTING UP THE SCROLLBARS MOVIE CLIP

As always, you should be on the lookout for elements in your movies that can be reused as instances of a single symbol instead of wasting precious file size with unnecessary bloat. In this case, you use the identical Scroll Bar symbol four times, performing four completely different functions.

1 Select the Scrollbars layer and drag four instances of the Scrollbar Movie Clip from the Movie Clips folder onto the Stage.

You'll name and position each instance and then edit the symbol to activate it.

2 Double-click an instance of Scrollbar, name the instance **Zoom**, and position and rotate it:

Object Inspector:	x: **112.1**
	y: **95.1**
Transform Inspector>Rotate:	**-90.0**

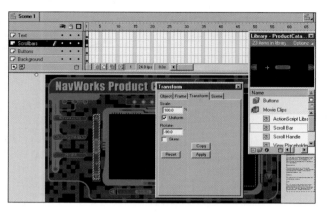

Name one of the Scrollbar instances Zoom and use the Transform Inspector to rotate it and the Object Inspector to position it.

3 Double-click another instance of Scrollbar, name the instance **ScrollX**, and position and rotate it:

Object Inspector:	x: **149.8**
	y: **276.9**
Transform Inspector>Rotate:	**0.0**

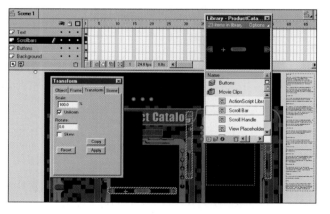

Name one of the other Scrollbar instances and rotate and position it.

4 Double-click another instance of Scrollbar, name the instance **ScrollY**, and, using inspectors, position and rotate it:

Object Inspector: x: **331.8**
                           y: **94.8**

Transform Inspector>Rotate: **90.0**

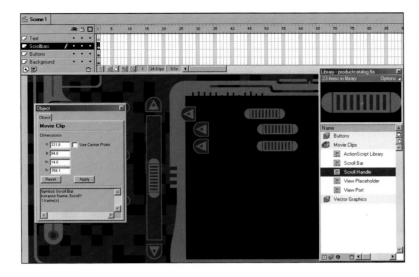

Name another Scrollbar instance and rotate and position it.

5 Double-click another instance of Scrollbar, name the instance **TextScroll**, and, using inspectors, position and rotate it:

Object Inspector: x: **515.8**
                           y: **94.8**

Transform Inspector>Rotate: **90.0**

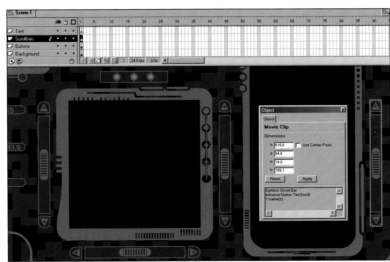

Name the fourth instance TextScroll and rotate and position it, using the inspectors.

EDITING THE SCROLLBAR

The Scroll Bar symbol consists of two scroll buttons and a middle "scroll handle" that is, in fact, a button nested within a Movie Clip. The Scrollbar works when users click the left or right buttons, or drag the scroll handle. Flash then uses the x coordinate information of the scroll handle to adjust the view, including zooming, scrolling, and text-scrolling.

1 Open your movie's Library and double-click the Scroll Bar symbol's icon to edit it.

Edit the Scroll Bar symbol to observe that it is made up of three components: two scroll buttons with a scroll handle between them.

2 Double-click the left button to open the Properties dialog box and, on the Actions tab, assign the following ActionScript statements to adjust the scroll handle's position:

This script checks to see if the scroll handle is within 5 pixels of the left end of the bar, and repositions it accordingly.

```
On (Release)
    If (GetProperty("ScrollHandle",_x) > 0)
        If (GetProperty("ScrollHandle",_x) > 5)
            Set Property ("ScrollHandle", X Position) =
                GetProperty("ScrollHandle",_x) - 5
        Else
            Set Property ("ScrollHandle", X Position) = 0
        End If
    End If
    Call ("/Library/:AdjustView")
End On
```

3 Double-click the other scroll button (to the far right) to open the Properties dialog box and, on the Actions tab, assign this complementary set of ActionScript statements:

This script is identical to the first except it moves the scroll handle right instead of left.

```
On (Release)
    If (GetProperty("ScrollHandle",_x) < 80)
        If (GetProperty("ScrollHandle",_x) < 75)
            Set Property ("ScrollHandle", X Position) =
                GetProperty("ScrollHandle",_x) + 5
        Else
            Set Property ("ScrollHandle", X Position) = 80
        End If
    End If
    Call ("/Library/:AdjustView")
End On
```

4 To enable the scroll handle itself, select the Scroll Handle symbol, name the instance **ScrollHandle**, right-click the symbol, and choose Edit in Place to access the symbol's contents.

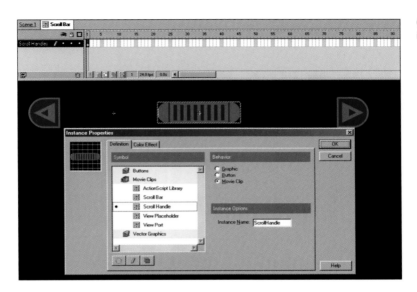

Give the scroll handle an instance name.

5 Select the Scroll Handle Button layer, double-click the instance of Scroll Handle Button on the Stage, and, on the Actions tab, assign the ActionScript.

As mentioned earlier, the Scroll Handle button allows the scroll handle to be draggable. Its positioning information is then used by the **AdjustView** function to set the zooming and scrolling of the product viewer and text area.

```
On (Press)
    Start Drag ("", L=0, T=0, R=80, B=0)
End On
On (Release, Release Outside, Drag Out)
    Stop Drag
    Call ("/Library/:AdjustView")
End On
```

6 Exit symbol-editing mode and return to the main Timeline.

CREATING THE TEXT AREA

Each product in the Product Catalog can have a block of accompanying text displayed to the right of the picture viewport. By taking advantage of the **.maxscroll** and **.scroll** properties of text fields, you can easily implement a scrollable text box.

First of all, you need the blocks of text for each product. The simplest way to do this is to have three separate text fields that sit offstage, storing all the data. Then, using

ActionScript, you can transfer the appropriate data into the main text box when a new product is selected.

In the Vector Graphics folder of ProductCatalog.fla, you'll find a symbol named Product Texts. This symbol contains three text fields: FlashPack1Text, FlashPack2Text and FlashPack3Text. The fields have been shrunk to make them more manageable.

1 To plug the data into your movie, select the Text layer and drag an instance of Product Texts off to the right of the Stage where it won't be seen.

The last text element required is the actual display field. You're going to set up its text properties.

These properties enable the text field to display data, be scrollable, and display consistently across platforms. Because you disabled editing but left selection enabled, users can copy and paste text about each product into an e-mail message or word processing document.

Drag an instance of the Product Texts symbol onto the Stage, but out of view.

2 Select the Text tool and set the following text properties, making certain that the Text Field modifier is selected:

Font: _sans
Font Size: 10 pt
Color: R: **0**, G: **153**, B: **255**

Selecting the Text Field modifier creates a text field, not a static text box.

3 Draw out your text field over the far right black section of the interface.

Your field should be approximately 225 pixels high and 113 pixels wide.

Place a text field over the large black area on the right side of the background.

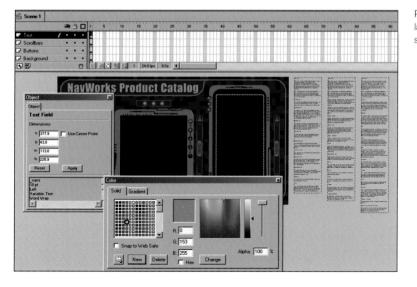

4 Select the Arrow tool, select your text field, open the Text Field Properties dialog box, and set the following properties:

Variable: **Text**

Selected Options: Multiline

Word Wrap

Disable Editing

Include All Font Outlines

Edit the properties of the text field as shown.

WORKING WITH THE VIEW PORT

The Product Catalog relies heavily on the **Load Movie** action. In other examples, you loaded additional .swf files into different levels, creating a stack of movies. You can also replace any Movie Clip target with the loaded movie, which is precisely what you'll be doing here. The View Port consists of a Movie Clip symbol containing a mask layer, on which you use **Load Movie** to replace the masked object (another Movie Clip) with the currently selected picture. Sound confusing? Don't worry, you'll get the hang of it.

1 Select the View Port layer, drag an instance of the View Port Movie Clip from the Movie Clips folder onto the Stage, position the instance at x: **149.0,** y: **94.2,** double-click the instance, and name the instance **ViewPort**.

2 Use Edit in Place to access the contents of ViewPort.

Inside, notice the two displaced black squares. The top left square is the symbol that will be replaced by the loaded pictures. It's a peculiarity of Flash that the loaded movie inherits the scale, position, and rotation of whatever symbol it's replacing; hence, the View Placeholder's center point is the top left corner of the masking square.

3 Double-click View Placeholder and name the instance **View**.

The point of using mask layers here is that the View instance can be zoomed and scrolled. By having a square mask, you can constrain the visible portion of the current picture.

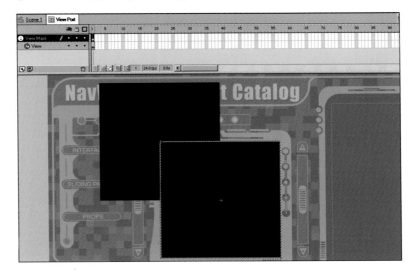

Use Edit in Place to view the contents of the ViewPort instance.

4 To enable the masking, select the View Mask layer, double-click the View Mask layer symbol to edit its Layer Properties, and set the Type property to Mask.

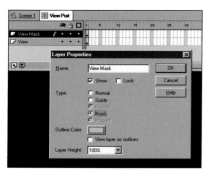

Use Layer Properties to change the View Mask layer's type to Mask.

5 Select the View layer, edit the Layer properties of the View layer, and set Type to Masked.

This completes the masking effect. Now only the parts of View covered by the View Mask will be visible to the user.

6 Exit symbol-editing mode.

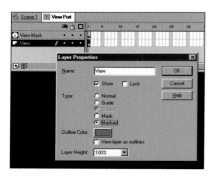

Use Layer Properties to change the View layer Type to Masked.

BUILDING THE ACTIONSCRIPT LIBRARY

In this application, the ActionScript Library symbol contains three functions: Initialize, AdjustView, and LoadView. You've already set up the **Call** statements for these elsewhere in the movie, so type them in now—you're nearly finished.

1 Select the ActionScript Library layer, ensure that no objects are selected on the Stage, and create a new Movie Clip symbol, naming it **ActionScript Library**.

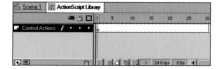

Name the layer in the ActionScript Library Movie Clip and add 29 frames to the layer.

2 In the symbol-editing mode of the ActionScript Library Movie Clip, name the existing layer **Control Actions** and insert an additional 29 frames, creating a total of 30.

3 Select keyframe 1, label the frame **Initialize**, open the Properties dialog box, and assign the ActionScript.

The Initialize script sets a number of key variables, including the current product, feature, and variant. It also loads the appropriate text and resets the text scroller before calling the LoadView and AdjustView keyframes.

```
Stop
FS Command ("AllowScale", False)
Set Variable: "/:Product" = "flashpack1"
Set Variable: "/:Feature" = "interface"
Set Variable: "/:Variant" = "1"
Set Variable: "/:Text" = /:FlashPack1Text
Set Property ("/TextScroll/ScrollHandle", X Position) = 0
Call ("LoadView")
Call ("AdjustView")
```

4 Insert a blank keyframe at frame 11, label the frame **AdjustView**, open the Properties dialog box, and, on the Actions tab, assign the ActionScript.

AdjustView takes scroll-handle positioning information from each of the four Scrollbars in turn and sets the properties of **View** and **Text** accordingly. By getting the information from all four each time, you eliminate the need for separate scripts.

The next step is the grand finale—**LoadView**. **LoadView** is the simplest of the functions. It simply assembles a filename based on the current product, feature, and variant values and then loads the file into the \ViewPort\View location, thereby replacing the previous picture with the current one.

```
If (GetProperty("/Zoom/ScrollHandle",_x) > 0)
    Set Property ("/ViewPort/View", X Scale) = GetProperty("/Zoom/ScrollHandle",_x) * 2.5
    Set Property ("/ViewPort/View", Y Scale) = GetProperty("/Zoom/ScrollHandle",_x) * 2.5
Else
    Set Property ("/ViewPort/View", X Scale) = 5
    Set Property ("/ViewPort/View", Y Scale) = 5
End If
Set Property ("/ViewPort/View", X Position) = 80 - ((GetProperty("/ViewPort/View",
    _xscale) / 100) * (GetProperty("/ScrollX/ScrollHandle",_x) * 2))
Set Property ("/ViewPort/View", Y Position) = 80 - ((GetProperty("/ViewPort/View",
    _xscale) / 100) * (GetProperty("/ScrollY/ScrollHandle",_x) * 2))
Set Variable: "/:Text.scroll" = Int((/:Text.maxscroll / 80) *
GetProperty("/TextScroll/ScrollHandle",_x))
```

5 Insert a blank keyframe at frame 21, label the frame **LoadView**, open the Properties dialog box, and assign the ActionScript.

```
Load Movie (/:Product & "_" & /:Feature & /:Variant & ".swf", "/ViewPort/View")
```

How It Works

The Product Catalog works in two ways. First, it has a series of buttons that set the current product, feature, and variant. After storing this information in variables, the buttons cause the appropriate file to be loaded into the main viewer.

The main viewing area is simply a masked area containing the picture of the current product. By using a mask layer, you make only a set area visible to the user.

Last, there are the scrollbars. Each of these acts as a trigger, causing the picture and text views to be updated based on the positions of all four scroll handles. By capturing the position data of the scroll handles, it's possible to set the zoom, horizontal, and vertical scroll of the picture and vertical scrolling of the text.

Modifications

Well, that's the Product Catalog. But wait! There's one last thing left to explain: the picture files. At the beginning of this project, you made copies of a bunch of .swf files. These are the additional movies loaded by this particular example of the Product Catalog. Notice the naming scheme: product_featurevariant.swf. To build your own custom catalog, create a similar set of files using product and feature names appropriate to your situation. For example, if your first product were named Eggs and its first feature named Color, your corresponding .swf filenames for that product and feature would be

Eggs_Color1.swf
Eggs_Color2.swf
Eggs_Color3.swf

This naming information is set by the product, feature, and variant buttons and is a snap to change, making the Product Catalog a very flexible and versatile application indeed. Plus, because the pictures are downloaded "on demand" rather than all at once, the Product Catalog is perfect for delivery over slower connections.

E-COMMERCE

"Some cause happiness

wherever they go; others

whenever they go."

—OSCAR WILDE

BUILDING A SHOPPING CART IN FLASH

The E-Commerce project uses several new

features found in Flash 4 to create a complete

e-commerce Web site within a Flash movie.

In this example, five products display in differ-

ent slide-out drawers. Items to be purchased

can simply be dragged and dropped into the

shopping cart.

PROJECT 12:

THE SHOPPING CART

Layers
Products
Cart
Misc1

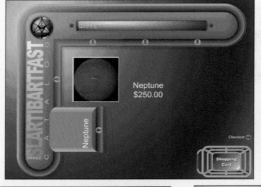
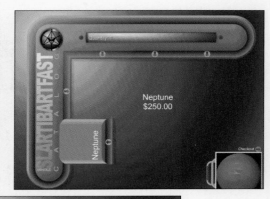

GETTING STARTED

You begin the project with NewCatalog.fla, a stripped-down version of the catalog, which contains just the interface, the drawers, and the navigation buttons. This means you don't have to align the drawers with the interface.

You might, however, appreciate a brief explanation of the working of the drawers. Each drawer is a Movie Clip with a **Stop** action and button in the first keyframe. When the user clicks a drawer button, a **Tell Target** statement indicates that the drawer is to open. The movie then goes to the corresponding keyframes, labeled 1 through 5, which contain displays for each product. Because another drawer could be open when this button is clicked, the ActionScript tells all the other drawers to close.

1 Open NewCatalog.fla from the Flash 4 Magic CD.

2 Insert three layers between the Overs and Body
layers, naming the new layers (from top to bottom)
Products, **Cart**, and **Misc1**.

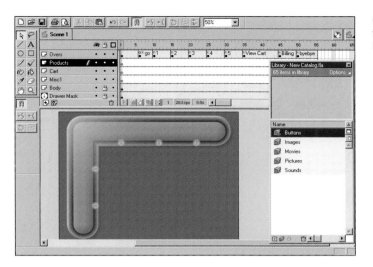

Open NewCatalog.fla and insert
three layers, naming them
Products, Cart, and Misc1.

SETTING UP THE PRODUCTS

In this section, you set up the five products: Earth, Jupiter, Mars, Neptune, and Saturn,
using the same process for each product. You begin by dragging an image onto the
Stage and converting it to a Button symbol. Then, you assign ActionScript to the button and convert the button to a Movie Clip.

1 In the Products layer, insert a keyframe at frame 10,
open the NewCatalogFin.fla Library, and drag an
instance of img_Earth.gif from the folder onto the
Stage, positioning it at x: **568** and y: **191.**

2 Press F8 to convert the instance into a Button
symbol, and name it **but_earth**.

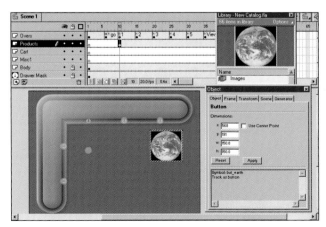

Insert a keyframe at frame
10 of the Products layer and
create a button, using
img_Earth.gif from the
Images folder.

145

3 Open the new button's Properties dialog box, and, on the Actions tab, assign the ActionScript.

The action inside **On (Press)** makes the button draggable. When the button is released, it is no longer draggable. If the product happens to be over the shopping cart when the button is released (determined by **_droptarget** and its following **If** statement), that product's count (**EarthCount** in the case of the Earth product) is increased by 1. The **Set Property** actions (X and Y position) move the product back from being dragged to the shopping cart. The **../cash Tell Target** plays a cash register sound file in the Cash Movie Clip.

```
On (Press)
    Start Drag ("")
End On
On (Release)
    Stop Drag
    Set Variable: "/:drop" = GetProperty("",_droptarget)
    If (/:drop eq "/cart")
        Set Variable: "/:EarthCount" = /:EarthCount + 1
        Set Property ("", X Position) = 643
        Set Property ("", Y Position) = 266
        Begin Tell Target ("../cash")
        Play
        End Tell Target
    End If
End On
```

4 Select the button on the Stage, press F8 to convert it to a Movie Clip, name the Movie Clip **mov_earth**, and name the instance **earth**.

Convert the button to a Movie Clip.

5 Insert blank keyframes at frames 15, 20, 25, and 30; drag an instance of each product image from the Images folder; and position the instances at the following coordinates:

Frame 15	img_Jupiter.gif	x: **220**	y: **191**
Frame 20	img_Mars.gif	x: **220**	y: **191**
Frame 25	img_Neptune.gif	x: **568**	y: **191**
Frame 30	img_Saturn.gif	x: **220**	y: **191**

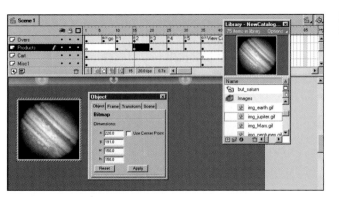

Instance each product image and position it.

6 Convert each image to a Button symbol, giving it a name that corresponds to its product name. For example, the button containing img_Jupiter.gif is **but_jupiter**.

7 Add the ActionScript commands from step 3 to each of the new buttons, modifying the **EarthCount** variable to reflect the name of the button (for example, **JupiterCount**) and the **Set Property** X and Y values to reflect the actual position of the button:

Jupiter	X: **295**	Y: **266**
Mars	X: **295**	Y: **266**
Neptune	X: **643**	Y: **266**
Saturn	X: **295**	Y: **266**

8 Convert each of the new buttons to a Movie Clip, substituting the appropriate product name for each instance name. For example, the name of the Movie Clip converted from the but_jupiter button is **mov_jupiter**, and its instance name is **jupiter**.

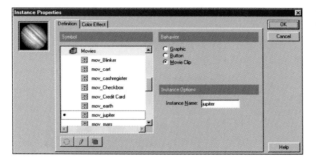

Convert each button to a Movie Clip.

SETTING UP THE CART

You don't have nearly as much work to do in the Cart layer. This layer contains the Movie Clip for the shopping cart that moves from the left to the right side of the Stage and sits there, waiting for products to be dragged to it.

1 Select frame 1 of the Cart layer, drag an instance of the mov_cart Movie Clip from the Movies folder onto the Stage, give it the instance name **cart**, and position it at x: **–115.2**, y: **488.5**.

2 Select frame 35 of the Cart layer and insert a blank keyframe.

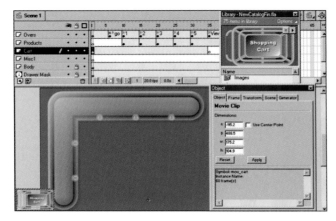

Instance the mov_cart Movie Clip and insert a blank keyframe.

CHECKING OUT

This project has a Checkout button that takes visitors to an invoice that tracks the items, quantities, prices, and totals of the purchase. In this section, you set up the Checkout button and the invoice.

1 Select frame 1 of the Misc1 layer, drag an instance of the but_checkout Button from the Buttons folder onto the Stage, and position the instance at x: **713.6**, y: **450.3.**

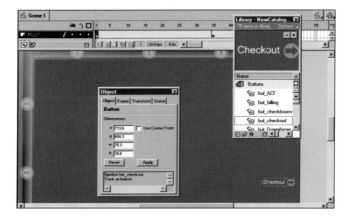

Instance the but_checkout Button.

2 Double-click the button to open its Properties dialog box, and, on the Actions tab, assign the ActionScript.

```
On (Release)
    Go to and Stop ("View Cart")
End On
```

3 Select the frame labeled View Cart and, on the Actions tab, assign the ActionScript.

```
Stop
Begin Tell Target ("/door2")
    Go to and Stop (1)
End Tell Target
Begin Tell Target ("/door3")
    Go to and Stop (1)
End Tell Target
Begin Tell Target ("/door4")
    Go to and Stop (1)
```

```
Stop
Begin Tell Target ("/door2")
    Go to and Stop (1)
End Tell Target
Begin Tell Target ("/door3")
    Go to and Stop (1)
End Tell Target
Begin Tell Target ("/door4")
    Go to and Stop (1)
End Tell Target
Begin Tell Target ("/door5")
    Go to and Stop (1)
End Tell Target
Begin Tell Target ("/door1")
    Go to and Stop (1)
End Tell Target
Set Variable: "SaturnTotal" = SaturnCount * 110
Set Variable: "MarsTotal" = MarsCount * 200
Set Variable: "EarthTotal" = EarthCount * 29.99
Set Variable: "JupiterTotal" = JupiterCount * 500
Set Variable: "NeptuneTotal" = NeptuneCount * 250
Set Variable: "subtotal" = SaturnTotal + MarsTotal + EarthTotal +
    JupiterTotal + NeptuneTotal
Set Variable: "GrandTotal" = Subtotal + 6.95 + Tax
```

4 In the Products layer, insert a blank keyframe at frame 35, drag an instance of pic_tables from the Pictures folder onto the Stage, and position the instance at x: **214.9**, y: **186.6**.

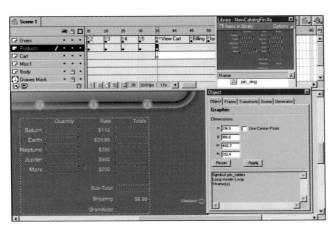

Add the pic_tables symbol to the Products layer.

149

SETTING UP THE BILLING SECTION

When the visitor clicks on the Billing button, the invoice shrinks and an area appears
for entering billing information. These are the elements you set up in this section.

1 In the Misc1 layer, insert a keyframe at frame 35, and
replace the instance of the Checkout button with one
of the but_billing button from the Buttons folder.

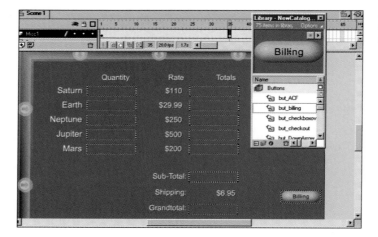

Replace the instance
of the Checkout button
with the but_billing button.

2 Double-click the but_billing Button to open its
Properties dialog box, and, on the Actions tab,
change the ActionScript.

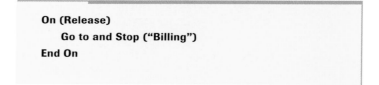

On (Release)
    Go to and Stop ("Billing")
End On

3 In the Products layer, insert a keyframe at frame 45
and drag an instance of the pic_billing symbol from
the Pictures folder onto the Stage, positioning it at x:
513.6, y: **178.5**.

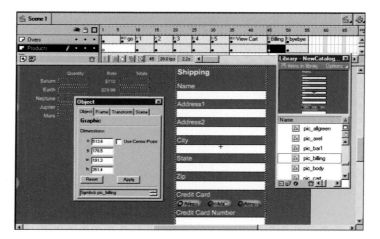

Add an instance of
the pic_billing symbol
to the Products layer.

150

4 Select the instance of the pic_tables symbol still on the Stage, and use the Object Inspector to resize the instance to w: **241.6**, h: **187.4**.

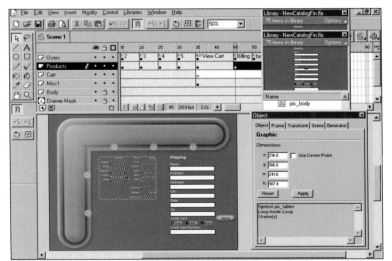

Resize the instance of the pic_tables symbol.

5 In the Misc1 layer, insert a blank keyframe at frame 45 and drag an instance of the but_order Button from the Buttons folder onto the Stage, positioning it below the instance of the pic_billing symbol in the Products layer.

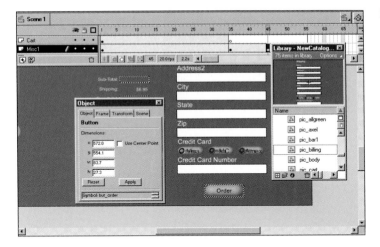

Instance the but_order Button.

6 Double-click the instance of the but_order Button to open its Properties dialog box, and, on the Actions tab, assign the ActionScript.

In the **Get URL** line, the **youraddress@your domain.com** should be your own email address.

> **On (Release)**
>   **Get URL ("mailto:youraddress@yourdomain.com",**
>   **vars=POST)**
>   **Go to and Stop ("byebye")**
> **End On**

ADDING THE FINISHING TOUCH

No order is complete until it is confirmed. In this section, you insert blank keyframes
and create a message confirming that orders have been processed.

1 In the Products layer, insert a blank keyframe
at frame 50.

2 In the Misc1 layer, insert a blank keyframe
at frame 50.

3 Select frame 50 of the Products layer and use the
Text tool to create a message telling your visitors
their orders have been sent.

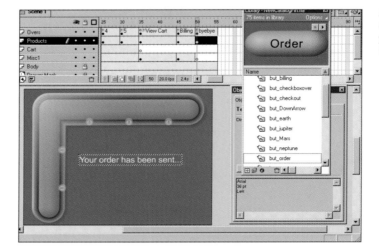

Add a message to frame 50
of the Products layer, telling
your customers their orders
have been sent.

HOW IT WORKS

When the Flash movie begins, the first frame has a **Stop** action. The shopping cart is
contained within its own movie, so it is not affected by this action, and the cart continues to roll out into place, even though the movie is stopped.

Keyframes labeled 1 through 5 are displays for each of the buttons. When the drawer
is shut, the movie jumps back to the Go keyframe. This happens because starting at
the beginning of the movie again would fire the shopping cart movie, so leaving it
out is preferred.

Dragging a planet into the shopping cart adds +1 to that product's variable. Clicking
Checkout takes you to the View Cart keyframe. The ActionScript in this keyframe
contains the price of each product, and it is here that the totals are compiled. Two
variables are contained in the format of **{product}Count** and **{product}Total**: **Count** is
the number of times a given product was dropped in the shopping cart, and **Total** is
the count multiplied by the cost of the product. **Place order** submits all your variables
as a form to an email address you specify.

MODIFICATIONS

You can customize this project in a number of ways. For example, you can add multiple products per drawer or even use the drawers for navigation to different "departments." Here are some other possibilities:

- Place an editable text field in the movie and name it **PRODUCTNAMECount**, where PRODUCTNAME is the name of the product. **PRODUCTNAMECount** shows the current quantity of that object in the cart at the given time.

- In the View Cart keyframe, add a button that subtracts 1 from the quantity of products ordered.

- Add a button to clear all variables and empty the cart completely.

- Use the mov_checkbox symbol to enable in-state customers to add the tax to their order. Enter an action in the first frame of mov_checkbox to set the variable **Tax = 0** and an action in the second to set the tax variable as the grand total times your tax rate (0.07, for example).

- Change the **Get URL mailto address** to include **?subject=Order** at the end. This change sends the email message with Order as the subject. Then, create an auto-reply message in your email program to confirm orders sent with Order in the subject.

- Variables can also be sent to other middleware such as CGI, ColdFusion, JavaScript, or Active Server Pages.

"Fall seven times,

stand up eight."

—JAPANESE PROVERB

24-HOUR
INTERNET
QUOTE CLOCK

USING EXTERNAL JAVASCRIPT TO BUILD A CLOCK

Flash 4 has a number of new scripting features that have enabled developers to create fresh presentations fueled by dynamic content. This project uses JavaScript to populate a Flash movie with two kinds of dynamic data: the current time and a famous or funny quote, randomly chosen each time the page loads.

JavaScript is ideal for this task because it is a client-side technology, meaning that when it is loaded, it executes only on your client machine. No communication is needed with any server for getting the current time. Flash 4 has no direct access to the system's clock, so JavaScript is required to query the system and relay the current time to the Flash movie.

Layers
Digits
Quote

GETTING STARTED

Because this movie's functionality is controlled with JavaScript, you need to create only the properly named clock and quote elements within Flash so that JavaScript can access them externally. The position, orientation, and size of the elements are not important, but JavaScript must be able to reference them by their Movie Clip instance names.

1   Load clock.fla as a regular Flash document, and open the movie's Library.

2   Examine the elements in the Library.

Symbols whose names start with *base* define the shape of each numeric digit, 0 through 9.

Symbols named with *num* define the tweened animations displayed when each new digit appears in the clock.

The *digit* symbol is a movie clip that contains each num symbol in a frame and is used for the hour, minute, and second. Instances of this symbol can be controlled with JavaScript's **GotoTarget()** call to change specific digits appropriately.

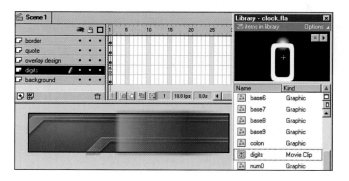

Open the Clock.fla file and Library.

SETTING UP THE DIGITS LAYER

In this section, you place the Digits Movie Clip instances to set up the hour, minutes, and seconds of the clock. This project uses the layout of the traditional digital clock. However, if you want an unusual clock, you can orient the digits any way you want, such as top-down, upside-down, or even backward.

1   On the Digits layer, click frame 1 on the Timeline, drag an instance of the Digits Movie Clip symbol onto the Stage, open the Instance Properties dialog box, and name the Movie Clip instance **hour1**.

2   Create five more instances of the Digits symbol and name them **hour2**, **minute1**, **minute2**, **second1**, and **second2**.

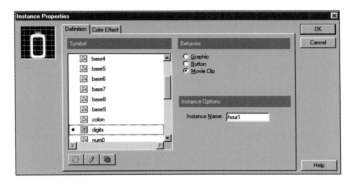

Use the Instance Properties dialog box to name the Digits Movie Clip instances.

3   Place and size each instance of the Digits symbol so that the project looks like a real clock.

4   Use the Align dialog box or the Object Inspector (Window>Inspectors>Object) to precisely align the elements with respect to each other and the Stage.

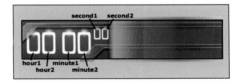

Place and size the instances of the Digits symbol.

5   On the Digits layer, drag an instance of the Ampm graphic symbol onto the Stage, press F8, convert the instance to a Movie Clip, open the Instance Properties dialog box, and name the instance **ampm**.

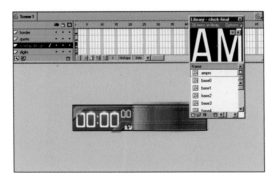

Set up the ampm instance.

6 On the Digits layer, drag an instance of the Colon graphic symbol onto the Stage, press F8, convert the instance to a Movie Clip, open the Instance Properties dialog box, and name the instance **Colon**.

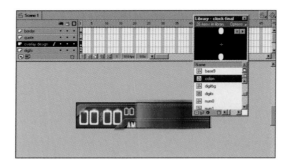

Use the Instance Properties dialog box to name the Colon instance.

SETTING UP THE QUOTE LAYER

In this section, you set up the area for displaying the quotations that randomly appear on the clock. You create the text object, set up its attributes, and then export the clock as a movie.

1 On the Quote layer, use the Text tool to create a text object in a blank area of the Flash movie, click the Text Field button to make the text field editable, and change the text attributes to

Font: Arial
Font Size: 10 pt
Text Color: White

In my example, I reserved space for the clock on the left and the quote on the right.

Set up the text field for quotes.

2 Select the text field and set the following attributes in the Text Field Properties dialog box:

Variable: **quotebox**
Options: Deselect Draw Border and Background
             Select Multiline
             Select Word Wrap
             Select Disable Editing
             Select Disable Selection
Outlines: Include only specified font outlines
             Numbers

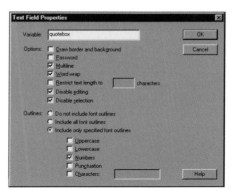

Set the attributes in the Quotebox Text Field properties dialog box.

3 Export the clock movie as clock.swf.

INSTALLING THE CLOCK IN YOUR DOCUMENT

Now that the proper Flash elements have been created, you can move on to plugging in the JavaScript code and customizing the quote randomizer.

1 In your favorite HTML or text editor, open the clock.html file, which contains three main code sections that are necessary for the clock to work:

- In the document's **<head>** tag, a JavaScript code section (enclosed by a **<script>**, **</script>** tag pair) makes the clock and quote generator work.

- The document's **<body>** tag includes an **onLoad** event handler that starts the clock running as soon as the page is loaded. For example, the body tag in this file is **<body onLoad="setflashclock();">.**

- The Flash movie is embedded in the document with the typical set of **<object>** and **<embed>** tags.

2 Copy these three code sections into the HTML file where you want the QuoteClock to appear, making sure that the **<script>** tag and **onLoad** event handler are in the **<head>** tag and **<body>** tag, respectively. Copy the Flash movie object code into the body of the new document where you want the clock to appear. For the clock to work, the **ID** and **NAME** parameters in the HTML should be set to **Clock** and the **PLAY** parameters should be **False**.

The <object> and <embed> tags used to insert the Flash movie into the Web page.

EDITING THE LIST OF QUOTES

Near the top of the clock's **\<script>** section is the quotes array that specifies the messages that can be randomly chosen for display. Quotes from famous people were used to give this clock an interesting theme, but you don't have to use any particular text format. You can change messages or add as many messages as you like—the JavaScript will automatically adjust its randomizer to pick from the list you provide.

1 Type each message you want to display at random within the parentheses of the **"var quotes = new Array();" statement**.

2 Check your message for the following syntax:

■ Make sure that each message is surrounded by single quotation marks at the beginning and end, and check that a comma separates each pair of messages.

■ For additional text control, you can type **"\n"** at any place in a message to mark the location of a new line. Flash will replace this character pair with a carriage return.

■ If your message contains a single quotation mark or an apostrophe that should be treated as such (instead of as the end of a character string), you must put a backslash character before it so it is treated literally (**\'**).

3 Save the HTML file and load it in your Web browser.

After saving the HTML file and loading it in your Web browser, the clock should function (with the correct time, no less!), and a random message from the quotes array should appear in your Quotebox symbol. Reloading the page will randomly select another message to display.

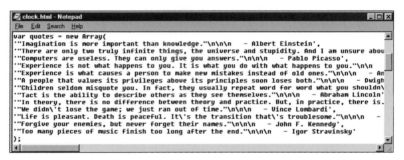

JavaScript code, defining the list of quotes to be chosen randomly.

Save the HTML file and load it in a Web browser.

160

How It Works

Most Flash movies are constructed by creating graphic elements and their corresponding animations within Flash, including all of the needed scripting and user interactivity to make the movie work. The QuoteClock uses a different approach by letting JavaScript handle the animation and content dynamically.

The Flash movie plug-in provides a way for an external scripting source, such as JavaScript or VBScript, to directly access some features of Flash—for example, playing or stopping a movie, setting ActionScript variables, and changing frames by using **Tell Target**.

After the Flash movie loads and the JavaScript begins execution, the script randomly picks a quote from a list and passes it to the movie's **Set Variable** method, causing the quote to appear in the text field. The JavaScript code then ascertains the current time by way of its own date functions and determines how each digit of the clock should change to reflect that time. **Call** statements are made to the movie's **Tell Target** function to change the frames of each digit. This process of getting the current time and setting the digits is repeated in a loop to maintain current time while the clock is visible.

Modifications

You might want to change the clock setup in this project. Here are two simple ways to adapt the clock to your purposes:

- If you'd prefer to have the clock display in military time rather than 12-hour form, set the military variable to **True** in the top of the JavaScript code segment.

- If you're feeling more adventuresome and would like to use your own clock symbols, re-create the clock element symbols in your own style, following the model used in clock.fla. Remember to give each symbol instance an appropriate hour/minute/second name. The figure shows a style of clock that was created by using new symbols but the same JavaScript code. This variation is available on the Flash 4 Magic CD as clock2.fla.

An alternative style for the QuoteClock.

P O L L

"The important thing is

not to stop questioning."

—ALBERT EINSTEIN

BUILDING A POLL USING FLASH AND PHP

Web surfers love to leave their mark! Give your

users a chance, and you can bet they'll do it.

What better way to give them such an oppor-

tunity than with a poll? Not only can they leave

their mark, they can also let you know what's

on their minds.

This poll combines the good looks of

Flash with the scripting power of PHP. It also

incorporates variable questions and answers,

which will enable you to change your poll with

a simple text file.

PROJECT 14:
WHAT'S YOUR TAKE?

After the first printing of this book, Macromedia made a modification in the Flash Player that causes attempts to load variables from a file on a remote server to fail. Now, when you put an .swf file on **http://www.mysite.com**, the URL of the text file (or other data source) must have the same domain. For additional information, check out the TechNote at **http://www.macromedia.com/support/flash/ts/documents/loadvars_security.htm**.

Scenes
Questions
Layers
Actions/Labels
Loading
Text fields
Buttons
Art
Results
Layers
Actions/Labels
Ring
Values
Text
Pie chart
Art

GETTING STARTED

If you want your results to match those of the finished project, follow the steps carefully. If you want to customize the project and are familiar with Flash 4, feel free to change the settings to those that meet your needs.

1 Starting with a new Flash movie, set the Stage dimensions to **220 × 310** and create five layers: **Actions/Labels**, **Loading**, **Text Fields**, **Buttons**, and **Art** (from top to bottom).

2 From the Flash 4 Magic CD, load poll.fla as a Library, select the Art layer, drag an instance of the Art graphic symbol from the Vector Graphics folder onto the Stage, and center the symbol.

3 In the Art layer, insert six more frames so that the Art graphic shows from frames 1 through 7.

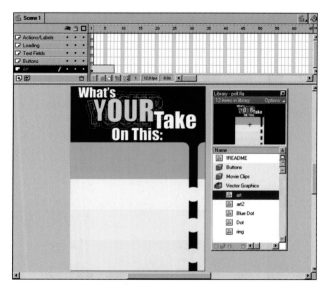

Set up the new movie with its layers and an Art instance.

164

SETTING UP THE QUESTIONS SCENE

In this section, you set up the Buttons layer, inserting three instances of the Poll
Button symbol, positioning them, and converting them to graphic symbols. Then you
set up the text boxes for the question and answers.

1   On the Buttons layer, select the Poll Button symbol
    from the Buttons folder and drag three instances of
    the symbol onto the Stage.

2   Use the Object Inspector to position these instances
    inside of the round areas in the Art layer, positioning
    the buttons at these x, y coordinates:

Top button	x: **188.1**	y: **168.4**
Middle	x: **188.1**	y: **219.9**
Bottom button	x: **188.1**	y: **271.4**

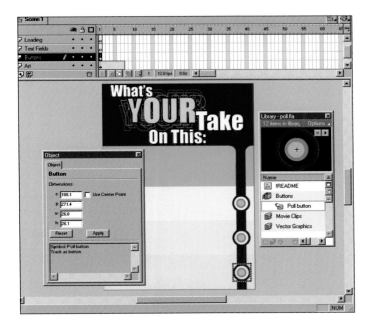

Use the Object Inspector
to position the three Poll
button instances.

3   On the Buttons layer, insert a keyframe on frame 6
    and change each of the Poll Button instances on
    frame 6 to graphic symbols
    (Modify>Instance>Definition<Graphic).

4   Insert a frame on the Buttons layer at frame 7.

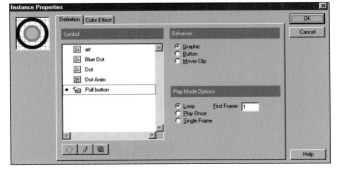

Use the Instance Properties
dialog box to change the Poll
Button instances on frame 6
to graphic symbols.

5 Insert a keyframe on frame 5 of the Text Fields layer, create a text field in the first colored block on the Art layer, and set these attributes:

Font: Arial

Font Size: 16 pt

Color: Dark blue

6 Set the following properties for this text field in the Text Field Properties dialog box, and click OK.

Variable: **question**

Options: Deselect Draw Border and
              Background
              Select Disable Editing
              Select Disable Selection

Outlines: Select Include All Font Outlines

7 Select and duplicate the text field, drag it down to the next colored block, change its name to **a1**, and use these attributes:

Font: Arial

Font Size: 12 pt

Color: Black

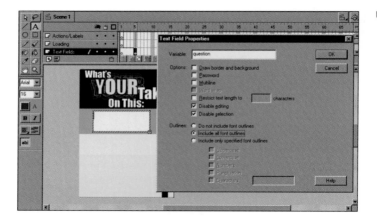

Use these Text Field properties.

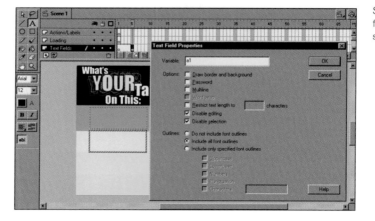

Set up the second text field with a different font size and color.

8 Select and duplicate the text field, drag it down to the next colored block, and change its name to **a2**, leaving the attributes as they are.

9 Repeat step 6, but name the text field **a3**, and then align the a1, a2, and a3 text fields so they line up on the left side.

Position the question, a1, a2, and a3 as text fields.

10 On the Text Fields layer, insert a normal frame at frame 7.

11 On the Text Fields layer, insert a keyframe on frame 6, make sure that frame 6 is selected, and change the color of all four text fields on the frame to a light gray.

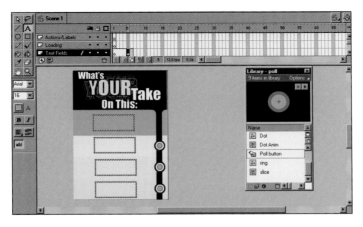

Add a keyframe to frame 6 and change the text fields to gray.

Note: You can change the color by Shift-selecting the text field, clicking on the Text tool, clicking the Text Color modifier button, and selecting a light gray color.

12 On the Loading layer, add a blank keyframe to frame 5, select frame 1, select the Text tool, make sure that the Text Field modifier is not selected, and type **Loading text**, using these attributes:

Font: Arial
Font Size: 16 pt
Color: Black

13 Save the file.

CREATING THE TEXT FILE

At this point, you will leave Flash for a moment. You need to create a text file to hold the values of the variables in the text fields you created in Flash. You will then add some actions to load the variables into the movie. The advantage of using a text file is that you can make the questions and answers for the poll more dynamic. If you use a text file, you can just edit the text file to change the questions and answers rather than editing the Flash file.

1 Create a new text file, using your favorite text editor (Notepad for the PC or SimpleText for the Mac is just fine).

2 Type the questions and answers in the text file.

The format to use in your text editor is **variable=value** pairs, separating each pair with an ampersand (**&**). The variables you need to add are

Question, the question in your poll
> Example: *question=What color should the sky be?*

a1, a2, a3, the answers to the question
> Example: *a1=The sky should definitely be blue!*

r1, r2, r2, the short descriptions of the answers, which will be in the results
> Example: *r1=Blue it is!*

3 Save this text file as **text.txt**, create a poll directory on your Web server, and upload the text.txt file to that directory.

Use a text editor such as Notepad on the PC or SimpleText on the Mac to enter the text.

SETTING UP THE SERVER SIDE

In this section, you upload the poll.php3 file to the poll directory and create an empty text file in the directory. You also set the read/write permissions for the files. Your server must support PHP for this poll to work.

1 On your Web server, upload the poll.php3 file (on the Flash 4 Magic CD) to the poll directory.

2 To hold the running tally of the values, create an empty text file named **poll.txt** in the poll directory, and upload the .txt file to your Web server.

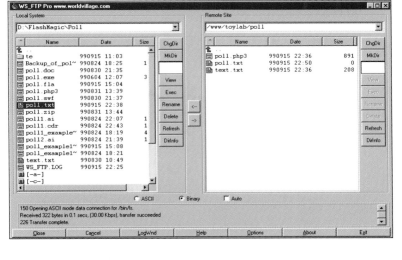

Use FTP to upload the text.txt, poll.php3, and poll.txt files to your Web server.

3 Set the read/write permissions on the directory and each file as follows:

chmod **755** poll

chmod **755** poll.php3

chmod **666** poll.txt

Have your server administrator set the read/write permissions of the directory that contains your poll files, as shown.

Note: If you are using the PHP module for IIS, you just need to give Script access to the directory in which you have all of your poll files.

4 Make sure that the PHP script is working by browsing to it.

You should see something like **value1=0&value2=0&value3=0**. If this doesn't come up, your server might not be running PHP; you'll have to find a server that is running PHP to make your poll work.

Test the PHP script to see if it is working properly.

SETTING UP THE BUTTONS

Now that you've uploaded these files to your Web server, you can go back into Flash and finish what you started. In this section, you assign the actions for the buttons. You can save time if you copy and paste the ActionScript.

1 Return to Flash, select frame 5 on the Buttons layer (which already has three buttons on it), and double-click the first button to open the Properties dialog box.

You're going to begin setting up the actions for the buttons. Don't forget that you access the **Load Variables** statement through the **Load Movies** option on the drop-down list of actions.

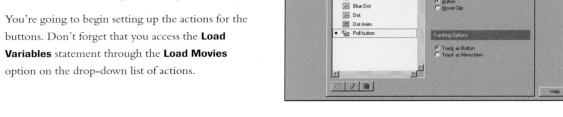

Open the Instance Properties dialog box for the Poll Button in frame 5 on the Buttons layer.

2 On the tab, assign the ActionScript.

The URL should be the URL of your PHP script. Note that **Send Using POST** works properly only when you run this movie from the Web. If you plan to run the poll from the standalone player, you need to set the Variables to **Send Using GET**.

```
On (Release)
    Set Variable: "choice" = 1
    Load Variables ("http://www.flashlite.net/poll/poll.php3", 0, vars=GET)
    Play
End On
```

3 Copy the entire ActionScript from this button, double-click the second button to open the Properties dialog box, paste the ActionScript on the Actions tab, and change the value of the **choice** variable to **2**.

4 Double-click the third button to open the Properties dialog box, paste the ActionScript on the Actions tab, and change the value of the **choice** variable to **3**.

That way, when the first button is clicked, it will send **choice=1** to the PHP script. When the second button is clicked, it will send **choice=2**, and so on.

Note: You can Shift-click each line of ActionScript to copy multiple lines at once.

170

SETTING UP THE RESULTS SCENE

In this section, you add a scene, naming it Results. Then you set up six layers that will range from having instances of graphic symbols and Movie Clips to text fields.

1 Open the Scene Inspector (Window>Inspectors>Scene), name your first scene **Questions**, add another scene after the Questions scene, and name it **Results**.

2 Making sure that you're in the Results scene, set up six layers and name them (from top to bottom) **Actions/Labels, Ring, Values, Text, Pie chart,** and **Art**.

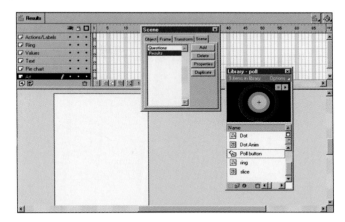

Generate a new Scene named Results that has six layers.

3 From the Flash 4 Magic CD, load poll.fla as a Library, select the Art layer, drag the Art2 graphic symbol onto the Stage, and align the symbol to the center of the Stage.

This symbol should look somewhat like the Art symbol, but with a large circle on the right side and three colored key boxes along the left side. These colored keys correspond with the colors in the pie chart.

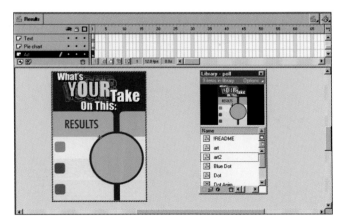

Center the Art2 Graphic symbol on the Art layer.

4 Select the Pie Chart layer, drag an instance of the Slice Movie Clip from the poll.fla Library onto the Stage, use the Object Inspector to position the Slice Movie Clip at x: **151.3** and y: **152.1**, and name the Movie Clip instance **slice1**.

Notice that the center point of the "slice" is actually at the bottom edge of the symbol.

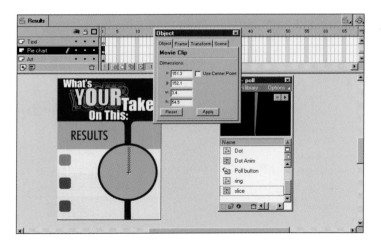

Place the Slice Movie Clip on the Pie Chart layer.

5 On the Text layer, draw a text field and place it in the colored area next to the first colored key box, using these font attributes:

Font: Arial
Font Size: 12 pt
Color: Black

6 Set the following properties for this text field in the Text Field Properties dialog box, and click OK.

Variable: **r1**
Options: Deselect Draw Border and
            Background
            Select Multiline
            Select Word Wrap
            Select Disable Editing
            Select Disable Selection
Outlines: Select Include All Font Outlines

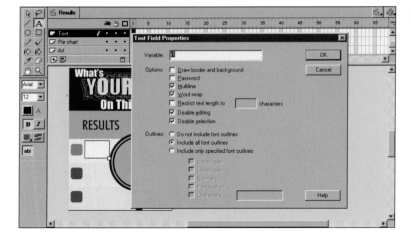

Set the Text Field Properties for the text field.

7 Select the r1 text field, duplicate it, place it in the colored area next to the second colored key box, and name it **r2**.

You might need to resize the text field so it doesn't overlap the circle on the right side of the Stage.

8 Select the r2 text field, duplicate it, place it in the colored area next to >the third colored key box, and name it **r3**.

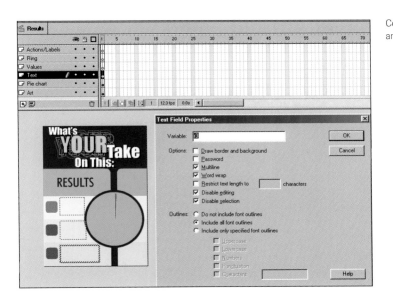

Copy and paste the text fields and position and name them.

9 On the Ring layer, drag an instance of the Ring Movie Clip symbol onto the Stage, name the instance **Ring**, and use the Object Inspector to position it at x: **95.5**, y: **152.1**.

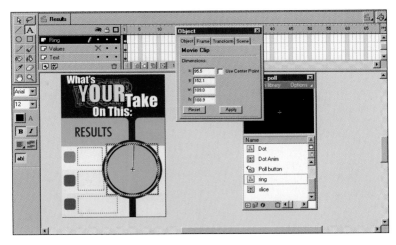

Instance the Ring Movie Clip symbol in the Ring layer.

SETTING UP THE QUESTIONS ACTIONSCRIPTS

You've already set up the layers of the Questions scene. The next step is to assign the ActionScript that checks the value returned from the PHP script.

1   Use the Scene Inspector to go back to the Questions scene and select the first keyframe in frame 1 of the Actions/Labels layer.

2   Open the Properties dialog box for the Loading keyframe, and, on the Actions tab, assign the ActionScript.

```
Load Variables ("./text.txt", 0)
```

The URL should be set to **./text.txt** if the text file will be in the same directory on the Web server as the poll movie. If you are planning to use the stand-alone player with this poll, type in the URL of the text file here.

3   On the Actions/Labels layer, insert a keyframe on frame 2. Open the Properties dialog box, label this keyframe **loading**, and, on the Actions tab, assign the ActionScript.

```
If Frame is Loaded ("done")
    If (r3 ne "")
        Go to and Stop ("done")
    End If
End Frame Loaded
```

This ActionScript first checks to ensure that the keyframe labeled "done" is the first keyframe in this movie to contain text fields with font outlines included, which is usually around 20–30 kilobytes of data—much more than the size of the questions text file. If Flash attempts to go to "done" before it is loaded, display problems may be experienced over a slower network connection.

If the loading status of "done" is found to be true, the script then runs a second test to see whether the value of the variable **r3** is empty. If the value is empty, the **If** statement will not be true, and the movie will continue to loop. If the value is not empty, the movie will go to the keyframe labeled "done" and stop. The content of the variable **r3** is significant because it is the last variable contained in the text file, and, therefore, acts as a loading indicator for the data that comes before it.

4 On the Actions/Labels layer, insert a keyframe on frame 3 of the Actions/Labels layer, and open the Properties dialog box.

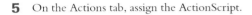

Insert a keyframe on frame 3 of the Actions/Labels layer.

5 On the Actions tab, assign the ActionScript.

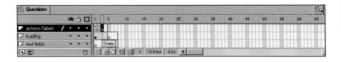

Go to and Play ("loading")

6 On the Actions/Labels layer, insert a keyframe on frame 5 of the Actions/Labels layer, and label the keyframe **done** .

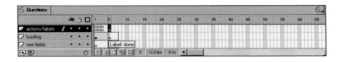

Insert and label a keyframe on frame 5 of the Actions/Labels layer.

7 On the Actions tab, assign the ActionScript.

Stop

8 On the Actions/Labels layer, insert a keyframe on frame 6 of the Actions/Labels layer, and label the keyframe **check**.

Insert and label a keyframe on frame 6 of the Actions/Labels layer.

9 On the Actions/Labels layer, insert a keyframe on frame 7 of the Actions/Labels layer, and open the Properties dialog box.

Insert and label a keyframe on frame 7 of the Actions/Labels layer.

10 On the Actions tab, assign the ActionScript.

This action checks the last value returned from the PHP script. It makes the movie loop until the value exists, because if the movie continues without it there could be problems. Note that the **Go to and Play** line is labeled "check." This keeps the movie looping between this keyframe and the Check keyframe until the value of the **value3** variable exists.

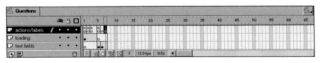

If (value3 eq "")
    Go to and Play ("check")
End If

SETTING UP THE RESULTS ACTIONSCRIPT

A major part of this project is the handling of the poll results. The ActionScript initializes the variables and creates the pie chart, coloring areas of the chart to indicate results.

1   Use the Scene Inspector to return to the Results
scene, select the keyframe on the Actions/Labels
layer, and label the keyframe **results.**

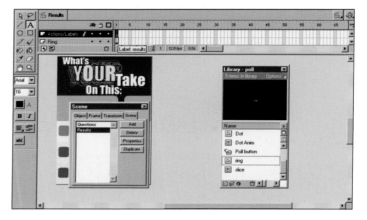

Return to the Results scene
and label the first keyframe
on the Actions/Labels layer.

2   Double-click the keyframe to open the Frame
Properties dialog box and, on the Actions tab, assign
the ActionScript.

This ActionScript is doing a great deal for your poll.
The first part of the ActionScript initializes variables
that will be used in later actions. The initialized variables are **angle** and **temp**.

The next part makes the pie chart. First, there is a
loop, which has actions to duplicate and rotate the
Slice Movie Clip, generating the circle for the pie
chart. This loop makes use of the **angle** and **temp**
variables you set in the first step. After the loop is
completed, the Ring Movie Clip is duplicated and
placed on top. This makes the pie chart's edge look
nicer, just in case the slices aren't all lined up.

The next part of the ActionScript initializes the **num**
variable and sets the value of the temp variable to
value1, which was sent to the poll by the PHP script.

```
Stop
Set Variable: "angle" = 0
Set Variable: "temp" = 2
Loop While (temp<=100)
      Set Variable: "angle" = angle+3.6
      Duplicate Movie Clip ("/slice1", "slice"&temp, temp)
      Set Property ("/slice"&temp, Rotation) = angle
      Set Variable: "temp" = temp+1
End Loop
Duplicate Movie Clip ("/ring", "ring"&top, temp+1)
Set Variable: "num" = 1
Set Variable: "temp" = Int(value1)
Loop While (temp>0)
      Begin Tell Target ("/slice"&num)
            Go to and Stop ("choice1")
      End Tell Target
      Set Variable: "temp" = temp-1
      Set Variable: "num" = num+1
End Loop
```

These variables will be used in the next part of the ActionScript.

Next are three more loops, used to color the slices of the pie chart based on the values of **value1**, **value2**, and **value3** from the PHP script. Each loop has a **Tell Target** statement that tells the appropriate duplicated Slice Movie Clip to go to the correct label.

Finally, there are three **Set Variable** statements, which designate the integer values of **value1**, value2, and **value3** from the PHP script. These values are used in the next part of this technique.

```
Set Variable: "temp" = Int(value2)
Loop While (temp>0)
    Begin Tell Target ("/slice"&num)
        Go to and Stop ("choice2")
    End Tell Target
    Set Variable: "temp" = temp-1
    Set Variable: "num" = num+1
End Loop
Loop While (num<=100)
    Begin Tell Target ("/slice"&num)
        Go to and Stop ("choice3")
    End Tell Target
    Set Variable: "num" = num+1
End Loop
Set Variable: "v1" = Int(value1)&"%"
Set Variable: "v2" = Int(value2)&"%"
Set Variable: "v3" = Int(value3)&"%"
```

TESTING THE MOVIE

At this point, it's time to test the movie. You can't test it in the editing environment, though, because you can't access the URLs. You must be connected to the Internet to reach your movie and the PHP script. After you are connected, you can export the movie, upload the .html and .swf files, and test it.

ADDING THE VALUES TO THE RESULTS

In this section, you create three text fields to contain the values. Then you assign properties to the text fields. To save time, you will want to duplicate the text fields rather than create each one from scratch.

1 Select the Values layer of the Results scene, create a text field on the layer, place the text field inside the first colored key box, and assign the following properties:

Variable: **v1**

Options: Deselect Draw Border and
               Background
               Select Disable Editing
               Select Disable Selection

Outlines: Select Include All Font Outlines

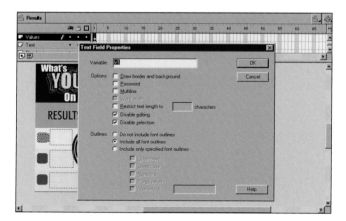

Add a new text field to the Values layer.

> **Note:** When you put this poll on the Web, you might want to change this to Do Not Include Font Outlines to reduce the size of the finished file.

2 Select the v1 text field, duplicate it, place it in the second colored key box, and name it **v2**.

3 Select the v2 text field, duplicate it, place it in the third colored key box, and name it **v3**.

4 Save your movie as **poll.fla**.

THE GRAND FINALE

You now have the moving parts of the Flash movie put together. All you have left to do is publish it.

1   Select File>Publish Settings>Formats, make sure that the Flash and HTML formats are selected, and click Publish.

2   Upload the published .swf and .html files to your server and test away!

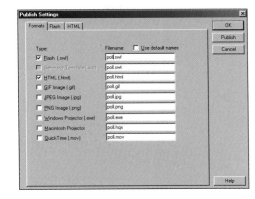

Use Publish Settings to publish the poll's .html and .swf files.

HOW IT WORKS

The poll is divided into two scenes—Questions and Results. The first scene consists of several text fields, which acquire their contents from a text file on the server, and three buttons. The buttons contain ActionScripts, each of which sends a variable **value** to a PHP script on the server.

The PHP script increments the value in the appropriate column of a database on the server by one. Then the PHP script sends the values of each column in the database back to the Flash movie, which forces the movie to continue to the Results scene. The Results scene consists of several text fields and a pie slice Movie Clip. Three of the text fields, the responses, get their values from a text file on the server. An ActionScript in the first frame of the Results scene processes the values sent by the PHP script and tells the pie slice Movie Clip to create a complete circle and divide it into three colors, based on the values from the PHP script. The ActionScript also provides the values for the remaining value text fields.

MODIFICATIONS

One of the great things about this poll is that you can easily modify it to suit your needs. If you decide you want to ask a new question or want to modify your answers, all you have to do is change the text file (text.txt) to reflect that. You don't have to even open the .fla file—only the text file.

You could even set up a dynamic system that pulls the questions and answers from a database by using PHP, ColdFusion, or ASP. Just change the URL of the text file from ./text.txt to the URL of the script that pulls the questions and answers from the database.

You can easily change the colors of your pie chart. You have to do this in only two places—the Slice Movie Clip and the Art2 graphic. The choice1, choice2, and choice3 labels in the Slice Movie Clip correspond to the first, second, and third color keys, respectively.

Finally, you don't have to use PHP to run this poll. If you know how to make a comparable script in ColdFusion, ASP, Perl, or some other scripting language, you can. Just make sure your script outputs the required values (value1, value2, and value3) and updates the poll.txt file as necessary. Then change the references to the PHP script to reflect the name of your custom script.

GUESTBOOK

"Happiness is not a

destination. It is a

method of life."

—BURTON HILLS

USING FLASH AND PHP TO BUILD A GUESTBOOK

As the Web grows, many different "widgets"

and gadgets are added to Web pages. One of

the most popular and useful of these widgets is

the Guestbook. This project explains how to

create a Guestbook with a new spin—it will be

animated with Flash 4!

PROJECT 15:

GUESTBOOK

Scenes
Read
  Layers
    Numbers
    Button
    Info.
    Background
    Loader
Sign
  Layers
    Button
    Text
    Background

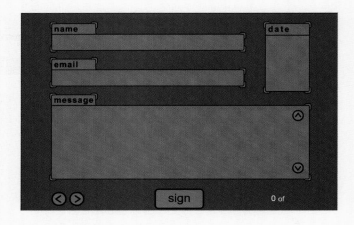

SETTING UP THE PHP BACK END

The Guestbook saves information submitted over the Web, so some sort of back-end script or program is required to parse the data and save it on the Web server. This project uses PHP as a back end because it's platform-independent, fast, and free; however, your Web server must have the PHP pre-parser installed for the project to function properly. If you are not sure whether your server supports PHP, try the first step of this tutorial. If it does not work, consult with your system administrator. Many hosting companies don't charge extra for PHP support because it doesn't directly cost them anything to install it. If you need more information about PHP, go to http://www.php.net.

If your system administrator or hosting company won't install PHP, you have another option. The features PHP uses to power the Guestbook are standard with just about any CGI-capable language, such as Perl, as well as Active Server Pages (ASP) and ColdFusion (CF). The conversion of the PHP to another back end is not particularly difficult, but it is beyond the scope of this book.

1 Upload the guestbook.php3 file from the Flash 4 Magic CD to your Web server.

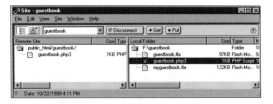

Upload guestbook.php3 to your Web server.

2 Make sure that the file has execute permissions turned on for all users. If you need help with this, consult your system administrator.

Set the permissions for guestbook.php3.

3 Create a new file, saved as guest.db, on your Web server and set the file permissions so that all users can write to it. Again, if you need help, consult your system administrator.

Create the new database file to store data.

4 Open a Web browser and go to the URL of the PHP script you uploaded to your Web server.

If you just see a blank screen, PHP and the Guestbook script are properly installed on your system. If you see something else, double-check the file permissions and consult your system administrator.

This is one time when you want to see a blank screen.

GETTING STARTED IN FLASH

Setting up a Flash file is probably old hat for you now. If you want your results to match those of the finished project, follow the steps carefully. If you want to customize the project and are familiar with Flash 4, feel free to change the settings to those that meet your needs.

1   Begin with a new Flash file, using these settings:

Frame rate:	**12 fps**
Stage dimensions:	**400 × 300**
Background color:	**Green**

2   From the Flash 4 Magic CD, open guestbook.fla as a Library.

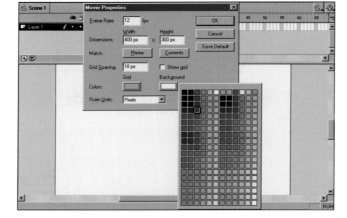

Use these settings for the new Flash file.

3   Use the Scene Inspector (Window>Inspectors>Scene) to set up two scenes, naming them (from top to bottom) **Read** and **Sign**.

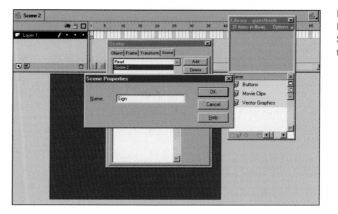

Load guestbook.fla as a Library and then use the Scene Inspector to set up two scenes.

4 Set up three layers in the Sign scene, naming them (from top to bottom) **Button**, **Text**, and **Background**.

5 Label the first keyframe of the Button layer in the Sign scene **sign**.

Set up the layers and the first keyframe of the Button layer in the Sign scene.

6 Set up five layers in the Read scene, naming them (from top to bottom) **Numbers**, **Buttons**, **Info**, **Background**, and **Loader**.

7 Label the first keyframe of the Loader layer in the Read scene **read**.

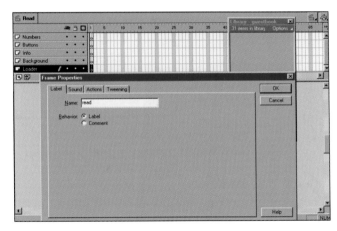

Set up the layers and the first keyframe of the Loader layer in the Read scene.

CREATING THE LOADER

In this section, you enter the ActionScript on the Loader layer of the Read scene. To do so, you need to insert three keyframes and set up an instance of the Loading Movie Clip.

1 Select the first keyframe of the Loader layer in the Read scene, open the Frame Properties dialog box, and, on the Actions tab, assign the ActionScript.

```
Set Variable: "max" = ""
Set Variable: "command" = "view"
Load Variables ("./guestbook.php3", 0, vars=GET)
```

2 Select the Loader layer, drag an instance of the Loading Movie Clip from the Library onto the Stage, and use the Object Inspector to position the instance at x: **194.5**, y: **71.2**.

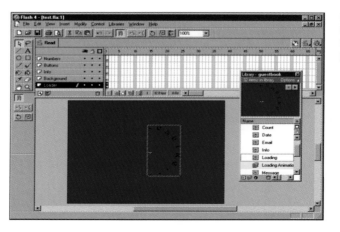

In the Loader layer, drag an instance of the Loading Movie Clip onto the Stage and position it.

3 Insert a keyframe in frame 2 of the Loader layer, open the Frame Properties dialog box and, on the Actions tab, assign the ActionScript.

```
If (max ne "")
    Go to and Stop (4)
End If
```

4 Insert a keyframe in frame 3 of the Loader layer, open the Frame Properties dialog box and, on the Actions tab, assign the ActionScript.

```
Set Variable: "/:name" = Eval("/:name"&/:count)
Set Variable: "/:email" = Eval("/:email"&/:count)
Set Variable: "/:date" = Eval("/:date"&/:count)
Set Variable: "/:year" = Eval("/:year"&/:count)
Set Variable: "/:time" = Eval("/:time"&/:count)
Set Variable: "/:message" = Eval("/:message"&/:count)
```

5 Insert a blank keyframe at frame 4 of the Loader layer, open the Frame Properties dialog box and, on the Actions tab, assign the ActionScript.

```
Stop
Set Variable: "count" = 0
If (max>0)
    Set Variable: "count" = 1
    Set Variable: "/:name" = Eval("/:name"&/:count)
    Set Variable: "/:email" = Eval("/:email"&/:count)
    Set Variable: "/:date" = Eval("/:date"&/:count)
    Set Variable: "/:year" = Eval("/:year"&/:count)
```

Set Variable: "/:time" = Eval("/:time"&/:count)

Set Variable: "/:message" = Eval("/:message"&/:count)

End If

CREATING THE INTERFACE

Creating the interface for this project requires that you drag several graphic symbols from the guestbook.fla Library onto the Stage. To reduce the number of decisions you have to make, we've included x, y coordinates for placing the symbols.

1 Select the Background layer in the Read Scene, insert a keyframe in frame 4, drag an instance of each of the following graphic symbols from the Library onto the Stage, and use the Object Inspector to position the instances at the specified coordinates.

Name	x: **11.4**	y: **12.4**
Date	x: **322.4**	y: **12.4**
Email	x: **11.4**	y: **65.7**
Message	x: **11.4**	y: **118.8**

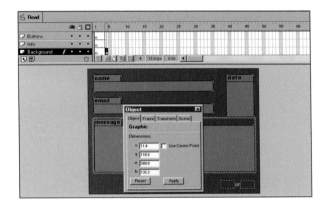

In the Background layer, drag and position an instance of each of the graphic symbols on the Stage.

3 Lock the Background layer.

4 Select the Info layer; insert a keyframe at frame 4; drag an instance of the Info Movie Clip from the Library onto the Stage; use the Object Inspector to position the instance at x: **17.4**, y: **32.0**; name the instance **info**; and then lock the Info layer.

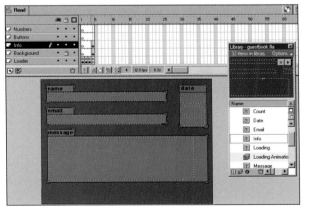

In the Info layer, drag and position an instance of the Info Movie Clip on the Stage.

CREATING THE DATA ENTRY MOVIE CLIP

In this section, you edit the Info Movie Clip, creating motion tweening on all the layers except the Actions layer. Then you move on to setting the Alpha of frame 10 in all the layers. You end this section by assigning the ActionScript to the Actions layer.

1 Open the Info Movie Clip in symbol-editing mode, select the first keyframe of the Actions layer, and, on the Actions tab, assign the ActionScript.

> **Note:** To enter the symbol-editing mode, right-click (Windows) or Control-click (Macintosh) on the instance, and choose Edit from the pop-up menu.

2 Select frame 10 of every layer and insert a new keyframe.

3 Create a motion tween between frames 1 and 10 in every layer except the Actions layer.

4 Select the Message Movie Clip in frame 10 of the Message layer and set its Alpha to 0.

5 Repeat step 4 for the Movie Clips in frame 10 of each of the other layers.

6 Select the keyframe in frame 10 of the Actions layer, open the Frame Properties dialog box, and, on the Actions tab, assign the ActionScript.

7 Choose Edit>Edit Movie to return to the main movie.

Stop

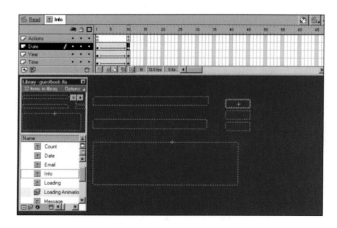

Create a motion tween on every layer except the Actions layer and then set the Alpha of the keyframe of frame 10 on every layer.

Set Variable: "/:name" = Eval("/:name"&/:count)
Set Variable: "/:email" = Eval("/:email"&/:count)
Set Variable: "/:date" = Eval("/:date"&/:count)
Set Variable: "/:year" = Eval("/:year"&/:count)
Set Variable: "/:time" = Eval("/:time"&/:count)
Set Variable: "/:message" = Eval("/:message"&/:count)

ADDING THE BUTTONS

In this section, you instance the Arrow Button four times, position each, and assign the appropriate ActionScript. Then you move on to the Sign and Email Buttons, positioning them and assigning the ActionScript. Be aware that although the instance of the Email button appears light blue, it is actually invisible to the user.

1   Select the Buttons layer in the Read scene, add a blank keyframe in frame 4, and drag four instances of the Arrow Button from the Library onto the Stage.

2   Select two of the instances of the buttons, scale them to 75% of their original size, and rotate them so one arrow faces up and the other faces down; position the up-facing arrow at x: **365**, y: **145** and the down-facing arrow at x: **365**, y: **224**.

3   Select one of the remaining instances of the buttons and rotate it so it points to the left; then select both of the remaining instances of the buttons and position them side by side in the lower left corner of the Stage.

4   Select the instance of the up arrow, open its Instance Properties dialog box, and, on the Actions tab, assign the ActionScript.

5   Select the instance of the down arrow, open its Instance Properties dialog box, and, on the Actions tab, assign the ActionScript.

Note: The previous two steps enable the user to scroll through text if there is more than enough to fill up the message box.

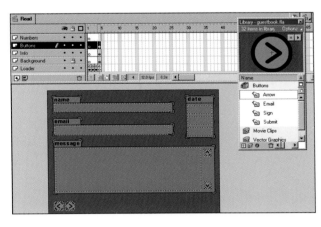

Add four instances of the Arrow Button symbol to the Buttons layer and position them appropriately.

```
If (/:message.scroll>1)
    Set Variable: "/:message.scroll" = /:message.scroll-1
End If
```

```
If (/:message.scroll</:message.maxscroll)
    Set Variable: "/:message.scroll" = /:message.scroll+1
End If
```

189

6 Select the instance of the left arrow, open its Instance Properties dialog box, and, on the Actions tab, assign the ActionScript.

```
On (Release)
    If (/:count>1)
        Set Variable: "/:count" = /:count-1
        Begin Tell Target ("/info")
            Play
        End Tell Target
    End If
End On
```

7 Select the instance of the right arrow, open its Instance Properties dialog box, and, on the Actions tab, assign the ActionScript.

```
On (Release)
    If (/:count</:max)
        Set Variable: "/:count" = /:count+1
        Begin Tell Target ("/info")
            Play
        End Tell Target
    End If
End On
```

8 Drag an instance of the Sign Button from the Library onto the Stage and position it so it's at the bottom of the Stage, centered horizontally.

9 Drag an instance of the Email Button from the Library onto the Stage and place it in the Email box.

The instance of the button will appear light blue to you, but it is in fact invisible.

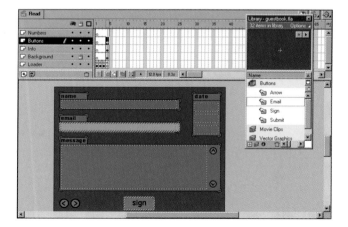

Add the Sign Button and the Email Button to the Buttons layer.

10 Select the instance of the Sign Button, open its Instance Properties dialog box, and, on the Actions tab, assign the ActionScript.

```
On (Release)
    Go to and Stop (Sign, "sign")
End On
```

11 Select the instance of the Email Button, open its Instance Properties dialog box, and, on the Actions tab, assign the ActionScript.

```
On (Release)
    Get URL ("mailto:"&/:email)
End On
```

ADDING THE NUMBERS

This section includes a handy little Count Movie Clip. Don't worry about having to enter complicated ActionScript to make it function properly—the Movie Clip is pre-fabricated and the only thing you have to do is place it in the Numbers layer.

1 Select the Numbers layer in the Read scene and add a keyframe at frame 4.

2 Drag an instance of the Count Movie Clip from the Library onto the Stage and position it in the bottom right corner of the Stage.

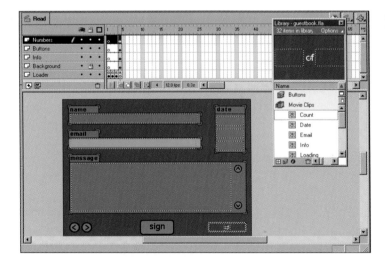

Add an instance of the Count Movie Clip to the Numbers layer.

SETTING UP THE SIGN SCENE

In this section, you set up the Background layer by creating an instance of the Sign graphic and assigning its ActionScript. In the Text layer, you instance the Sign Text Movie Clip and assign ActionScript to it. Finally, you add the Submit Button and the Submitting graphic symbol and assign ActionScript to the Button layer.

1 Select the Background layer of the Sign scene and drag an instance of the Sign graphic from the Library onto the Stage, positioning it at x: **10.0**, y: **10.0**.

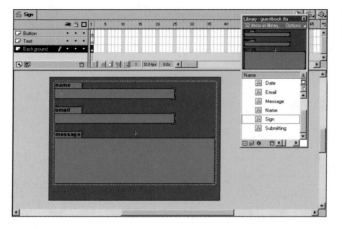

Insert an instance of the Sign graphic symbol to the Background layer.

2 Select the first frame of the Background layer, open the Properties dialog box, and, on the Actions tab, assign the ActionScript.

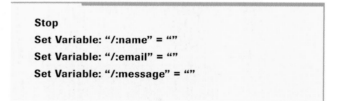

```
Stop
Set Variable: "/:name" = ""
Set Variable: "/:email" = ""
Set Variable: "/:message" = ""
```

3 Select the Text layer in the Sign scene and drag an instance of the Sign Text Movie Clip from the Library onto the Stage, positioning it at x: **13.9**, y: **30.1**.

4 Select the Button layer in the Sign scene and drag an instance of the Submit Button onto the bottom of the Stage, centering it horizontally.

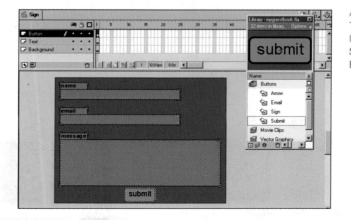

Add an instance of the Sign Text Movie Clip to the Text layer and an instance of the Sign Button symbol to the Button layer.

192

5   Select the Submit Button, open the Instance Properties dialog box, and, on the Actions tab, assign the ActionScript.

```
On (Release)
    Set Variable: "command" = "sign"
    Set Variable: "done" = 0
    Load Variables ("./guestbook.php3", 0, vars=GET)
    Play
End On
```

6   Insert a blank keyframe in frame 2 of the Button layer, drag an instance of the Submitting graphic symbol from the Library onto the Stage and center it horizontally and vertically; open the Instance Properties dialog box, and, on the Actions tab, assign the ActionScript.

```
If (done ne "0")
    Go to and Play (Read, "read")
End If
```

7   Insert a keyframe at frame 3 of the Button layer, open the Frame Properties dialog box, and, on the Actions tab, assign the ActionScript.

```
Go to and Play (2)
```

How It Works

When a user reads the Guestbook, Flash firsts connects to the server and waits until it receives all the Guestbook entries. Flash then proceeds to display the variables that represent the first entry in the database (name, date, and so on). The data is stored in a format in which the actual field of the data—the message— is followed by the number of the entry (for example, 1). If Flash received three messages from the Guestbook, they'd be numbered message1, message2, and message3. The entry the user is currently viewing is defined by a variable that controls the number that precedes the field name. The user can view the next Guestbook entry or go to a previous one by pressing the appropriate arrow, which increments or decrements the aforementioned number.

When a user writes to the Guestbook, Flash passes the information to the server, where the PHP script timestamps it and adds it to the list of entries.

Modifications

You can modify the Guestbook in these ways:

- Create scrollbars (such as those provided with Flash 4) for the entries so that the user can simply scroll to see a particular entry.
- Change the order of the scenes so that a user is always prompted to sign the Guestbook first.
- Create a scrolling list of all entries and set it up in such a way that when the user clicks on a signer's name, the information the signer provided displays.

Here are a couple of ways you can modify the PHP:

- Whenever an entry is added, the owner of the Guestbook receives an email notification of the addition.
- Every user who signs the Guestbook automatically receives an email message thanking them.

PART II

GAMES

Quiz Game 196

Memory Game 220

Wack-a-Mole Game 232

Pong Game 244

Hangman Game 260

Dodge Game 274

QUIZ GAME

MAKING A QUIZ GAME IN FLASH

Games make great Web content, and quiz games are especially great. A quiz can be used as a contest, a survey, or just for fun. This flexible Flash Quiz allows for three levels of four multiple-choice questions and even allocates points for each question based on how long the user takes to answer.

PROJECT 16:
QUIZ

Layers
> ActionScript Library
> Retry Screen
> Level Screens
> Buttons
> Indicators
> Questions
> Background

GETTING STARTED

Setting up a Flash file is probably old hat for you now. If you want your results to match those of the finished project, follow the steps carefully. If you want to customize the project and are familiar with Flash 4, feel free to change the settings to those that meet your needs.

1   Begin with a new Flash Movie, open Quiz.fla (on the Flash 4 Magic CD) as a Library, and use these settings for the Stage:

Frame rate:	**24 fps**
Stage dimensions:	**400 × 300**
Background color:	**Black**

2   Set up seven layers, naming them (from top to bottom) **ActionScript Library**, **Retry Screen**, **Level Screens**, **Buttons**, **Indicators**, **Questions,** and **Background**.

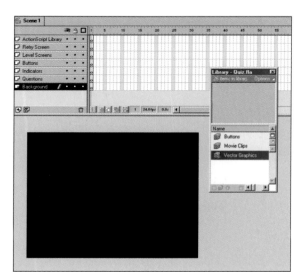

Open Quiz.fla as a Library and set up the layers.

3 Select the Background layer, drag an instance of the Background graphic symbol from the Vector Graphics folder onto the Stage, center it, and lock the layer.

You're locking the layer because you won't be dealing with it again.

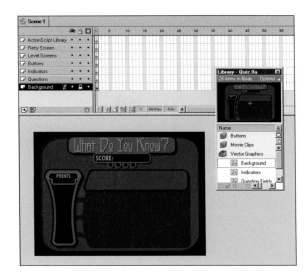

Center the Background graphic on the Stage.

SETTING UP THE QUESTIONS AND ANSWERS

In this section, you instance the Question Fields graphic symbol and set up a text field for questions. Then you set up the text fields for the three multiple-choice answers.

1 Select the Questions layer, drag an instance of the Question Fields graphic symbol from the Vector Graphics folder onto the Stage, select the instance, and use the Object Inspector (Window>Inspectors> Object) to set its coordinates to x: **127.0**, y: **96**.

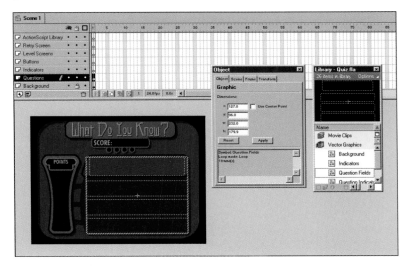

Create an instance of the Question Fields symbol and position it on the Stage.

2 Select the Question Fields instance, enter its symbol-editing mode, select the first (top) text field, open the Text Field Properties dialog box, and type **Question** in the Variable field.

> **Note:** To enter the symbol-editing mode, right-click (Windows) or Control-click (Macintosh) on the Question Fields instance, and choose Edit from the pop-up menu.

3 Repeat step 2 with the remaining three fields, naming them (from top to bottom) **AnswerA**, **AnswerB**, and **AnswerC**.

4 Exit symbol-editing mode and return to Scene 1.

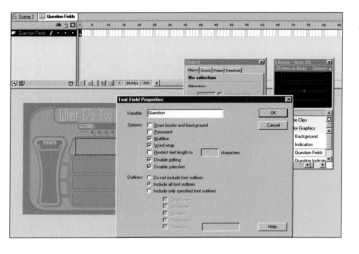

Give the first text field the variable name Question.

INDICATING THE PROGRESS

The Indicators layer is your next focus. It contains a field that displays the number of points the player has accumulated. You also work with two Movie Clip symbols. To the left is the Points indicator. Each time a question displays, the player starts off with 1000 points, and this value decrements over time until it reaches 0 and the player fails one more question.

The final indicator object appears as a small white dot below the Score field. (A small white dot denotes a graphic or Movie Clip symbol with a blank first frame.) This particular symbol is a visual indicator that displays a series of red lights, with the number of lights corresponding to the number of questions answered in the current level.

1 Select the Indicators layer, drag an instance of the Indicators graphic symbol from the Vector Graphics folder onto the Stage, and use the Object Inspector to set its coordinates to x: **52**, y: **57**.

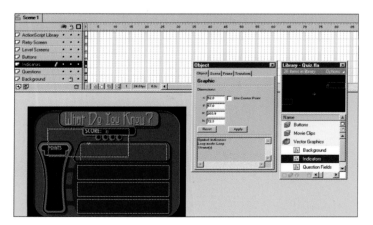

Position the Indicators symbol at x: 52, y: 57.

2 Use Edit in Place to edit the Indicators symbol, open the Text Field Properties dialog box of the text field near the word Score, and assign the Variable Name **Score**.

3 While still in the symbol-editing mode for the Indicators symbol, select the Points Indicator symbol on left of the Stage, open its Instance Properties dialog box, and name the instance **Points**, enabling the other symbols to reset the points count later.

4 To make the Questions Indicators instance a target, open its Instance Properties dialog box and name the instance **QuestionIndicators**.

5 Exit symbol-editing mode and return to Scene 1.

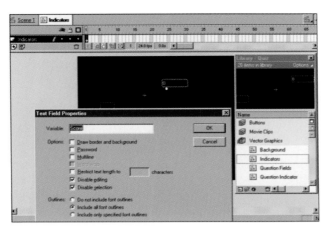

Set up the variable Score.

Button It—As Easy as A, B, C

You now have everything you need to display the questions, answers, scores, and progress. The next important ingredient is a method for accepting user input. This project uses buttons for accepting the input.

1 In the Buttons layer, drag an instance of the A Button from the Buttons folder onto the Stage, and use the Object Inspector to position the instance at x: **57.2**, y: **153.3**.

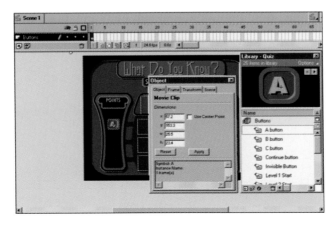

Position an instance of the A Button alongside the AnswerA text field.

2 Double-click the instance of the A Button to open the Instance Properties dialog box, and, on the Actions tab, assign the ActionScript.

> **Note:** You can select the ActionScript, copy it, paste it onto the Actions tabs for the other two buttons, and then change the value of **CurrentAnswer**.

This script sets the value of **CurrentAnswer** to **A** and then calls the **AnswerQuestion** function contained in the ActionScript Library symbol. **AnswerQuestion** handles the comparison between **CurrentAnswer** and the correct answer for each question, and triggers a series of events accordingly.

To make things interesting, you must nest each answer button inside a Movie Clip symbol so you can make each one visible or invisible, depending on whether the player chooses the correct answer. After the player answers each question, only the correct answer is left visible and the remaining two are hidden.

3 Select the instance of the A button and press F8 to convert it to a Movie Clip symbol.

```
On (Release)
    Set Variable: "/:CurrentAnswer" = "A"
    Call ("/Library/:AnswerQuestion")
End On
```

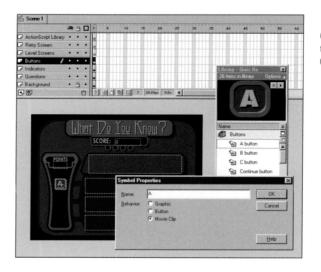

Convert the instance of the A Button to a Movie Clip symbol.

4 Open the Instance Properties dialog box for A, and name the instance **A**.

Naming the instance enables you to manipulate the visibility properties of the symbol with the **Set Property** action.

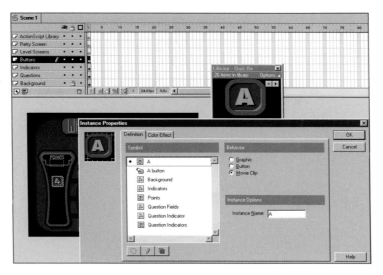

Give the A Movie Clip instance the name "A."

5 In the Buttons layer, drag an instance of the B Button from the Buttons folder onto the Stage, and use the Object Inspector to position it at x: **57.2**, y: **196.3**.

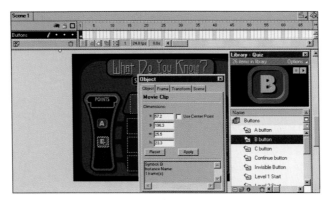

Drag an instance of the B Button alongside the AnswerB text field.

6 Assign the same script as in step 2 to the B Button and replace the **"A"** literal with the **"B"** literal.

7 Select the instance of the B button and press F8 to convert it to a Movie Clip symbol.

8 Open the Instance Properties dialog box for B, and name the instance **B**.

```
On (Release)
    Set Variable: "/:CurrentAnswer" = "B"
    Call ("/Library/:AnswerQuestion")
End On
```

9 In the Buttons layer, drag an instance of the C
Button from the Buttons folder onto the Stage, and
use the Object Inspector to position the C Button
instance at x: **56.2**, y: **238.3**.

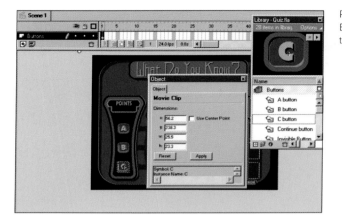

Position an instance of the C
Button alongside the AnswerC
text field.

10 Assign the same script as in step 2 to the C Button
and replace the **"A"** literal with the **"C"** literal.

11 Select the instance of the C button and press F8
to convert it to a Movie Clip symbol.

12 Open the Instance Properties dialog box for C,
and name the instance **C**.

```
On (Release)
    Set Variable: "/:CurrentAnswer" = "C"
    Call ("/Library/:AnswerQuestion")
End On
```

CONTINUING ON WITH BUTTONS

Before moving on, you need to add the Continue button. After answering a question and
viewing the correct response, players must click Continue to progress to the next question.

1 Drag an instance of Continue from the Movie Clips
folder (not the Buttons folder) onto the Stage, open
the Object Inspector, position the instance at x: **310**,
y: **280**.

2 Open the Instance Properties dialog box and name
the instance **Continue**.

Similar to A, B and C, Continue is a button that has
been nested within a Movie Clip symbol so you can
set its visibility property.

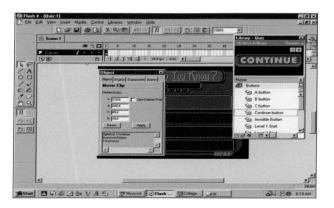

Position an instance of the
Continue Movie Clip symbol
at x: 310, y: 280.

3 Select the Continue instance and, in symbol-editing mode, select the Continue Button instance, open its Instance Properties dialog box, and, on the Actions tab, assign the ActionScript.

The Continue Button script performs a number of tasks. First, it sets the visibility of the parent Movie Clip to **False**, making Continue invisible. The script then prompts for the next question to be displayed and checks to see whether the current level has been completed, and completed correctly. The script plays **LevelScreens** or **RetryScreen**, depending on the outcome of the current level.

4 Exit symbol-editing mode and return to Scene 1.

```
On (Release)
    Set Property ("", Visibility) = False
    Call ("/Library/:DisplayQuestion")
    If (/:CurrentQuestion = 5)
        If (/:CorrectCount = 4)
            Begin Tell Target ("/LevelScreens")
                Play
            End Tell Target
        Else
            Begin Tell Target ("/RetryScreen")
                Play
            End Tell Target
        End If
    End If
End On
```

ADDING THE LEVEL AND RETRY SCREENS

The Quiz game has the capacity for three different levels, each containing four questions. The Quiz is set to progress to the next level only if the player gets all four questions correct in the current level. When the player makes an error, a Retry Screen displays and the level does not progress until all the questions are answered correctly. To control the flow of the game, you need to create a set of Level Screens. The three Level Screens set the current level and give the player information about the preceding questions.

1 In the Level Screens layer, drag an instance of Level 1 Start from the Buttons folder onto the Stage and center it.

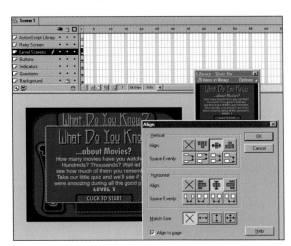

Create an instance of Level 1 Start and center it on the Stage.

2 Double-click Level 1 Start to open the Instance Properties dialog box, and, on the Actions tab, assign the ActionScript.

Each of the Level buttons will share a similar script, setting the current level and count of correct answers and then resetting the current question to **1**. The functions **Level1** and **DisplayQuestion** are also called here, which in turn reset all the question-and-answer variables and then display the current question.

Note: You can select the ActionScript, copy it, paste it onto the Actions tabs for the other two levels, and then make the necessary changes.

3 Select the Level 1 Start instance and press F8, converting the instance to a Movie Clip symbol named **LevelScreens**.

4 Open the Instance Properties dialog box and name the instance **LevelScreens**.

5 Enter the symbol–editing mode of the Level Screens symbol; name the existing layer **Level Screens**; add one upper layer, naming it **Control Actions**; and add 39 frames to both layers, making a total of 40 frames on each layer.

6 In the Level Screens layer, insert blank keyframes at positions 2, 11, 12, 21, 22, 31, and 32.

```
On (Release)
    Set Variable: "/:CurrentLevel" = 1
    Set Variable: "/:CorrectCount" = 0
    Set Variable: "/:CurrentQuestion" = 1
    Call ("/Library/:Level1")
    Call ("/Library/:DisplayQuestion")
    Play
End On
```

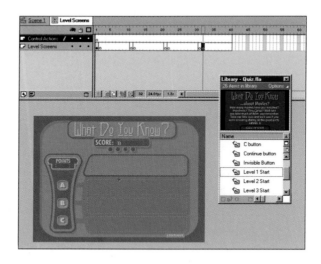

Add blank keyframes to the Level Screens layer.

7 Move the playhead to frame 11, drag an instance of Level 2 Start from the Buttons folder onto the Stage, and center it.

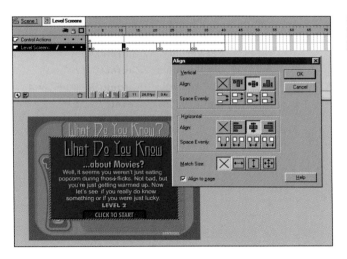

Create an instance of Level 2 Start and center it on the Stage.

8 Select the Level 2 Start instance, open its Instance Properties dialog box, and, on the Actions tab, assign the ActionScript.

```
On (Release)
    Set Variable: "/:CurrentLevel" = 2
    Set Variable: "/:CorrectCount" = 0
    Set Variable: "/:CurrentQuestion" = 1
    Call ("/Library/:Level2")
    Call ("/Library/:DisplayQuestion")
    Play
End On
```

9 Move the playhead to frame 21, drag an instance of Level 3 Start from the Buttons folder onto the Stage, and center it.

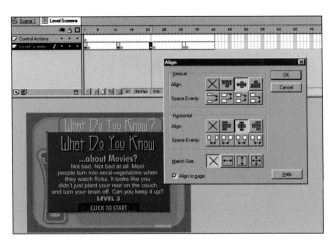

Create an instance of Level 3 Start and center it on the Stage.

10 Select the Level 3 Start instance, open its Instance Properties dialog box, and, on the Actions tab, assign the ActionScript.

Notice that a similar script was used each time—only the level number was changed.

```
On (Release)
    Set Variable: "/:CurrentLevel" = 3
    Set Variable: "/:CorrectCount" = 0
    Set Variable: "/:CurrentQuestion" = 1
    Call ("/Library/:Level3")
    Call ("/Library/:DisplayQuestion")
    Play
End On
```

THE WIN BUTTON

Sometimes you win, sometimes you lose. In this short section, you participate in a winning activity: creating the instance of the Win Button symbol and assigning ActionScript to it.

1 Move the playhead to frame 31, drag an instance of Win from the Buttons folder onto the Stage, and center it.

Win is different from the other buttons in that it shows only after all three levels are completed. The Win Button's actions call the **Initialize** function stored in the ActionScript Library symbol and then set the current Level Screens frame to **Level1**, thereby restarting the game.

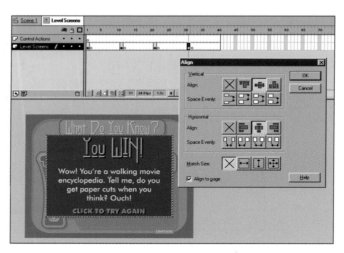

Create an instance of the Win Button symbol and center it on the Stage.

2 Open the Instance Properties dialog box of the Win button, and, on the Actions tab, assign the ActionScript.

```
On (Release)
    Call ("/Library/:Initialize")
    Go to and Stop ("Level1")
End On
```

SETTING UP THE CONTROL ACTIONS LAYER

The Control Actions layer simply controls the flow of the Timeline. You need to
insert blank keyframes on the layer, label them, and assign the ActionScript.

1   In the Control Actions layer, insert blank keyframes
    at frames 10, 11, 20, 21, 30, and 31.

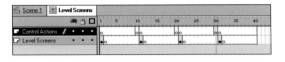

Insert blank keyframes on the
Control Actions layer.

2   Open the Frame Properties dialog box for keyframes
    1, 10, 11, 20, 21, 30, and 31, and, on each Actions
    tab, assign the ActionScript.

3   In the Control Actions layer, add the following labels:

    | Keyframe 1 | **Level1** |
    | Keyframe 11 | **Level2** |
    | Keyframe 21 | **Level3** |
    | Keyframe 31 | **Win** |

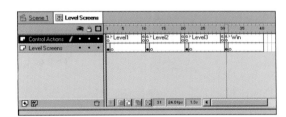

Assign labels to keyframes 1,
11, 21, and 31 in the Control
Actions layer.

4   Exit symbol-editing mode and return to Scene 1.

SETTING UP THE RETRY SCREEN

Now it's time to set up the Retry Screen that displays when the player makes an error.
You need to create a new Movie Clip and set up two layers in it before you can create an
instance of the Retry Button, insert keyframes, and assign the ActionScript. When it's
all finished, you need to place an instance of the Retry Screen Movie Clip in Scene 1.

1   In the Retry Screen layer, ensure that nothing on the
    Stage is selected and then create a new Movie Clip
    symbol, naming it **Retry Screen**.

    Because you're creating a new empty symbol, Flash
    automatically switches to symbol-editing mode.

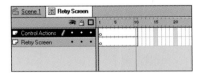

Create a new Movie Clip and
insert additional frames in the
Control Actions and Retry
Screen layers.

2 In the symbol-editing mode of the Retry Screen Movie Clip, rename the existing empty layer **Retry Screen**, add a new layer above it, name the new layer **Control Actions**, and add an extra nine frames to both layers, making a total of 10 frames.

3 In the Retry Screen layer, insert blank keyframes at positions 2 and 3. Move the playhead to keyframe 2, drag an instance of the Retry button from the Buttons folder onto the Stage, and center it.

Create an instance of Retry and center it on the Stage.

4 Double-click the instance of the Retry Button to open the Instance Properties dialog box, and, on the Actions tab, assign the ActionScript.

This script is similar to that of Level Screens, except it doesn't alter the value of the current level, which is appropriate because the player has to repeat the same set of questions.

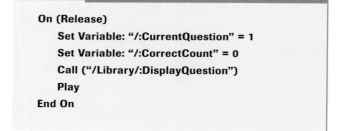

```
On (Release)
    Set Variable: "/:CurrentQuestion" = 1
    Set Variable: "/:CorrectCount" = 0
    Call ("/Library/:DisplayQuestion")
    Play
End On
```

5 In the Control Actions layer, insert additional blank keyframes at positions 2 and 10, and label keyframe 1 **Retry**.

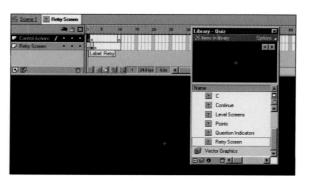

Insert additional blank keyframes in the Control Actions layer.

210

6 Double-click keyframe 1 to open the Frame Properties dialog box, and, on the Actions tab, assign the ActionScript.

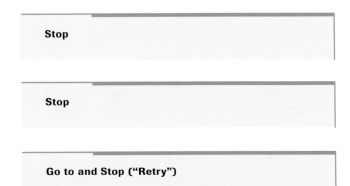

Stop

Stop

7 Double-click keyframe 2 to open the Frame Properties dialog box, and, on the Actions tab, assign the ActionScript.

8 Double-click keyframe 10 to open the Frame Properties dialog box, and, on the Actions tab, assign the ActionScript.

Go to and Stop ("Retry")

This script causes the Retry Screen symbol to reset itself after it is played.

9 Exit symbol-editing mode and return to Scene 1.

10 Drag an instance of Retry Screen from your movie's Library onto the Stage, double-click the Retry Screen instance to open its Instance Properties dialog box, name the instance **RetryScreen**, and use the Object Inspector to position the instance at x: **200.0**, y: **150.0**.

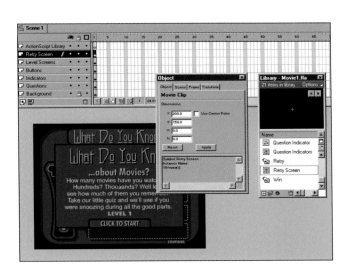

Create an instance of the Retry Screen symbol and position it on the Stage.

BUILDING THE ACTIONSCRIPT LIBRARY

The final step is to build the ActionScript functions to drive the rest of the movie. The main functions are designed to display a question, process an answer, or set the question and answer variables for the current level.

1 In the ActionScript Library layer, ensure that no objects are selected on the Stage, and create a new Movie Clip symbol, naming it **ActionScript Library**.

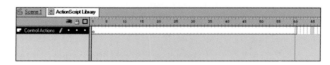

Create a new Movie Clip and insert additional blank frames in the Control Actions layer.

2 In the symbol-editing mode of the ActionScript Library Movie Clip, name the existing layer **Control Actions**, and insert an additional 59 frames, creating a total of 60.

3 Insert blank keyframes at positions 11, 21, 31, 41, and 51, and then, beginning with keyframe 1, work your way over to the right, assigning these frame labels:

Assign frame labels to the new blank keyframes on the Control Actions layer.

Keyframe 1	**Initialize**
Keyframe 11	**DisplayQuestion**
Keyframe 21	**AnswerQuestion**
Keyframe 31	**Level1**
Keyframe 41	**Level2**
Keyframe 51	**Level3**

4 Double-click keyframe 1 (labeled Initialize) to open its Frame Properties dialog box, and, on the Actions tab, assign the ActionScript.

To begin the game, Initialize sets a few important variables and ensures that the Continue button is not visible. It also resets the **QuestionIndicators** symbol and calls the **Level1** function, which sets the question-and-answer variables for the current level.

```
Stop
FS Command ("AllowScale", False)
Set Property ("/Continue", Visibility) = False
Set Variable: "/:CurrentLevel" = 1
Set Variable: "/:CurrentQuestion" = 1
Set Variable: "/:CurrentAnswer" = ""
Begin Tell Target ("/QuestionIndicators")
    Go to and Stop ("Question1")
End Tell Target
Call ("Level1")
```

212

5 Double-click keyframe 11 (labeled DisplayQuestion) to open its Frame Properties dialog box, and, on the Actions tab, assign the ActionScript.

DisplayQuestion makes each of the answer buttons visible and then sets the question-and-answer fields to display the current question. It also resets the points counter and progresses the question indicator lights.

```
If (/:CurrentQuestion <= 4)
    Set Property ("/A", Visibility) = True
    Set Property ("/B", Visibility) = True
    Set Property ("/C", Visibility) = True
    Begin Tell Target ("/Points")
        Go to and Play (1)
    End Tell Target
    Begin Tell Target ("/QuestionIndicators")
        Go to and Stop ("Question" & /:CurrentQuestion)
    End Tell Target
    Set Variable: "/:Question" = Eval("Q" & /:CurrentQuestion & "_Question")
    Set Variable: "/:AnswerA" = Eval("Q" & /:CurrentQuestion & "_A")
    Set Variable: "/:AnswerB" = Eval("Q" & /:CurrentQuestion & "_B")
    Set Variable: "/:AnswerC" = Eval("Q" & /:CurrentQuestion & "_C")
End If
```

6 Double-click keyframe 21 (labeled AnswerQuestion) to open its Frame Properties dialog box, and, on the Actions tab, assign the ActionScript.

AnswerQuestion is called after one of the answers is chosen or when the points count reaches zero. It stops the points counter and compares the selected answer with the correct one. If the answer is correct, the correct count is incremented by one; otherwise, the correct count stays the same. This script also hides the incorrect answers and tells players whether they got it right. Last, it increases the current question variable by one and makes the Continue button visible.

```
Begin Tell Target ("/Points")
    Stop
End Tell Target
If (/:CurrentAnswer eq Eval("Q" & /:CurrentQuestion & "_CorrectAnswer"))
    Set Variable: "/:Score" = /:Score + /:Points
    Set Variable: "Correct" = True
    Set Variable: "/:CorrectCount" = /:CorrectCount + 1
Else
    Set Variable: "Correct" = False
End If
If (Correct = True)
    Set Variable: "/:Question" = "Right on! The correct answer was:"
Else
    Set Variable: "/:Question" = "Wrong! The correct answer was:"
End If
Set Property ("/A", Visibility) = False
Set Property ("/B", Visibility) = False
Set Property ("/C", Visibility) = False
Set Property ("/" & Eval("Q" & /:CurrentQuestion & "_CorrectAnswer"), Visibility) = True
If (Eval("Q" & /:CurrentQuestion & "_CorrectAnswer") eq "A")
    Set Variable: "/:AnswerB" = ""
    Set Variable: "/:AnswerC" = ""
Else If (Eval("Q" & /:CurrentQuestion & "_CorrectAnswer") eq "B")
    Set Variable: "/:AnswerA" = ""
    Set Variable: "/:AnswerC" = ""
Else If (Eval("Q" & /:CurrentQuestion & "_CorrectAnswer") eq "C")
    Set Variable: "/:AnswerA" = ""
    Set Variable: "/:AnswerB" = ""
End If
Set Variable: "/:CurrentQuestion" = /:CurrentQuestion + 1
Set Property ("/Continue", Visibility) = True
```

7 Double-click keyframe 31 (labeled Level1) to open its Frame Properties dialog box, and, on the Actions tab, assign the ActionScript.

Level1, as with all three of the Levelx frames, contains all the necessary question-and-answer data. It sets question-and-answer values for all four questions and provides the value of the correct responses. After you've added all the actions for Level1, it's recommended that you copy and paste the list of statements into Level2 and Level3 and then just change the values. This will save quite a bit of work—and time, of course.

Notice how easy it is to change the questions displayed by the Quiz. To put in your own questions, simply substitute each of the values in these level frames.

```
Set Variable: "Q1_Question" = "In Mary Poppins, what does Uncle Albert need to do to get
    down from the ceiling?"
Set Variable: "Q1_A" = "burp"
Set Variable: "Q1_B" = "think of something sad"
Set Variable: "Q1_C" = "walk down the wall till he reaches the floor"
Set Variable: "Q1_CorrectAnswer" = "B"
Set Variable: "Q2_Question" = "Which invention finally made a fortune for Caractacus Potts,
    the father in "Chitty Chitty Bang Bang"?"
Set Variable: "Q2_A" = "candy for dogs"
Set Variable: "Q2_B" = "vacuum cleaner"
Set Variable: "Q2_C" = "automatic hair cutting machine"
Set Variable: "Q2_CorrectAnswer" = "A"
Set Variable: "Q3_Question" = "In "Willy Wonka and the Chocolate Factory," what happens
    to Violet?"
Set Variable: "Q3_A" = "she gets sucked into a big tube of liquid chocolate"
Set Variable: "Q3_B" = "she turns into a big blueberry"
Set Variable: "Q3_C" = "she marries Willy Wonka and they live happily ever after"
Set Variable: "Q3_CorrectAnswer" = "B"
Set Variable: "Q4_Question" = "In "E.T.," the little alien just wants to:"
Set Variable: "Q4_A" = "eat a really juicy steak"
Set Variable: "Q4_B" = "pick up some new clothes"
Set Variable: "Q4_C" = "phone home"
Set Variable: "Q4_CorrectAnswer" = "C"
```

8 Double-click keyframe 41 (labeled Level2) to open its Frame Properties dialog box, and, on the Actions tab, assign the ActionScript.

Set Variable: "Q1_Question" = "In "Chitty Chitty Bang Bang," the queen of Vulgaria really hates"

Set Variable: "Q1_A" = "big dogs"

Set Variable: "Q1_B" = "her husband"

Set Variable: "Q1_C" = "children"

Set Variable: "Q1_CorrectAnswer" = "C"

Set Variable: "Q2_Question" = "In "Kiki's Delivery Service," Kiki leaves home as part of her training as a:"

Set Variable: "Q2_A" = "witch"

Set Variable: "Q2_B" = "babysitter"

Set Variable: "Q2_C" = "dirigible co-pilot"

Set Variable: "Q2_CorrectAnswer" = "A"

Set Variable: "Q3_Question" = "Goofy is a:"

Set Variable: "Q3_A" = "really weird cow"

Set Variable: "Q3_B" = "rather unusual dog"

Set Variable: "Q3_C" = "quite unfriendly coyote"

Set Variable: "Q3_CorrectAnswer" = "B"

Set Variable: "Q4_Question" = "Frosty the Snowman comes to life with the help of:"

Set Variable: "Q4_A" = "a magician's hat"

Set Variable: "Q4_B" = "a really warm scarf"

Set Variable: "Q4_C" = "a pair of enchanted snowboots"

Set Variable: "Q4_CorrectAnswer" = "A"

9 Double-click keyframe 51 (labeled Level3) to open its Frame Properties dialog box, and, on the Actions tab, assign the ActionScript.

Relax, that's the last of it!

10 Exit symbol-editing mode, return to Scene 1, drag an instance of ActionScript Library from your movie's own Library onto the Stage, and name the instance **Library**.

The Quiz will now be completely functional!

Set Variable: "Q1_Question" = "The Brave Little Toaster finds his master with the help of a radio, a lamp, a vacuum cleaner, and :"

Set Variable: "Q1_A" = "a blender"

Set Variable: "Q1_B" = "a coffee maker"

Set Variable: "Q1_C" = "an electric blanket"

Set Variable: "Q1_CorrectAnswer" = "C"

Set Variable: "Q2_Question" = "Pinocchio only turns into a donkey on two parts of his body, which are:"

Set Variable: "Q2_A" = "his feet and hands"

Set Variable: "Q2_B" = "his ears and tail"

Set Variable: "Q2_C" = "his nose and legs"

Set Variable: "Q2_CorrectAnswer" = "B"

Set Variable: "Q3_Question" = "Cinderella's two little mice friends are named:"

Set Variable: "Q3_A" = "Bill and Ted"

Set Variable: "Q3_B" = "Harry and George"

Set Variable: "Q3_C" = "Gus and Jag"

Set Variable: "Q3_CorrectAnswer" = "C"

Set Variable: "Q4_Question" = "In "Beauty and the Beast," Belle's father in an inventor, whose latest invention is:"

Set Variable: "Q4_A" = "a wood-chopping machine"

Set Variable: "Q4_B" = "a mirror that can show what someone is doing"

Set Variable: "Q4_C" = "a coach that walks on legs"

Set Variable: "Q4_CorrectAnswer" = "A"

MODIFICATIONS

Although our sample quiz is lighthearted and fun, you can use the same method to create a more serious survey or even a test. By adding a few script statements, you could have the player's results submitted to a Web database and stored for marketing purposes or an academic assessment, perhaps. Thanks to Flash's capability to send and receive data from a Web server, even the questions could become dynamic, with Level1, Level2, and Level3 loading variables from a database or text file rather than being set manually. The possibilities are practically endless—all it takes is some good planning and a little experimentation.

MEMORY GAME

"A smooth sea never made

a skillful mariner."

—ENGLISH PROVERB

MAKING A CONCENTRATION GAME IN FLASH

Matching games—or Memory games, as they're

more commonly known—have long been a

favorite for passing the time or testing one's

brain power. Thanks to Flash, you can take the

time-honored Memory game and turn it into an

animated gadget for your desktop or Web site.

Notable features of this application include a

random layout of all the pieces on the board

and completely cheat-proof game play to pro-

vide a genuine challenge.

PROJECT 17:
CONCENTRATION

Layers
    Control Actions
    Game Screens
    Background

GETTING STARTED

If you want your results to match those of the finished project, follow the steps carefully. If you want to customize the project and are familiar with Flash 4, feel free to change the settings to those that meet your needs.

1   Begin with a new Flash Movie, using these settings:

Frame rate:	**12 fps**
Stage dimensions:	**320 × 240**
Background color:	**White**

2   Create three layers, naming them (from top to bottom) **Control Actions**, **Game Screens**, and **Background**.

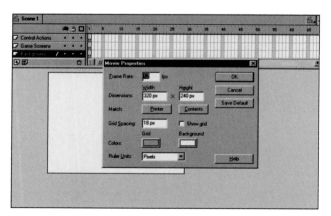

Begin with three layers on the main Timeline.

3 From the Flash 4 Magic CD, load MatchingGame.fla as a Library.

4 In the Background layer, drag an instance of the Tiled Background symbol from the Vector Graphics folder of the MatchingGame.fla Library onto the Stage and center it.

5 Lock the Background layer now because you won't be dealing with it again, and save your file as **concentration.fla**.

6 Insert an additional 29 blank frames to all three layers, creating a total of 30.

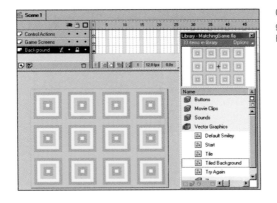

Center the Tiled Background symbol in the Background layer.

CREATING THE SMILES

The key to the Matching game is the individual game pieces—in this case, animated smiley faces. The game consists of 12 smileys: six different types with two copies of each. Before you set out the game board, you need to create the smiley symbols. The code contained in each symbol is the same, so after you complete the example in this section, you'll find that we've included the other five types already put together.

1 Press Control+L (PC) or Command+L (MAC) to open your movie's Library.

You should have two Libraries open now—the Library from the MatchingGame.fla file and the Library from your concentration.fla file.

2 In the Game Screens layer, drag the Chewy symbol from the Movie Clips\Smileys folder of the MatchingGame.fla Library to the concentration.fla Library.

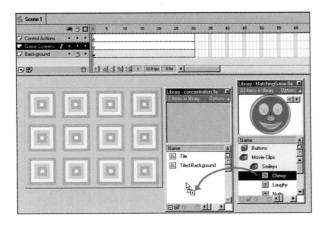

Drag and drop the Chewy Movie Clip from the MatchingGame.fla Library to the concentration.fla Library.

Note: You cannot edit a Movie Clip that is located in a Library you've opened from an external Flash file. To edit a Movie Clip from a Movie you've opened as a Library, copy that Movie Clip to your new movie.

3 Double-click the Chewy Movie Clip icon in the concentration.fla Library to enter the symbol-editing mode for the Movie Clip.

Notice that the Movie Clip currently contains only one layer (Chewy)—essentially a series of keyframes that make up this smiley's particular animation. Your job is to add a set of keyframes and an ActionScript that will enable this symbol to be used in the game.

4 Add two layers above the Chewy label and label them **Control Actions** and **Button**.

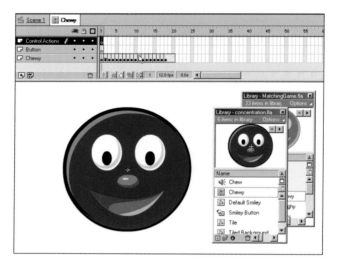

Add two layers to the Chewy Movie Clip and name them Control Actions and Button.

5 In keyframe 1 in the Button layer, drag an instance of the Smiley Button from the Buttons folder onto the Stage, and use the Object Inspector to position the Smiley Button symbol at x: **−33.1**, y: **−33.2**.

The instance should be centered precisely over the blue smiley face in the layer below.

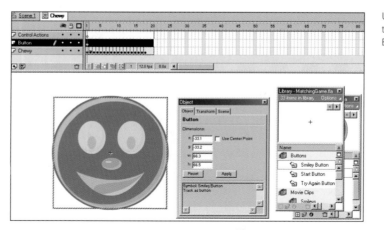

Use the Object Inspector to position the Smiley Button symbol.

6 Double-click the instance of Smiley Button you just created to open Instance Properties, and, on the Actions tab, assign the ActionScript.

Only two smileys should be active at a time. A variable named **Count** tracks the number of game pieces the user has clicked. This script checks the value of

```
On (Release)
    If (/:Count < 2)
        Play
    End If
End On
```

Count and plays the animation only if its value is less than two.

7 In the Button layer, insert a blank keyframe at frame 2 to remove the button from the Stage and prevent the user from clicking the same smiley twice in the same turn.

8 In the Control Actions layer, double-click the blank keyframe in frame 1 to open the Frame Properties dialog box, and, on the Actions tab, assign the ActionScript.

```
Stop
Set Variable: "SmileyType" = "Chewy"
```

These actions stop play at the first frame, which is important so that the invisible button is always displayed in the default state. The second action sets a variable named **SmileyType** within this Movie Clip. **SmileyType** keeps track of what kind of smiley has been clicked so the movie can determine whether the two currently active pieces match.

9 With the Control Actions layer still selected, insert a second blank keyframe at frame 2, double-click the frame to open the Frame Properties dialog box, and, on the Actions tab, assign the ActionScript.

```
Set Variable: "/:Count" = /:Count + 1
Set Variable: "/:Smiley" & /:Count & "Type" = SmileyType
Set Variable: "/:Smiley" & /:Count & "Name" = GetProperty( "", _name )
```

> **Note:** The Variable portions of the last two Set Variable actions are Expressions. Throughout this project, you need to pay close attention to whether values are Literals or Expressions: accuracy is crucial to retaining the script's functionality.

Here's where things start to get a little tricky. First of all, the variable **Count** is incremented by 1 to show that an additional smiley has just been clicked. Second, a variable is dynamically created to store the value of **SmileyType**. For example, if **Count** currently equals 1 and **SmileyType** equals Chewy, the variable will be created as **Smiley1Type = Chewy**.

Last, a variable is created to store the name of the particular instance that was just clicked. Because symbols are reusable, you don't hardcode one instance name into this code—rather, you obtain it on the fly by using the **GetProperty** action. If **Count** is 1 and the instance name is Smiley8, the third line of code will evaluate as **/:Smiley1Name = Smiley8**.

10 Insert blank keyframes at frames 18, 19, and 20; double-click keyframe 18 to open the Frame Properties dialog box; and, on the Actions tab, assign the ActionScript.

```
Set Variable: "/:DoneCount" = /:DoneCount + 1
```

DoneCount makes sure that both animations are completed before the matching process takes place. It is incremented by 1 at frame 18 in Chewy (the end of this particular animation), but because the animation lengths vary from smiley to smiley, you'll see that **DoneCount** is set at whatever keyframe contains the final animated frame for each example.

11 Double-click keyframe 19 to open the Frame Properties dialog box, and, on the Actions tab, assign the ActionScript.

In a nutshell, this script checks to see whether **DoneCount** equals 2, indicating that the user has clicked two smileys. If **DoneCount** does equal 2, Flash hides the two clicked smileys when they match and resets them for the next turn when they don't match. If **DoneCount** doesn't equal 2, the script plays to the next frame.

A variable named **Pairs** is used to determine whether all the smileys have been matched. If a match is detected, Pairs is decremented by one. When **Pairs** equals 0, the main Timeline is instructed to go to another keyframe that prompts the user to play again.

```
Stop
If (/:DoneCount < 2)
    Play
Else
    Set Variable: "/:DoneCount" = 0
    If (/:Count = 2)
        If (/:Smiley1Type eq /:Smiley2Type)
            Set Property ("/" & /:Smiley1Name, Visibility) = False
            Set Property ("/" & /:Smiley2Name, Visibility) = False
            Set Variable: "/:Pairs" = /:Pairs - 1
            If (/:Pairs = 0)
                Begin Tell Target ("..")
                    Go to and Stop ("Try Again")
                End Tell Target
            End If
        Else
            Begin Tell Target ("/" & /:Smiley1Name)
                Go to and Stop (1)
            End Tell Target
            Begin Tell Target ("/" & /:Smiley2Name)
                Go to and Stop (1)
            End Tell Target
        End If
        Set Variable: "/:Count" = 0
    End If
End If
```

12 Double-click keyframe 20 to open the Frame Properties dialog box, and, on the Actions tab, assign the ActionScript.

This action causes the playhead to cycle between keyframes 19 and 20 while the movie waits for **DoneCount** to reach 2.

```
Go to Previous Frame
```

13 Exit the symbol-editing mode for the Chewy Movie Clip and go back to the main Timeline.

POPULATING THE GAME SCREENS

In this section, you lay out the symbols that constitute the visible part of the movie before proceeding to the Control Actions layer, where you'll add the remaining scripts.

1 In the Game Screens layer, insert blank keyframes at frames 11 and 21.

2 In the blank keyframe on frame 1, drag an instance of the Start Button symbol from the Buttons folder of MatchingGame.fla onto the Stage and center it.

In the main Timeline, add blank keyframes to frames 11 and 21 and a Start Button instance on frame 1 of the Game Screens layer.

3 Double-click the instance of the Start Button to open the Instance Properties dialog box, and, on the Actions tab, assign the ActionScript.

The **Go to** command used here refers to a frame label that will be added to the Control Actions layer in later steps.

```
On (Release)
    Go to and Stop ("Game")
End On
```

4 Move the playhead to keyframe 11, and, from your movie's own Library, drag two instances of the Chewy Movie Clip symbol onto the Stage.

The placement of these symbols is unimportant because they'll be randomly repositioned by an ActionScript routine when the game is played.

5 From the Movie Clips\Smileys folder in MatchingGame.fla, drag two instances each of Laughy, Nutty, Scary, Sneezy, and Wacky.

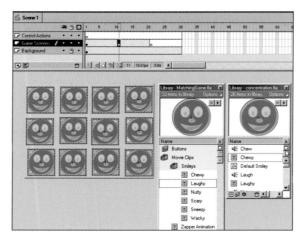

Be careful to use the symbols from the correct Library.

6 Double-click each of the 12 smiley symbols, and give each one an instance name, using the names **Smiley1** through **Smiley12**.

These instance names enable **Tell Target** and **Set Property** control over these Movie Clips by other parts of the game.

Give each Smiley Movie Clip an instance name.

7 In the Game Screens layer, double-click the blank keyframe 21 to open its Frame Properties dialog box, and, on the Actions tab, assign the ActionScript.

Stop

8 In the Game Screens layer, drag an instance of the Try Again graphic symbol from the Vector Graphics folder and an instance of the Try Again Button symbol from the Buttons folder in the MatchingGame.fla Library onto the Stage.

9 Use the Align feature to align Try Again to the bottom center of the page, and then use the Object Inspector to position the Try Again Button at x: **10.4**, y: **25.1**.

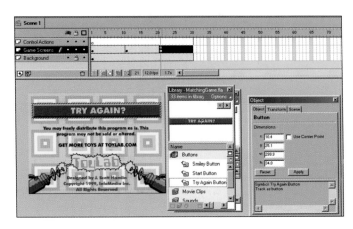

Position the Try Again symbol and button on the Stage.

10 Double-click the Try Again Button instance to open Instance Properties, and, on the Actions tab, assign the ActionScript.

Once again, Game is a frame label that will appear in the Control Actions layer.

On (Release)
    Go to and Stop ("Game")
End On

ADDING THE FINISHING TOUCHES

1 In the Control Actions layer, insert blank keyframes at frames 11 and 21 and, beginning with keyframe 1, label the three keyframes **Initialize**, **Game**, and **Try Again**.

Label the three blank keyframes Initialize, Game, and Try Again.

2 Double-click keyframe 1 to open its Frame Properties dialog box, and, on the Actions tab, assign the ActionScript.

These actions control playback and initialize all the major game variables.

```
Stop
Set Variable: "Count" = 0
Set Variable: "DoneCount" = 0
Set Variable: "Pairs" = 6
Set Variable: "Smiley1Type" = ""
Set Variable: "Smiley2Type" = ""
Set Variable: "Smiley1Name" = ""
Set Variable: "Smiley2Name" = ""
FS Command ("AllowScale", "False")
```

3 Double-click keyframe 11 to open its Frame Properties dialog box, and, on the Actions tab, assign the ActionScript.

The Game script does a number of things. First, it creates an array (or list) of variables, one for each smiley. Each variable in the array is used to indicate whether that smiley has been assigned a place on the game board. The initial value for each variable is **False**, denoting that none of them have been positioned.

The remainder of the script cycles through each grid position in turn and selects a random smiley to go to that position. Before moving the smiley, however, Flash checks the corresponding array variable to see if that smiley has already been taken. If it has, the script repeats the selection process until a "free" smiley is chosen.

```
Stop
Set Variable: "SmileyCounter" = 0
Loop While (SmileyCounter < 12)
        Set Variable: "SmileyCounter" = SmileyCounter + 1
        Set Variable: "Smiley" & SmileyCounter = False
End Loop
Set Variable: "SmileyCounter" = 0
Set Variable: "Row" = 0
Set Variable: "Column" = 0
Loop While (SmileyCounter < 12)
        Set Variable: "SmileyCounter" = SmileyCounter + 1
        If ((SmileyCounter >= 1) and (SmileyCounter <= 4))
                Set Variable: "Row" = 1
                Set Variable: "Column" = SmileyCounter
        Else If ((SmileyCounter >= 5) and (SmileyCounter <= 8))
                Set Variable: "Row" = 2
                Set Variable: "Column" = SmileyCounter - 4
```

Although the smileys are being repositioned dynamically each time the game is played, all this work takes
place in one frame so the movement is never visible
to the player.

```
Else If ((SmileyCounter >= 9) and (SmileyCounter <= 12))
    Set Variable: "Row" = 3
    Set Variable: "Column" = SmileyCounter - 8
End If
Set Variable: "Done" = False
Loop While (Done = False)
    Set Variable: "CurrentSmiley" = Random(12) + 1
    If (Eval("Smiley" & CurrentSmiley) = False)
        Set Property ("Smiley" & CurrentSmiley, X Position) = ((Column - 1) * 80) + 40
        Set Property ("Smiley" & CurrentSmiley, Y Position) = ((Row - 1) * 80) + 40
        Set Variable: "Done" = True
        Set Variable: "Smiley" & CurrentSmiley = True
    Else
        Set Variable: "Done" = False
    End If
End Loop
End Loop
```

4   Double-click keyframe 21 to open its Frame
    Properties dialog box, and, on the Actions tab, assign
    the ActionScript.

```
Stop
```

The game is now complete and ready to play!

MODIFICATIONS

Because the Matching Game (and most other examples in this book, for that matter) is
built strictly with symbols, you can easily substitute new graphics and animations and
create a range of customized versions. When you're familiar with the scripting
involved, you can even extend the size of the game board to increase the difficulty of
game play. By creating a strong Library of symbols whenever you author a Flash movie,
you can save on file size, complexity, and development time.

WACK-A-MOLE
GAME

"Creativity is allowing

yourself to make mistakes.

Art is knowing which

ones to keep."

—SCOTT ADAMS

MAKING A WACK A-MOLE GAME IN FLASH

This project covers the creation of a Wack-A-Mole style game. Before you actually start building the game, you need to understand its parameters. First, the game has 16 holes from which 50 targets can appear. The 50 targets are of six types—four target types award one point, one target type deducts one point from the score, and one target type resets the score to 0. The amount of time that the targets are "wackable" is random, ranging from .5 to 3 seconds. After 50 targets have displayed, the game is over.

PROJECT 18:
WACK-A-MOLE

Scenes
Start
Game Play
End

GETTING STARTED

This section sets up a new Flash file. If you want your results to match those of the finished project, follow the steps carefully. If you want to customize the project and are familiar with Flash 4, feel free to change the settings to those that meet your needs.

1 Begin with a new Flash Movie, using these settings:

Frame rate:	**18 fps**
Stage dimensions:	**440 × 320**
Background color:	**Light blue**

2 Set up three scenes, naming them (in order) **Start**, **Game Play**, and **End**.

3 Select the Start scene and set up three layers, naming them (from top to bottom) **Foreground**, **Start Animation**, and **Background**.

4 Select the Game Play scene and set up five layers, naming them (from top to bottom) **Foreground**, **Controllers**, **Variables**, **Background**, and **Apertures**.

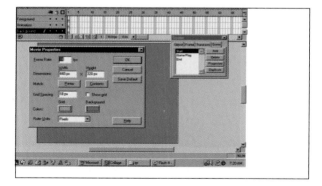

Set up the new movie, its scenes, and the layers in the Start scene.

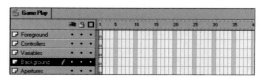

Label the five layers in the Game Play scene.

234

5 Select the End scene and set up three layers, naming them (from top to bottom) **Foreground**, **End Animation**, and **Background**.

6 From the Flash 4 Magic CD, open Wack.fla as a Library.

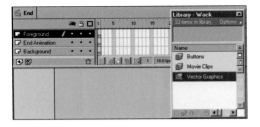

Set up the three layers in the End scene and open the Library.

CREATING THE TARGET TIMER

The Target Timer is the Movie Clip used to determine when to make a target unavailable if it has not been hit. This Movie Clip uses two variables, Start and End, both of which are set by the Movie Clip in which the Target Timer will reside.

1 In the Game Play scene, choose Insert>New Symbol to create a new Movie Clip, and name it **Timer**.

Flash opens this new Movie Clip symbol in symbol-editing mode.

Insert a new Movie Clip named Timer.

2 Open the Properties dialog box for the first keyframe and, on the Actions tab, add the ActionScript.

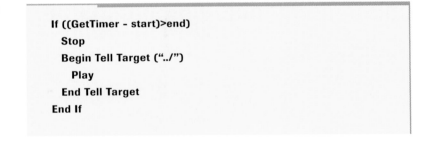

```
If ((GetTimer - start)>end)
    Stop
    Begin Tell Target ("../")
        Play
    End Tell Target
End If
```

3 Right-click or Control+click on the first keyframe, select Copy Frame, select the second frame, right-click or Control+click on it, and choose Paste Frames.

You should now have two identical keyframes. If you somehow end up with extra keyframes in the Movie Clip, make sure that you delete them.

4 Choose Edit>Main Movie to return to the main movie.

Copy and paste the frame so that the Timer Movie Clip has two identical keyframes.

CREATING THE TARGETLIST MOVIE CLIP

The list of targets (TargetList Movie Clip) is a six-frame Movie Clip that has one of the six target buttons in each frame. The Hole Movie Clip displays one of these frames whenever the aperture is opened.

1 Choose Insert>New Symbol to make new Movie Clip, naming it **TargetList**.

Flash opens this new Movie Clip in symbol-editing mode.

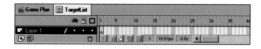

Insert a new Movie Clip named TargetList.

2 Open the Properties dialog box for the first keyframe and, on the Actions tab, add the ActionScript.

Stop

3 Select the first keyframe, copy it, and paste it in the next five frames so that the Movie Clip has six keyframes.

4 In the first keyframe, drag an instance of the Approval symbol from the Target Buttons folder in the Buttons folder of the Wack.fla Library onto the Stage, and center the instance horizontally and vertically on the page.

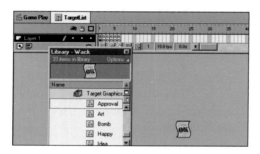

Copy and paste so that the TargetList Movie Clip has six keyframes, and create an instance of the Approval symbol.

5 In the second keyframe, drag an instance of the Art symbol from the Target Buttons folder as in step 4.

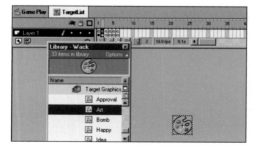

Instance the Art symbol in the second keyframe.

6 Continue dragging instances of the other buttons from the Target Buttons folder to the remaining keyframes.

Place an instance of a button on each of the six keyframes.

7 Select the instance of the Approval button in the first keyframe, open its Properties dialog box, and, on the ActionScript, assign the ActionScript.

8 Copy and paste the same ActionScript on the Actions tabs of the five remaining buttons in the Movie Clip.

9 Choose Edit>Main Movie to return to the main movie.

```
On (Press)
    If (wackable=True)
        Set Variable: "/:score" = /:score+1
        Begin Tell Target ("../")
            Play
        End Tell Target
    End If
End On
```

CREATING THE HOLE MOVIE CLIP

The Hole Movie Clip is the hole in the game that opens to reveal the targets you just made. This Movie Clip will contain the two previous Movie Clips.

1 Copy the Hole Movie Clip from the Wack.fla Library into your movie Library.

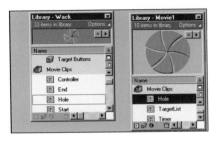

Drag an instance of the Hole Movie Clip from the Wack.fla Library into your own movie's Library.

Note: Copying a Movie Clip from one Library to another is simple: Open the Library for your movie (Window>Library), select the Hole symbol from the Wack.fla Library, and drag it into the Library for your movie.

2 Select the copy of the Hole Movie Clip in your movie's Library and open it in symbol-editing mode.

The Movie Clip already has a single layer named Apertures with 13 frames in it.

3   Create two new layers in the Movie Clip, name them **Actions** and **Targets,** and place the layers in this order (from top to bottom): Actions, Apertures, and Targets.

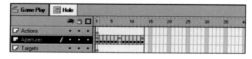

Create three layers in the Hole Movie Clip.

4   Create a new blank keyframe in frame 2 of the Targets layer, open the Library for your movie, drag an instance of the TargetList Movie Clip from your movie's Library onto the Stage, center it horizontally and vertically on the page, and name the instance **TargetList.**

Instance the TargetList Movie Clip.

5   Make sure that the Target layer has a total of 13 frames so it ends where the Aperture layer ends.

6   In the Actions layer, open the Properties dialog box of the first keyframe, and, on the Actions tab, assign the ActionScript.

```
Stop
Set Variable: "open" = False
```

7   Insert a keyframe in frame 2 of the Actions layer, open the Frame Properties dialog box and, on the Actions tab, assign the ActionScript.

```
Set Variable: "open" = True
Set Variable: "/:numUp" = /:numUp+1
Set Variable: "TargetList/:wackable" = True
Begin Tell Target ("TargetList")
   Go to and Play (Random(6)+1)
End Tell Target
```

8 In the Actions layer, insert a blank keyframe at frame 7, drag an instance of the Timer Movie Clip from your Library (not the Wack.fla Library) onto the Stage, and name the instance **Timer**.

The positioning of this Movie Clip is not important because it is not visible.

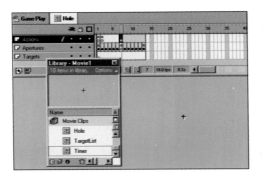

Instance the Timer Movie Clip from your Library in frame 7.

9 Open the Properties dialog box for frame 7 and, on the Actions tab, assign the ActionScript.

```
Stop
Set Variable: "Timer/:start" = GetTimer
Set Variable: "Timer/:end" = Random(3000)+500
```

10 In the Actions layer, insert a blank keyframe at frame 8, open its Properties dialog box, and, on the Actions tab, assign the ActionScript.

```
Set Variable: "TargetList/:wackable" = False
Set Variable: "/:numUp" = /:numUp-1
```

11 Choose Edit>Main Movie to return to the main movie.

CREATING THE CONTROLLER MOVIE CLIP

The workhorse of the game is the Controller Movie Clip. It controls the opening of each of the holes and signals when the game is finished.

1 Choose Insert>New Symbol to create a new Movie Clip, naming it **Controller**.

Flash enters symbol-editing mode.

Insert a new Movie Clip named Controller.

2 Select the only keyframe in the Controller Movie Clip, open its Properties dialog box, and, on the Actions tab, assign the ActionScript.

```
If (Random(3) = 1 and /:numUp<3 and /:total<>50)
    Set Variable: "found" = False
    Set Variable: "num" = Random(16)+1
```

continues

continued

```
              Loop While (found=False)
            If (Eval("/target"&num&"/:open")=False)
                 Set Variable: "found" = True
            Else
                 Set Variable: "num" = Random(16)+1
            End If
              End Loop
              Set Variable: "/:total" = /:total+1
              Begin Tell Target ("/target"&num)
                   Play
              End Tell Target
        End If
        If (/:total=50 and /:numUp=0)
          Begin Tell Target ("/")
            Play
          End Tell Target
        End If
```

3 Select the first keyframe, copy it, and paste it in the second frame.

Make sure that no other blank frames are in the Timeline.

PUTTING THE START AND END SCENES TOGETHER

1 In the Background layer of the Start scene, drag the Background symbol from the Vector Graphics folder in the Wack.fla Library onto the Stage, centering it horizontally and vertically.

2 In the Foreground layer of the Start scene, drag the Foreground symbol from the Vector Graphics folder in the Wack.fla Library onto the Stage, using the Object Inspector to position it at x: **0**, y: **4**.

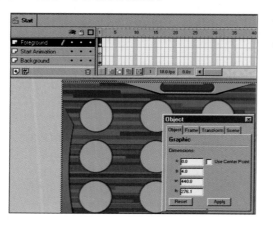

Add the Background and Foreground graphics to the appropriate layers.

240

3 In the Start Animation Layer, drag the Start Movie Clip from the Movie Clips folder in the Wack.fla Library onto the Stage, and center it horizontally and vertically.

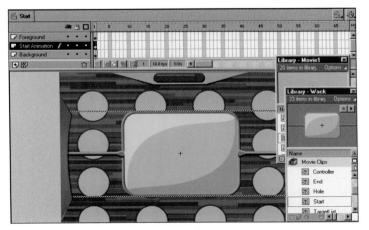

Center the Start Movie Clip on the Stage.

4 Select the first frame of the Foreground layer, open its Properties dialog box, and, on the Actions tab, assign the ActionScript.

Stop

5 In the Background layer of the End scene, drag the Background symbol from the Vector Graphics folder in the Wack.fla Library onto the Stage, centering it horizontally and vertically.

6 In the Foreground layer of the End scene, drag the Foreground symbol from the Vector Graphics folder in the Wack.fla Library onto the Stage, and use the Object Inspector to position it at x: **0**, y: **4**.

7 In the End Animation layer of the End scene, drag the End Movie Clip from the Movie Clips folder of the Library to the Stage and use the Object Inspector to position the symbol at exactly x: **219**, y: **162**, making sure that the Use Center Point option is selected.

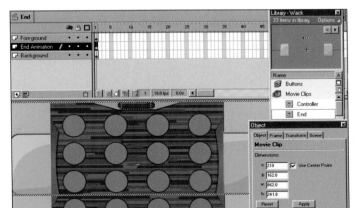

Add the Background and Foreground graphics, and then instance the End Movie Clip.

8 In the first keyframe of the Foreground layer of the End scene, open the Properties dialog box, and, on the Actions tab, assign the ActionScript.

The actual game play will be located in the Game Play scene.

Stop

PUTTING THE GAME PLAY SCENE TOGETHER

1   In the Background layer of the Game Play scene,
drag an instance of the Background symbol from the
Vector Graphics folder in the Wack.fla Library onto
the Stage, and center it horizontally and vertically on
the Stage.

2   In the Foreground layer of the Game Play scene, drag
an instance of the Foreground symbol from the
Vector Graphics folder in the Wack.fla Library onto
the Stage, and align it so that it fits with the
Background graphic.

3   In the Controller layer of the Game Play scene,
drag an instance of the Controller Movie Clip from
your movie's Library (not the Wack.fla Library) onto
the Stage.

The positioning of this Movie Clip is not important
because it's not visible.

4   In the Apertures layer, drag 16 instances of the Hole
Movie Clip from your movie's Library onto the Stage
and align the instances so they fit in the holes in the
Background layer.

5   Name the instances (from the upper left corner to
the lower right corner) **target1** through **target16**.

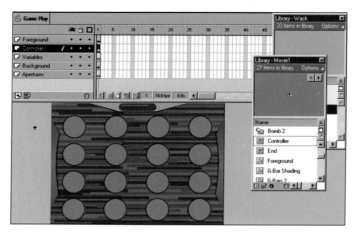

Set up the Background,
Foreground and
Controller layers.

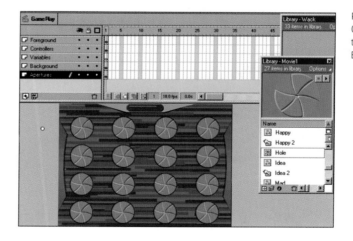

Position the Hole Movie
Clips so they can be seen
through the holes in the
Background layer.

6 In the Variables layer, create a new text box, select the Text Field button to make it an editable text field, draw the text field to fit inside the space, and give it the following attributes and properties:

Font:	Arial
Font Size:	14 pt
Font Color:	Light green
Variable:	**/:score**
Options:	Deselect Draw Border and Background
	Select Disable Editing and Disable Selection
Outlines:	Select Include only specified font outlines (Numbers)

7 In the Variables layer, open the Properties dialog box of the first keyframe, and, on the Actions tab, assign the ActionScript.

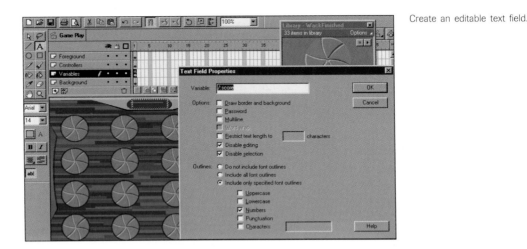

Create an editable text field.

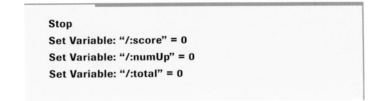

Stop
Set Variable: "/:score" = 0
Set Variable: "/:numUp" = 0
Set Variable: "/:total" = 0

MODIFICATIONS

This game is one you can modify into an educational tool relatively easily. Instead of using purely graphical images, you could set the game up to display math facts, images of historical figures, or any other bits of information students could learn just by sight.

PONG GAME

> "The only time you don't
>
> fail is the last time you try
>
> anything—and it works."
>
> **—WILLIAM STRONG**

MAKING A PONG GAME IN FLASH

Care for a little game of ping pong—digitally,

that is? Although you won't get as much

exercise from this version of the game,

Flash can give you a run for your brain

and digital dexterity.

PROJECT 19:
PONG

Scenes
- Lose
  - Layers
    - Button
    - Graphic
    - Background
- Win
  - Layers
    - Button
    - Graphic
    - Background
- Game
  - Layers
    - Controllers
    - Trig
    - Paddles
    - Ball
    - Score
    - Background
- Intro
  - Layers
    - Button
    - Graphic
    - Background

GETTING STARTED

This section sets up a new Flash file. If you want your results to match those of the finished project, follow the steps carefully. If you want to customize the project and are familiar with Flash 4, feel free to change the settings to those that meet your needs.

1 Create a new movie, using these settings:

Frame rate:	**25 fps**
Stage dimensions:	**550 × 400**
Background color:	**Black**

2 Open the Scene Inspector; create three additional scenes, bringing your total to four; and name them (from top to bottom) **Intro**, **Game**, **Lose**, and **Win**.

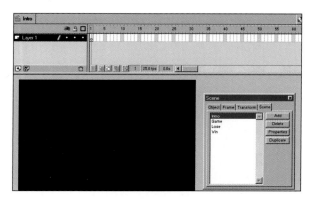

Create a total of four scenes, named Intro, Game, Lose, and Win.

3 In the Win scene, set up three layers, naming them (from top to bottom) **Button**, **Graphic,** and **Background**.

4 Repeat step 3 with the Lose scene.

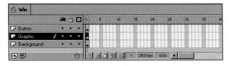

Set up a total of three layers, naming them Button, Graphic, and Background.

5 In the Game scene, set up six layers, naming them (from top to bottom) **Controllers**, **Trig**, **Paddles**, **Ball**, **Score**, and **Background**.

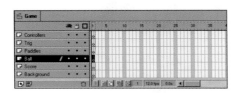

Set up the layers for the Lose and Game scenes.

6 In the Intro scene, set up three layers, naming them (from top to bottom) **Button**, **Graphic,** and **Background**.

7 From the Flash 4 Magic CD, open the Pong.fla file as a Library.

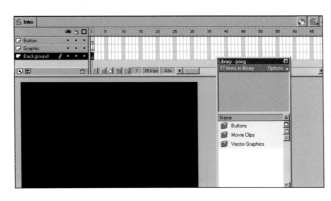

Create three layers in the Intro scene and then open the Pong Library.

SETTING UP THE INTRO SCENE

In this section, you instance the graphic symbols for the Background and Graphic layers. Then, on the Button layer, you set up the ClickToPlay Button, instancing it and assigning its ActionScript.

1 In the Background layer of the Intro scene, drag an instance of the Background symbol from the Vector Graphics folder onto the Stage, centering it horizontally and vertically.

2 In the Graphic layer, drag an instance of the Intro symbol from the Vector Graphics folder onto the Stage, centering it horizontally and vertically.

Add graphics to the Background and Graphic layers of the Intro scene.

3 In the Button layer, drag an instance of the ClickToPlay Button from the Buttons folder onto the Stage and use the Object Inspector to position it at x: **78.8**, y: **315.4**.

Add the ClickToPlay Button to the Button layer.

4 Double-click the ClickToPlay instance to open its Properties dialog box, and, on the Actions tab, assign the ActionScript.

```
On (Release)
        Go to and Play (Game, "newgame")
End On
```

5 Double-click the keyframe in frame 1 of the Button layer to open the Properties dialog box and, on the Actions tab, assign the ActionScript.

```
Stop
```

6 Select the ClickToPlay Button and choose Edit>Copy.

SETTING UP THE LOSE SCENE

It sure would be nice if everyone won every round of every game played. Unfortunately, that never happens, so you have to set up your game to have a Lose scene. The Lose scene contains an instance of the Background symbol, the Lose symbol, and the ClickToPlay button.

1   In the Background layer of the Lose scene, drag an instance of the Background symbol from the Vector Graphics folder onto the Stage, centering it horizontally and vertically.

2   In the Graphic layer, drag an instance of the Lose symbol from the Vector Graphics folder onto the Stage and center it horizontally and vertically.

3   In the Button layer, choose Edit>Paste in Place to paste the ClickToPlay Button from the Intro scene.

Add the symbols to the appropriate layers in the Lose scene.

4   Double-click the keyframe in frame 1 of the Button layer to open the Properties dialog box, label the keyframe **Lose**, and, on the Actions tab, assign the ActionScript.

Stop

SETTING UP THE WIN SCENE

Believe it or not, the Win scene is quite similar to the Lose scene. Both scenes have an instance of the Background symbol and the ClickToPlay Button. The only differences are that the Graphic layer has an instance of the Win symbol and the label of the keyframe in the Button layer is Win.

1   In the Background layer of the Win scene, drag an instance of the Background symbol from the Vector Graphics folder onto the Stage, centering it horizontally and vertically.

2   In the Graphic layer, drag an instance of the Win symbol from the Vector Graphics folder onto the Stage, centering it horizontally and vertically.

3   In the Button layer, choose Edit>Paste in Place to paste a copy of the ClickToPlay Button into it.

Add the symbols to the appropriate layers in the Win scene.

4 Double-click the first keyframe of the Button layer to open the Properties dialog box, label the keyframe **Win**, and, on the Actions tab, assign the ActionScript.

SETTING UP THE GAME SCENE'S BACKGROUND

This short section is important. In it, you instance the Background symbol one more time. However, you also add frames and then lock the Background layer so that you can work on the Game scene without messing up the Background layer.

1 In the Background layer of the Game scene, drag an instance of the Background symbol from the Vector Graphics folder onto the Stage, centering it horizontally and vertically.

2 Insert two additional frames (**not** keyframes) on the Background layer and lock the layer.

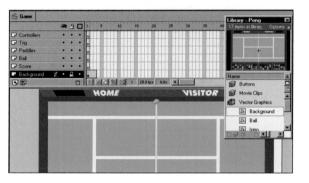

Add the Background symbol to the Background layer and then add two frames and lock the layer.

ADDING THE GAME ELEMENTS

You have quite a bit of work to do in the other layers of the Game Scene. In this section, you instance several Movie Clips, using the Object Inspector to position them correctly. Then you set up text boxes and insert frames in the layers.

1 In the Paddles layer of the Game scene, drag an instance of the Player Movie Clip from the Movie Clips folder onto the Stage, name the instance **player**, and position it at x: **510**, y: **166**, making sure that the Use Center Point option is selected.

2 In the Paddles layer, drag an instance of the Computer Movie Clip from the Movie Clips folder onto the Stage, name the instance **computer**, and

Set up the instance of the Player Movie Clip.

250

position it at x: **40**, y: **166**, making sure that the Use Center Point option is still selected.

3   In the Ball layer, drag an instance of the Ball Movie Clip from the Movie Clips folder onto the Stage, name the instance **ball**, and position it so that its center point is at x: **275**, y: **166**.

4   In the Trig layer, drag an instance of the Trig Movie Clip from the Movie Clips folder onto the Stage, and name the instance **trig**.

You can place this invisible Movie Clip anywhere on the Stage.

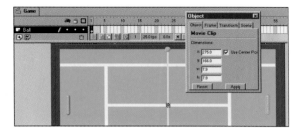

Set up the Ball Movie Clip.

5   Select the Score layer and create two text fields with the following attributes:

Font:	Arial
Font Size:	12 pt
Font Color:	White

6   Position the text fields so they fit inside of the spaces provided in the Background graphic.

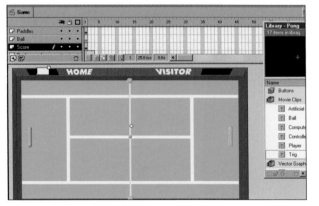

Create two text fields in the Score layer.

7   Select the text field next to the Home label in the Background graphic and set the following properties:

Variable: **cscore**

Options: Deselect Draw Border and Background
                  Select Disable Editing
                  Select Disable Selection

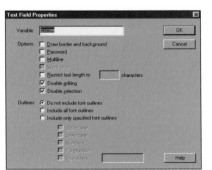

Set the properties for the text field next to the Home label.

8 Select the text field next to the Visitor label in the Background graphic and set the following properties:

Variable: **pscore**

Options: Deselect Draw Border and Background
              Select Disable Editing
              Select Disable Selection

Outlines: Select Include All Font Outlines

9 Create two new frames (not keyframes) in the Trig, Ball, Paddles, and Score layers so that they each have three frames.

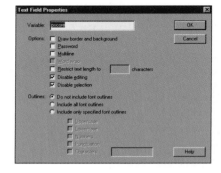

Set the properties for the text field next to the Visitor label.

ADDING THE ACTIONSCRIPT TO THE GAME SCENE

The Movie Clip instances and text boxes are in place. Now it's time to initialize the player and computer scores and assign the ActionScript that drives each round of play.

1 Double-click the keyframe in the first frame of the Controllers layer in the Game scene to open the Frame Properties dialog box, and label the frame **newgame**.

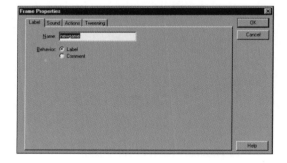

Set up the newgame frame.

2 On the Actions tab, assign the ActionScript.

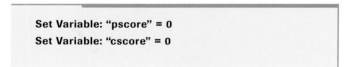

Set Variable: "pscore" = 0
Set Variable: "cscore" = 0

3 Insert a new keyframe in frame 2 of the Controllers layer and label the keyframe **round**.

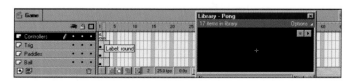

Label the new keyframe in frame 2.

252

4   Insert a new keyframe in frame 3 of the Controllers
    layer, double-click the keyframe to open its
    Properties dialog box, and, on the Actions tab, assign
    the ActionScript.

```
Set Variable: "horz" = -1
Set Variable: "vert" = Random(2)
If (vert=0)
    Set Variable: "vert" = -1
End If
Set Variable: "speed" = 20
Set Variable: "/trig:angle" = Random(70)
Set Variable: "cspeed" = 0
Call ("/trig:cos")
Call ("/trig:sin")
Set Variable: "xspeed" = (speed*/trig:cos)
Set Variable: "yspeed" = (speed*/trig:sin)
Set Variable: "ballx" = 275
Set Variable: "bally" = 166
Set Property ("/ball", X Position) = ballx
Set Property ("/ball", Y Position) = bally
Set Property ("/computer", X Position) = 40
Set Property ("/computer", Y Position) = 166
Set Property ("/player", X Position) = 510
Set Property ("/player", Y Position) = 166
Start Drag ("/player", L=510, T=55, R=510, B=290, lockcenter)
Stop
```

CREATING THE CONTROLLER AND ARTIFICIAL IDIOT MOVIE CLIPS

Roll up your sleeves. It's time to wade into the real workings of this game. In this section, you assign the lines of ActionScript that control the movement of the balls. Not
only that, you set up the Artificial Idiot against which human players do battle.

1 Choose Insert>New Symbol to create a new movie clip, naming it **Controller**.

Flash automatically takes you into symbol-editing mode for the new Movie Clip.

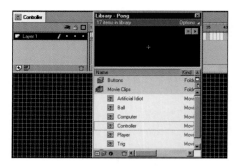

Set up the new Controller Movie Clip.

2 Double-click the keyframe in frame 1 of the Controller Movie Clip to open the Properties dialog box and, on the Actions tab, assign the ActionScript.

```
If (/:bally<30 and /:vert=-1)
    Set Variable: "/:vert" = 1
End If
If (/:bally>315 and /:vert=1)
    Set Variable: "/:vert" = -1
End If
If (/:ballx>=(GetProperty ("/player", _x)-(/:speed)) and /:ballx<=(GetProperty ("/player",
_x)+(/:speed)) and /:horz=1 )
    Set Variable: "paddle" = GetProperty ("/player", _y)
    If ((paddle-/:bally)<=25 and (paddle-/:bally)>=-25)
        If ((paddle-/:bally)>=0)
            Set Variable: "/:vert" = -1
        Else
            Set Variable: "/:vert" = 1
        End If
        Set Variable: "/trig:angle" = ((-1*/:vert*(paddle-/:bally))/25)*75
        Call ("/trig:sin")
        Call ("/trig:cos")
        Set Variable: "/:xspeed" = /trig:cos*/:speed
        Set Variable: "/:yspeed" = /trig:sin*/:speed
        Set Variable: "/:horz" = -1
    End If
End If
If (/:ballx>=(GetProperty ("/computer", _x)-(/:speed)) and /:ballx<=(GetProperty
        ("/computer", _x)+(/:speed)) and /:horz=-1)
    Set Variable: "paddle" = GetProperty ("/computer", _y)
    If ((paddle-/:bally)<=25 and (paddle-/:bally)>=-25)
```

```
              If ((paddle-/:bally)>=0)
                    Set Variable: "/:vert" = -1
              Else
                    Set Variable: "/:vert" = 1
              End If
              Set Variable: "/trig:angle" = ((-1*/:vert*(paddle-/:bally))/25)*75
              Call ("/trig:sin")
              Call ("/trig:cos")
              Set Variable: "/:xspeed" = /trig:cos*/:speed
              Set Variable: "/:yspeed" = /trig:sin*/:speed
              Set Variable: "/:horz" = 1
        End If
  End If
  If (/:ballx<20)
        Set Variable: "/:pscore" = /:pscore+1
        If (/:pscore=10)
              Begin Tell Target ("/")
                    Go to and Stop ("win")
              End Tell Target
        Else
              Begin Tell Target ("/")
                    Go to and Play ("round")
              End Tell Target
        End If
  End If
  If (/:ballx>530)
        Set Variable: "/:cscore" = /:cscore+1
        If (/:cscore=10)
              Begin Tell Target ("/")
                    Go to and Stop ("lose")
              End Tell Target
        Else
              Begin Tell Target ("/")
                    Go to and Play ("round")
              End Tell Target
        End If
  End If
```

continues

255

continued

Set Variable: "/:ballx" = /:ballx+(/:xspeed*/:horz)

Set Variable: "/:bally" = /:bally+(/:yspeed*/:vert)

Set Property ("/ball", X Position) = /:ballx

Set Property ("/ball", Y Position) = /:bally

3 Select the keyframe in frame 1, choose Edit>Copy
Frames and then Edit>Paste Frames to paste a copy
into frame 2 of the same layer.

4 Choose Edit>Main Movie to return to the
main movie.

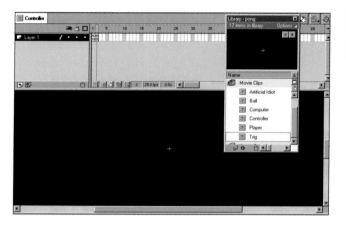

Set up the two keyframes
in the Controller Movie Clip,
each with the same
ActionScript.

5 Select the keyframe in frame 3 of the Controllers
layer in the Game scene, choose Window>Library
to open the Library for your movie, and drag
an instance of the Controller Movie Clip onto
the Stage.

The positioning of this Movie Clip is not important
because it doesn't actually show up on the Stage.

6 Choose Insert>New Symbol to create a new Movie
Clip, naming it **Artificial Idiot**.

Flash automatically takes you into symbol-editing
mode for this Movie Clip.

7 Double-click the keyframe in frame 1 to open its
Properties dialog box and, on the Actions tab, assign
the ActionScript.

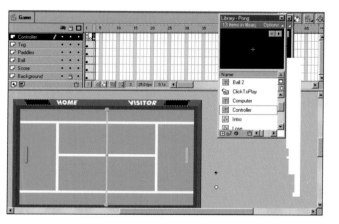

Add the Controller Movie Clip
to the third keyframe of the
Controllers layer in the
Game scene.

If (/:horz=-1)

Set Variable: "/:cspeed" = Random(15)+20

If (GetProperty ("/computer", _y)>/:bally and /:cspeed>=0)

```
            Set Variable: "/:cspeed" = /:cspeed*-1
      End If
      If (/:cspeed<0)
            Set Variable: "sign" = 1
      Else
            Set Variable: "sign" = -1
      End If
      If ((GetProperty ("/computer", _y)-/:bally)<60 or (GetProperty ("/computer", _y)-
            /:bally)>-60)
            Set Variable: "dspeed" = /:cspeed*(((GetProperty ("/computer", _y)-
                  /:bally)*sign)/60)
      Else
            Set Variable: "dspeed" = /:cspeed
      End If
      Set Property ("/computer", Y Position) = GetProperty ("/computer", _y)+dspeed
      If (GetProperty ("/computer",_y)<55)
            Set Property ("/computer", Y Position) = 55
      End If
      If (GetProperty ("/computer",_y)>290)
            Set Property ("/computer", Y Position) = 290
      End If
End If
```

8 Copy the first keyframe (Edit>Copy Frames) and
paste it (Edit>Paste Frames) into the second frame
of the same layer.

9 Choose Edit>Main Movie to return to the main
movie, select the keyframe in frame 3 of the
Controllers layer in the Game scene, and drag an
instance of the Artificial Idiot symbol from your
movie's Library onto the Stage.

The positioning of this Movie Clip is unimportant.

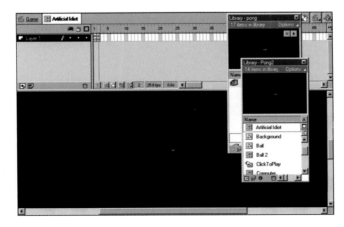

Set up the two keyframes in
the Artificial Idiot Movie Clip,
each with the same
ActionScript.

257

MODIFICATIONS

To change the difficulty of the game, just change the values in the **Set Variable: "/:cspeed" = Random(15)+20** ActionScript. That line (in the code found at the bottom of page 256) modifies the max speed of the computer's paddle. To make the game much easier than it is in this project, for example, change the line to **Set Variable: "/:cspeed" = Random(5)+30**. However, make certain that the values total 35.

HANGMAN GAME

"Clothes make the man.

Naked people have little or

no influence on society."

—MARK TWAIN

MAKING A HANGMAN GAME IN FLASH

Despite its macabre origins, Hangman and its

many variations remain perennial favorites.

In this project, you build a Flash version of

Hangman called Don't Konk the Giggle. You'll

incorporate dynamic duplication and positioning

of symbols, keyboard input, and a big wooden

mallet. Now it's time to get cracking!

PROJECT 20:

HANGMAN

Layers
> ActionScript Library
> Game Screens
> Win Animation
> Lose Animation
> Letter Buttons
> Letter
> Giggle Animation
> Background

GETTING STARTED

If you want your results to match those of the finished project, follow the steps carefully. If you want to customize the project and are familiar with Flash 4, feel free to change the settings to those that meet your needs.

1 Begin with a new Flash Movie, using these settings:

Frame rate:	**24 fps**
Stage dimensions:	**300 × 150**
Background color:	**White**

2 Create eight layers, naming them (from top to bottom) **ActionScript Library**, **Game Screens**, **Win Animation**, **Lose Animation**, **Letter Buttons**, **Letter**, **Giggle Animation**, and **Background**.

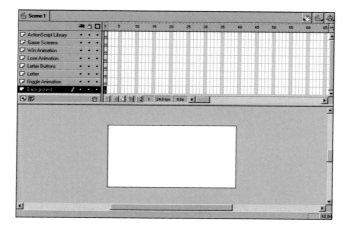

Set up the new movie file.

262

3 From the Flash 4 Magic CD, load Hangman.fla as a Library.

4 In the Background layer, drag an instance of the Background symbol from the Vector Graphics folder onto the Stage, center it horizontally and vertically, and lock the Background layer because you won't be dealing with it again.

5 In the Giggle Animation layer, drag an instance of Giggle Animation from the Movie Clips folder onto the Stage, name the instance **Giggle**, and use the Align tool to center the instance vertically and left-align it on the Stage.

6 In the Letter Buttons layer, drag an instance of the Letter Buttons symbol from the Movie Clips folder onto the Stage, name the instance **LetterButtons,** and use the Object Inspector to position it at x: **132**, y: **14**, making sure that you do not have Use Center Point selected.

7 In the Lose Animation layer, drag an instance of the Lose Animation symbol from the Movie Clips folder onto the Stage, name the instance **Lose**, and use the Object Inspector to position it at x: **59.8**, y: **75**.

8 In the Win Animation layer, drag an instance of the Win Animation symbol from the Movie Clips folder, name the instance **Win,** and use the Object Inspector to position it at x: **59.8**, y: **75.3**.

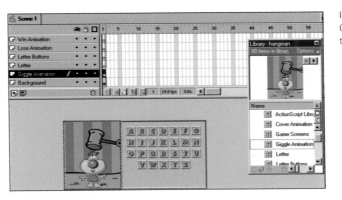

Instance the Background and Giggle Animation symbols in the appropriate layers.

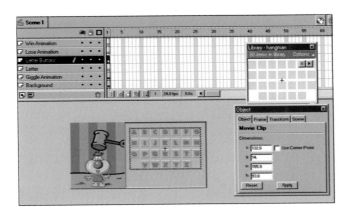

Position the Letter Buttons symbol.

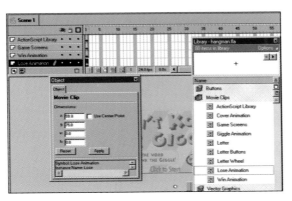

Set up the Lose instance.

CREATING DYNAMIC LETTERS

This game is driven predominantly by routines contained in the ActionScript Library symbol. Each time the game is played, one of five possible words is chosen, and the letters are displayed along the bottom of the game board. The five words are easily changeable—they're just text variables—but first, you need to build a single Letter symbol that can be duplicated a number of times and then set to display the appropriate letter.

The basis of the Letter symbol is a Movie Clip symbol named Letter Wheel. It has a series of keyframes containing all 26 letters of the alphabet.

1   In the Letter layer, drag an instance of the Letter Wheel symbol from the Movie Clip folder onto the Stage and name the instance **Wheel**.

2   Select the Wheel instance, press F8 to convert it to a Movie Clip symbol, name it **Letter**, and move it off the Stage and onto the gray background area.

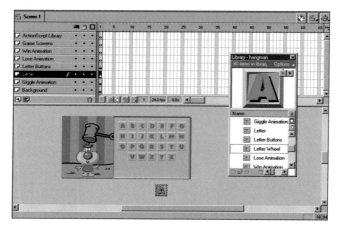

Instance the Letter Movie Clip and move it onto the gray background area.

3   Enter symbol-editing mode for the new Letter Movie Clip, name the existing layer **Letter Wheel**, and insert two additional layers above it, naming them **Control Actions** and **Cover Animation**.

> **Note:** To enter the symbol-editing mode, right-click (Windows) or Control-click (Macintosh) on the new instance, and choose Edit from the pop-up menu.

4   Insert nine frames in each layer so that each has 10 frames.

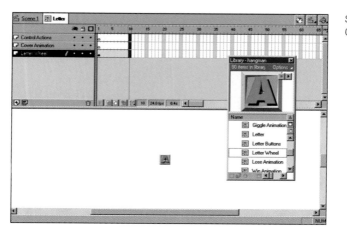

Set up the Letter Movie Clip symbol.

5 Select the first keyframe in the Control Actions layer, label the keyframe **On**, and, on the Actions tab, assign the ActionScript.

6 Insert a blank keyframe in frame 6 of the Control Actions layer, label the keyframe **Off**, and, on the Actions tab, assign the ActionScript.

7 In the Cover Animation layer, drag an instance of the Cover Animation symbol from the Movie Clips folder onto the Stage, and center it horizontally and vertically on the Stage so that it covers the Letter Wheel Movie Clip in the Letter Wheel layer.

8 Insert a keyframe in frame 6 of the Cover Animation layer, automatically duplicating the contents of keyframe 1.

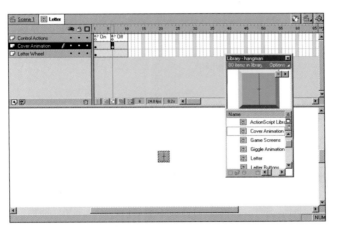

Place the Cover Animation Movie Clip over the Letter Wheel Movie Clip, and insert a keyframe in frame 6.

9 Return to keyframe 1, open the Cover Animation Instance Properties dialog box, and on the Definition tab, change the Behavior setting to Graphic and Play Mode Options to Single Frame.

These changes prevent the Letter Cover animation from playing and revealing the letter beneath before the player has a chance to guess it.

Make this instance of Cover Animation a graphic symbol, not a Movie Clip.

265

BUILDING THE ACTIONSCRIPT LIBRARY

You can simplify the task of designing and debugging your Flash documents by storing most of your scripts in a single location. Using the **Call** statement, you can then reuse script routines over and over, cutting down on complexity and file bloat.

In this particular game, you put together a number of routines: scripts to initialize or clear the game board, to handle mouse clicks and keystrokes, and to play the winning and losing animations.

1 Choose Insert>New Symbol to create a new Movie Clip symbol, naming it **ActionScript Library**.

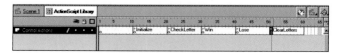

Set up the layers and keyframes for the ActionScript Library Movie Clip.

2 Name the existing layer of this new symbol **Control Actions** and insert 59 additional frames, creating a total of 60.

3 Insert blank keyframes at positions 11, 21, 31, 41, and 51 and label the frames **Initialize**, **CheckLetter**, **Win**, **Lose**, and **ClearLetters**.

Keyframe 1 shouldn't have a label.

4 Open the Frame Properties dialog box for keyframe 1 of the Control Actions layer and, on the Actions tab, assign the ActionScript.

The Visibility property of **/Letter** is set to **False** to hide the original instance of the Letter Movie Clip. The user may resize the Flash Player movie so it can be seen offstage.

```
Stop
FS Command ("AllowScale", False)
Set Property ("/Letter", Visibility) = False
```

5 Open the Frame Properties dialog box for the Initialize keyframe and, on the Actions tab, assign the ActionScript.

```
Set Variable: "Word1" = "CHUCKLE"
Set Variable: "Word2" = "SNICKER"
Set Variable: "Word3" = "CRAZY"
Set Variable: "Word4" = "GOOFY"
Set Variable: "Word5" = "COMEDY"
Set Variable: "CurrentWord" = Eval("Word" & (Random(5) + 1))
Set Variable: "WordLength" = Length(CurrentWord)
Set Variable: "/:LettersRemaining" = WordLength
```

Initialize is a crucial frame. It chooses a random word from the available choices and duplicates as many letters as required to display that word on the gameboard. The letters are then lined up in order and the word is centered in the right-hand portion of the screen.

The Letter symbol actually contains another symbol, the Letter Wheel, that contains all 26 letters of the alphabet. This way, one symbol can be reused and dynamically told to display one portion of the current word.

The Win, Lose, and Giggle animations are all set to their initial state, and the Letter Buttons are switched on so keyboard and mouse input that the movie can accept.

```
Set Variable: "LetterCounter" = 0
Loop While (LetterCounter < WordLength)
    Set Variable: "LetterCounter" = LetterCounter + 1
    Set Variable: "Letter" & LetterCounter = Substring (CurrentWord, LetterCounter, 1)
    Duplicate Movie Clip ("/Letter", "Letter" & LetterCounter, LetterCounter)
    Set Variable: "LeftBound" = 210 - (WordLength * 12.5)
    Set Property ("/Letter" & LetterCounter, X Position) = LeftBound + ((LetterCounter - 1) *
        25) + 12.5
    Set Property ("/Letter" & LetterCounter, Y Position) = 130
    Set Variable: "/Letter" & LetterCounter & "/Wheel:CurrentLetter" =
        Eval("/Library:Letter" & LetterCounter)
    Set Variable: "/Letter" & LetterCounter & "/Wheel:On" = True
    Begin Tell Target ("/Letter" & LetterCounter & "/Wheel")
        Go to and Stop (CurrentLetter)
    End Tell Target
End Loop
Begin Tell Target ("/Win")
    Go to and Stop (1)
End Tell Target
Begin Tell Target ("/Lose")
    Go to and Stop (1)
End Tell Target
Begin Tell Target ("/Giggle")
    Go to and Stop (1)
End Tell Target
Begin Tell Target ("/LetterButtons")
    Go to and Stop ("On")
End Tell Target
```

6 Open the Frame Properties dialog box for the CheckLetter keyframe and, on the Actions tab, assign the ActionScript.

CheckLetter is executed every time one of the Letter Buttons is clicked (or its corresponding key is pressed on the keyboard). It takes the letter selected by the

```
Set Variable: "WordLength" = Length(CurrentWord)
Set Variable: "LetterCounter" = 0
Set Variable: "Correct" = False
Loop While (LetterCounter < WordLength)
    Set Variable: "LetterCounter" = LetterCounter + 1
```

continues

player and compares it to each letter in the current word. When it finds a match, the appropriate letters are revealed and the player progresses in the game. If no match is found, the wooden mallet rises one notch higher and the Giggle begins to look a little more nervous.

CheckLetter also tracks the number of letters left to be guessed. When LettersRemaining reaches zero, the Win frame is called.

continued

```
        Set Variable: "LoopCount" = LoopCount + 1
        If ((Eval("/Letter" & LetterCounter & "/Wheel:CurrentLetter") eq
            /LetterButtons:CurrentLetter) and (Eval("/Letter" & LetterCounter & "/Wheel:On") =
            True) )
            Set Variable: "Correct" = True
            Begin Tell Target ("/Letter" & LetterCounter)
                Set Variable: "/:LettersRemaining" = /:LettersRemaining - 1
                Set Variable: "Wheel:On" = False
                Go to and Stop ("Off")
            End Tell Target
        End If
    End Loop
    If (Correct = False)
        Begin Tell Target ("/Giggle")
            Go to Next Frame
        End Tell Target
    End If
    If (/:LettersRemaining = 0)
        Call ("Win")
    End If
```

7 Open the Frame Properties dialog box for the Win keyframe and, on the Actions tab, assign the ActionScript.

The Win script essentially does the following three things: plays the Win animation, turns off the Letter Buttons to prevent further input, and sends the GameScreens symbol to display a "You Won! Play again?" message.

```
Begin Tell Target ("/Win")
    Play
End Tell Target
Begin Tell Target ("/LetterButtons")
    Go to and Stop ("Off")
End Tell Target
Begin Tell Target ("/GameScreens")
    Go to and Play ("Win")
End Tell Target
```

8 Open the Frame Properties dialog box for the Lose keyframe and, on the Actions tab, assign the ActionScript.

Obviously, Lose is the opposite of Win. The Lose frame is called when the Giggle Animation symbol reaches its final frame. At that point, the player has run out of guesses and the Lose animation plays, showing the Giggle character being konked by the wooden mallet.

```
Begin Tell Target ("/Lose")
    Play
End Tell Target
Begin Tell Target ("/LetterButtons")
    Go to and Stop ("Off")
End Tell Target
Begin Tell Target ("/GameScreens")
    Go to and Play ("Lose")
End Tell Target
```

9 Open the Frame Properties dialog box for the ClearLetters keyframe and, on the Actions tab, assign the ActionScript.

ClearLetters removes all the duplicate Movie Clips used to construct the word laid out on the game board. Doing this is important because duplicated symbols always appear above any other objects on the Stage, obscuring the Win or Lose messages you want to display. **ClearLetters** is to be called from within the GameScreens symbol, which you'll create now.

```
Set Variable: "LetterCounter" = 0
Loop While (LetterCounter < WordLength)
    Set Variable: "LetterCounter" = LetterCounter + 1
    Remove Movie Clip ("/Letter" & LetterCounter)
End Loop
```

10 Exit symbol-editing mode, return to Scene 1, drag an instance of ActionScript Library from your document's Library onto the Stage, and name the instance **Library**.

ActionScript Library is invisible on playhead because all of its frames are empty, so you can position it any-where without affecting its function.

Instance and name the ActionScript Library.

269

SETTING UP THE GAME SCREENS

The Game Screens technique controls the game play and gives simple Start/Win/Lose feedback to the player.

1 In the Game Screens layer, drag an instance of the Start Screen symbol from the Game Screens folder of the Vector Graphics folder onto the Stage, and center it horizontally and vertically.

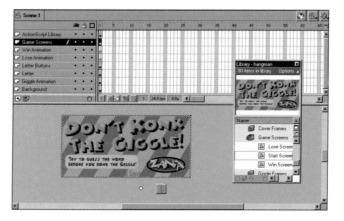

Add the Start Screen symbol to the main movie.

2 Select the instance and press F8 to convert it to a Movie Clip symbol, naming it **Game Screens**.

3 Enter symbol-editing mode for the new Game Screens symbol, name the existing layer **Game Screens**, and add two layers above it, naming them **Control Actions** and **Button**.

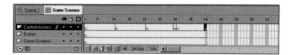

Set up the Game Screens Movie Clip.

4 Insert 39 frames in each layer, giving each layer a total of 40 frames.

5 In the Control Actions layer, insert blank keyframes at frames 11, 21, 30, 31, and 40.

6 Label keyframe 1 **Start**, open its Properties dialog box, and, on the Actions tab, assign the ActionScript.

Stop

7 Label keyframe 11 **Play**, open its Properties dialog box, and, on the Actions tab, assign the ActionScript.

Stop

8 Label keyframe 21 **Win**, go to keyframe 30, open its Properties dialog box, and, on the Actions tab, assign the ActionScript.

```
Stop
Call ("/Library/:ClearLetters")
```

9 Label keyframe 31 **Lose**, go to keyframe 40, open its Properties dialog box, and, on the Actions tab, assign the ActionScript.

```
Stop
Call ("/Library/:ClearLetters")
```

You'll notice a gap between the Win and Lose keyframes and the ones that call the Movie Clip with the instance name ClearLetters. This gap is intentional because you want a small piece of animation to play before the Win or Lose message appears. In the ActionScript Library symbol, the GameScreens symbol is told to go to either Win or Lose and then **Play**, so the script creates a pause long enough for the Win or Lose animations to play through.

10 In the Button layer, drag an instance of the Start Button symbol from the Buttons folder onto the Stage and center it horizontally and vertically on the stage.

This button triggers the game play to start.

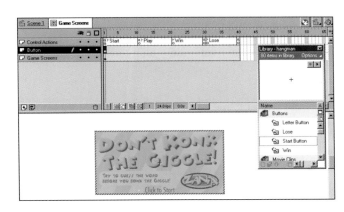

Add an instance of the Start Button symbol to the Button layer.

11 Open the Start Button Properties dialog box, and, on the Actions tab, assign the ActionScript.

12 Insert a keyframe at frame 21 of the Button layer and insert a blank keyframe at frame 11.

Inserting the frames in this order is important so that the button is visible in the **Start**, **Win**, and **Lose** states, but not in the **Play** state.

```
On (Release)
    Go to and Stop ("Play")
    Call ("/Library/:Initialize")
End On
```

ADDING THE GAME SCREEN GRAPHICS

In this section, you set up the Game Screens layer of the Game Screens Movie Clip. You're creating an instance of the Win Screen and Lose Screen symbols, and then you're hiding the layer.

1   In the Game Screens layer of the Game Screens Movie Clip, insert blank keyframes at frames 11, 21, 30, 31, and 40.

2   Move the playhead to keyframe 30, drag an instance of the Win Screen symbol from the Vector Graphics folder onto the Stage, and center it horizontally and vertically on the page.

3   Go to keyframe 40 and repeat step 2 with the Lose Screen symbol from the Vector Graphics folder.

4   Exit symbol-editing mode and return to Scene 1.

5   Double-click the copy of the Game Screens symbol, name the instance **GameScreens**, and hide the Game Screens layer so that you can continue to deal with objects beneath it.

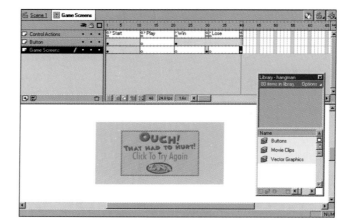

Add the Win Screen and Lose Screen symbols to the Game Screens Movie Clip.

ADDING THE BUTTONS

By now, you might be wondering how all the preceding elements are tied together. The primary driving force in this game is the Letter Buttons symbol that takes guesses from the player. Most of the buttons contained in the Letter Buttons symbol have been pre-wired, but to finish setting up the game, you need to activate the letter A.

1   Right-click (PC) or Control+click (Mac) the Letter Buttons instance, choose Edit In Place, double-click the button marked A to open the Properties dialog box, and, on the Actions tab, assign the ActionScript.

This script is crucial to the functioning of the game. When the user clicks a letter button or presses a key on the keyboard, a variable named **CurrentLetter** is

```
On (Release, Key: a)
    Set Variable: "CurrentLetter" = "A"
    Call ("/Library/:CheckLetter")
End On
```

set to that letter. When **CheckLetter** is called, the value of **CurrentLetter** is compared to each letter in the current word. If the user clicks the A button, for example, the game checks for any available As in the current word and either reveals them or raises the mallet a notch higher.

2   Exit symbol-editing mode and return to the main Timeline.

MODIFICATIONS

The name of the game might sound silly, but as you can see, the underlying mechanics are quite powerful. Most notably, the available words in the puzzle can be changed simply by altering five text variables in your Flash document. Combine that with the capability to easily replace the graphics used in the game and you have a highly customizable product.

Once again, a strongly organized symbol and script Library is the key to a clean movie that you can easily update. A little extra effort is required at the beginning, but it's more than worth it down the line.

DODGE GAME

"All your dreams come

true, if you have the

courage to pursue them."

—WALT DISNEY

MAKING A DODGE GAME IN FLASH

Dodge games are classic kids' favorites. Using

a clever combination of Flash features, you can

bring such a game to life on the Web or as a

standalone Flash projector. The Dodge game

you will create in this project also introduces

a movie flow-control mechanism called Game

Screens that's useful for creating randomized,

single-level games.

PROJECT 21:

BITZO IN SPACE

Scenes
    Introduction
        Layers
            Control Actions
            Intro Graphic
    Game
        Layers
            Control Actions
            Black Mask
            Game Screens
            Sprites
            Lives
            Score
            Background

GETTING STARTED

If you want your results to match those of the finished project, follow the steps carefully. If you want to customize the project and are familiar with Flash 4, feel free to
change the settings to those that meet your needs.

1 Begin with a new Flash Movie, using these settings:

Frame rate:	**24 fps**
Stage dimensions:	**264 × 216**
Background color:	**Black**

2 Set up two scenes, naming them **Introduction**
and **Game**.

3 Select the Game scene and set up seven layers, nam-
ing them (from top to bottom) **Control Actions**,
Black Mask, **Game Screens**, **Sprites**, **Lives**,
Score, and **Background**.

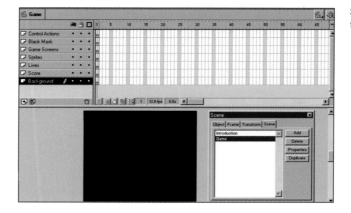

Set up the new movie and
the Game scene.

276

4 Select the Introduction scene and set up two layers, naming them **Control Actions** and **Intro Graphic**.

5 From the Flash 4 Magic CD, load BitzoInSpace.fla as a Library.

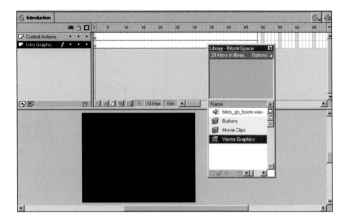

Set up the layers of the Introduction scene and open the BitzoInSpace.fla file as a Library.

BUILDING THE INTRODUCTION

The introduction scene serves two purposes. First, it can display a copyright or disclaimer message for a preset length of time before the game starts. Second, you can add preloader logic into this scene to display loading status for Web delivery. (If you don't understand preloading, check out Preloader, the first project in this book.)

1 Select both layers in the Introduction scene and set up a total of 48 blank frames in each.

Because the movie's frame rate is 24 frames per second, these 48 frames equal two seconds of movie time.

Set up 48 frames in the two layers.

2 Select the first keyframe in the Control Actions layer of the Introduction scene, open its Properties dialog box, and, on the Actions tab, assign the ActionScript.

Bitzo uses relatively complex vector graphics, making it unsuitable for full-screen playback on most systems. If you set **AllowScale** to **False**, the movie can be played back at any dimension and the graphics will stay positioned in the center at the original dimension. This **FSCommand** action is appropriate only to the standalone Flash player and will have no effect

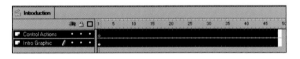

```
FS Command ("allowscale", "false")
```

when the movie is embedded in an HTML document. Rather, the dimensions of the Flash player in a Web page are set by the HTML code used to embed it.

3   Select the Intro Graphic layer, drag an instance of the Intro Graphic symbol from the Vector Graphics folder of the BitzoInSpace.fla Library onto the Stage, and center the image vertically and horizontally on the Stage.

Instance and place the Intro Graphic symbol.

LAYING THE GAME FOUNDATIONS

Bitzo In Space is driven by two main components: the flying missile array and the Bitzo sprite that follows the mouse cursor. Secondary to these are the Score and Lives indicators and the Game Screens. In this section, you lay out the supporting artwork and scripting before building the active components. Because all the game action is driven by self-contained Movie Clip symbols, each layer of this scene has only one frame. The purpose of the Black Mask layer is to obscure the missiles that fly in from the left and exit on the right.

1   Select the Background layer in the Game scene, drag an instance of the Space Background graphic from the Vector Graphics folder onto the Stage, and center the image vertically and horizontally on the Stage.

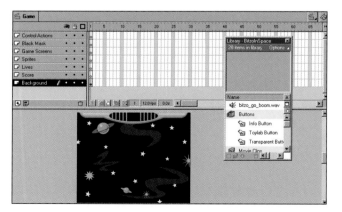

Instance and place the Space Background graphic.

2 Select the Black Mask layer, drag an instance of the Black Mask graphic symbol in the Vector Graphics folder onto the Stage, and position the instance so that the transparent region is neatly positioned above the Background image.

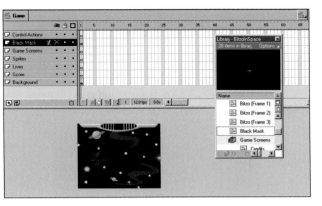

Set the Black Mask layer to be invisible.

3 Select the Black Mask layer, open the Layer Properties dialog box, and deselect Show.

In the first keyframe of the Control Actions layer, you need to make the Bitzo sprite draggable so that the game can function. To make the Bitzo sprite draggable, you need to assign the **Drag Movie Clip** action to a keyframe instead of a button. When you use a keyframe, the Clip becomes "sticky"—it follows the mouse cursor full-time and doesn't require manual clicking and dragging.

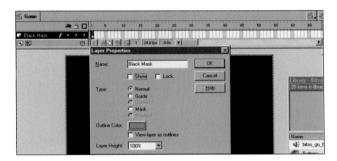

Deselect the Show option for the Black Mask layer.

4 Select the first keyframe in the Control Actions layer, open its Properties dialog box, and, on the Actions tab, assign the ActionScript.

Adding the Constrain to Rectangle parameters prevents the Bitzo sprite from following the mouse cursor outside the playable game region. No cheating allowed in this game!

Stop
Start Drag ("/bitzo", L=0, T=0, R=260, B=220, lockcenter)

BUILDING BITZO

The completed Bitzo sprite consists of several symbols that combine to form one.
Bitzo's spaceship is animated during game play. When the spaceship is struck, the
explosion is animated. The explosion is accompanied by a sound. You'll create the
individual pieces first and then assemble them into the final Bitzo.

1   In the Sprites layer, drag an instance of Bitzo from
    the Movie Clips folder onto the Stage.

Instance the Bitzo Movie Clip.

2   Select the Bitzo Movie Clip in the Sprites layer of the
    Game scene, press F8, convert the symbol into a
    Movie Clip symbol, and name it **Moving Bitzo**.

Note: The next step asks you to enter the symbol-
editing mode. Right-click (Windows) or Control-click
(Macintosh) on the new instance, and choose Edit
from the pop-up menu.

Create the new instance
of Moving Bitzo.

3   Enter symbol-editing mode for Moving Bitzo, name
    the only layer **Moving Bitzo**, select the first
    keyframe (which should contain the animated Bitzo
    symbol), and, on the Actions tab, assign the
    ActionScript.

```
Stop
```

4   In the Moving Bitzo layer, insert an additional 24
    frames (making a total of 25), insert a keyframe at
    frame 2, and insert a blank keyframe at frame 10.

5   Move the playhead to frame 2 and drag an instance of
    the Explosion Movie Clip from the Movie Clips
    folder of the BitzoInSpace.fla library onto the Stage.

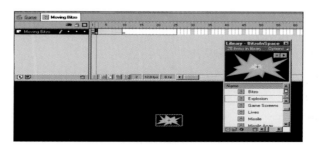

Center the Explosion Movie
Clip on the stage.

6 Delete the instance of the Bitzo Movie Clip and center the instance of the Explosion Movie Clip horizontally and vertically on the Stage.

The last step in building the Moving Bitzo symbol is to add the sound effect to keyframe 2.

7 Make sure that the playhead is positioned at frame 2 and drag bitzo_go_boom.wav over the Stage.

You should see the waveform added to the Timeline.

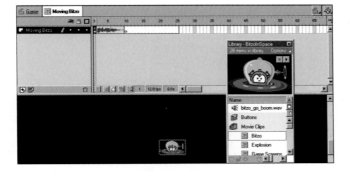

Drag the sound file over the Stage.

8 Exit symbol-editing mode, return to the Game scene, select the Moving Bitzo symbol in the Sprites layer, and name the instance **bitzo**.

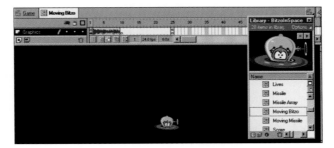

Name the Instance Bitzo.

All done! Before moving on, have a look at why Moving Bitzo is structured the way it is. During the game—that is, before being struck by a missile—Bitzo and his ship follow the mouse cursor around, displaying a looping animation of the engine firing.

This is represented by keyframe 1. That frame is displayed and then playhead is halted by the **Stop** action. This means that further intervention is required in the form of a **Tell Target** action before the Movie Clip plays on. The **Tell Target...Play** action is provided by the next part of the game—the missiles—when they strike the Moving Bitzo.

When the Moving Bitzo is told to play, the ship animation changes to an explosion and sound that plays for .5 seconds before disappearing. At this point, the playhead reaches the last blank keyframe in Moving Bitzo and then returns to frame 1, which is again the animated Bitzo.

BUILDING THE MISSILES

Although Bitzo is the main character, the Missiles are the more complex and crucial players. The Missile symbol does a number of things: First, it sets a random latitude for itself on the game board. The Missile symbol also sets a random speed and then moves at that speed. This jack-of-all-trades symbol also detects collisions with Bitzo, sets Score and Lives counters, detects when it has exited right of screen, and resets itself.

1   In the Sprites layer of the Game scene, choose Insert>New Symbol, name the new symbol **Moving Missile,** and give it Movie Clip behavior.

2   In the symbol-editing mode of Moving Missile, set up two layers: **Control Actions** and **Missile Graphics**.

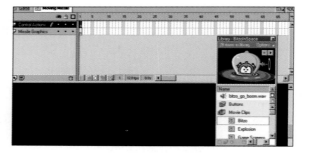

Set up the new Moving Missile Movie Clip.

3   Select the keyframe in the Control Actions layer, label it **Initialize Missile**, and, on the Actions tab, assign the ActionScript.

This frame is the initialization frame. First of all, it sets two of its own properties, X position and Y position. X position is set to −45 pixels, just enough left of the Stage to be concealed by the Black Mask. Y position is set to a random number, so that the Missile flies in from a different Y position each time. A random variable named **xStep** is also set to control the speed at which the Missile moves.

Last, this frame checks to see whether the number of remaining Missiles (score) is zero, in which case the game ends and the Win screen is displayed.

```
Set Property ("", Y Position) = Random ( 160 ) + 30
Set Property ("", X Position) = -45
Set Variable: "xStep" = Random (6) + 6
If (Eval("/score:count") = 0 and (GetProperty ( "/gamescreens", _currentframe ) = 2))
  Begin Tell Target ("/gamescreens")
    Go to and Stop ("Win")
  End Tell Target
Else
  Set Variable: "/score:count" = Eval("/score:count") - 1
End If
```

4 Insert a blank keyframe in frame 2 of the Control Actions layer, label it **Draw Missile,** and, on the Actions tab, assign the ActionScript.

This script moves the Missile to the right xStep number of pixels and then retrieves the position data of both itself and the Moving Bitzo symbol. The script then compares the two positions and determines whether a collision has occurred. If the collision has occurred (yes), the Moving Bitzo is told to play (triggering the explosion), and a life is removed. If a collision hasn't occurred (no), nothing happens, and the Missile continues.

```
Set Property ("", X Position) = GetProperty ( "", _x ) + xStep
Set Variable: "shipX" = GetProperty("/bitzo",_x)
Set Variable: "shipY" = GetProperty("/bitzo",_y)
Set Variable: "missileX" = GetProperty("",_x)
Set Variable: "missileY" = GetProperty("",_y)
If ((missileX > (shipX - 38)) and (missileX < shipX) and (missileY > (shipY - 23))  and
    (missileY < (shipY + 23)) and (GetProperty ( "/bitzo", _currentframe ) = 1) and
    (GetProperty ( "/gamescreens", _currentframe ) = 2))
  Begin Tell Target ("/bitzo")
    Play
  End Tell Target
  Begin Tell Target ("/lives")
    Go to Next Frame
  End Tell Target
End If
```

5 Insert a blank keyframe in frame 3 and assign the ActionScript commands.

This frame determines whether the Missile has moved beyond the right side of the game area and then either reinitializes the Missile or simply returns to frame 2, moving the Missile again to the next position.

```
Go to and Play ("Draw Missile")
If (GetProperty ( "", _x )  >= 300)
  Go to and Play ("Initialize Missile")
End If
```

6 Select the Missile Graphics layer, leave the first keyframe blank, and insert a blank keyframe in frame 2.

7 Drag an instance of the Missile Movie Clip from the Movie Clips folder onto the Stage, center the instance horizontally and vertically on the Stage, and return to the Game scene.

Center the instance of the Missile Movie Clip on the Stage.

CREATE THE ARRAY OF MISSILES

In this section, you instance one Missile and then replicate another four so that the game has a total of five Missiles. (You can have more than or fewer than five if you want to change the difficulty of the game.) Instance names aren't required for these symbols because they're completely self-contained, sending only **Tell Target** commands and not receiving any.

1   In the Sprites layer of the Game scene, drag an instance of the Moving Missile Movie Clip from your Library to the left of the Stage.

2   Copy and paste the original Moving Missiles symbol to create more arrays.

    The positioning of these instances isn't important, but for better organization of the workspace, simply move them off to the left side of the Stage.

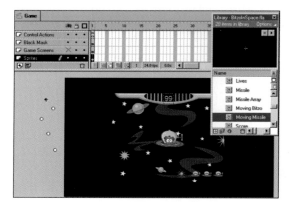

Set up the instances of the Moving Missile Movie Clip.

ADDING THE SCORE COUNTER

The Score Counter is quite simple—it's just a text field with the capacity to display a two-digit number representing the Missiles left to dodge. As each Missile initializes, this number diminishes by one.

1   In the Game scene, select the Score layer.

2   Drag an instance of the Score Movie Clip from the Movie Clips folder of the BitzoInSpace.fla library onto the Stage, and name the instance **score**.

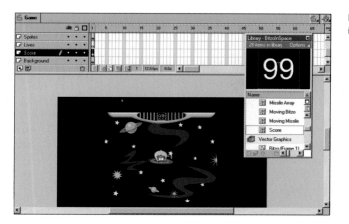

Place the Score Movie Clip in the space provided.

ADDING THE LIVES COUNTER

The Lives Counter represents the number of lives remaining before the game ends. A life is removed each time a missile collides with Bitzo, causing him to explode. When no lives are left, a short pause occurs before the Lose screen is displayed.

1   In the Game scene, select the Lives layer and find the Lives Movie Clip in the Movie Clips folder of the BitzoInSpace.fla Library.

2   Drag an instance of the Lives Movie Clip onto the lower right of the Stage in the space provided, double-click it to open the Instance Properties dialog box, and name the instance **lives**.

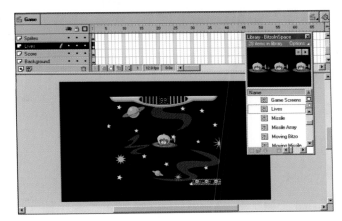

Place the Lives Movie Clip in the lower right corner of the Stage.

BUILDING THE GAME SCREENS

Last but not least come the Game Screens. This symbol controls the flow of game play and displays feedback such as "You Win" or "You Lose."

1   Create a new empty Movie Clip symbol, naming it **Game Screens.**

2   Make sure that you're in the symbol-editing mode of the Game Screens Movie Clip, and set up four layers, naming them (from top to bottom) **Control Actions, Foreground Buttons, Buttons,** and **Game Messages**.

With the Game Messages, you build the symbol from the bottom up.

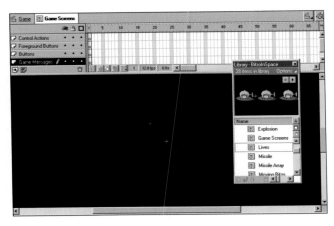

Set up four layers in the Game Screens Movie Clip.

285

3 Select frame 1 of the Game Messages layer, label the frame **Start,** drag an instance of the Start graphic symbol (in the Game Screen folder inside the Vector Graphics folder) onto the Stage, and center the instance horizontally and vertically on the Stage.

4 Insert blank keyframes at frames 2, 3, 4, and 5 in the Game Messages layer, and, referring to the table, label each frame and drag its instance onto the Stage, centering each horizontally and vertically on the Stage—just as you did with frame 1 in step 3.

Keyframe	Graphic Symbol	Label
2	None	**Play**
3	Lose	**Lose**
4	Win	**Win**
5	Credits	**Credits**

Labeling the keyframes is essential to ensuring that the movie functions correctly: they are used in **Go To Label** actions.

5 In keyframe 1 of the Buttons layer, drag an instance of the Transparent Button in the Buttons folder onto the Stage, center it horizontally and vertically on the Stage, and, on the Actions tab, assign the ActionScript.

6 In the Buttons layer, insert keyframes in frames 2 and 3, select keyframe 2, and delete the transparent button, leaving a blank keyframe.

The purpose of these buttons is to enable the user to click once from any of the game screens and enter play mode. You'll notice that all the keyframes at position 2 (Play position) are empty, allowing the gameboard underneath to show through. When any of the game screens is visible, the action underneath is concealed.

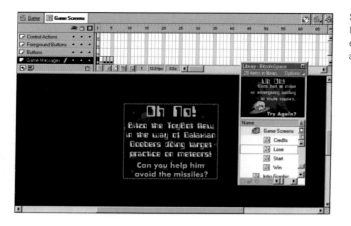

Set up the Game Messages layer with five keyframes, each with a different label and graphic.

On (Release)
Go to and Stop ("Play")
End On

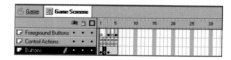

Delete the transparent button in the Buttons layer.

7 Select frame 1 in the Control Actions layer and, on the Actions tab, assign the ActionScript.

Stop

8 Insert blank keyframes in frames 3 through 5 and, on the Actions tab for each of the new keyframes, assign the ActionScript.

Stop

9 Insert a blank keyframe in frame 2 and, on the Actions tab, assign the ActionScript.

This script resets the number of Missiles remaining to 99 and sends the Lives and Moving Bitzo symbols back to their first keyframes.

```
Stop
Set Variable: "/score:count" = 99
Begin Tell Target ("/lives")
  Go to and Stop (1)
End Tell Target
Begin Tell Target ("/bitzo")
  Go to and Stop (1)
End Tell Target
```

THE CREDITS SCREEN

Credits screens usually have a link to the author's Web site, so why not add them to the Game Messages layer of the Game Screens Movie Clip? Well, with the transparent button sitting on top of all the game screens, the link buttons wouldn't work. You need to add an uppermost layer especially for these additional buttons.

1 In the Foreground Buttons layer of the Game Screens Movie Clip, insert blank keyframes in frames 3, 4, and 5.

2 Select frame 3 of the Foreground Buttons layer and drag an instance of the Info Button in the Buttons folder onto the Stage (between the Lose text and the Play Again text).

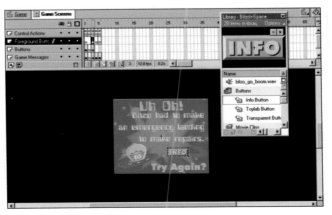

Insert blank keyframes and instance the Info Button in frame 3 of the Foreground Buttons layer.

3 Select the Info Button instance, open its Properties dialog box, and, on the Actions tab, assign the ActionScript.

This makes the Game Screens symbol skip to Credits when the button is clicked.

```
On (Release)
    Go to and Stop ("Credits")
End On
```

4 In the frame 5 keyframe, drag an instance of the Toylab Button symbol onto the Stage (beneath the text "Another game from").

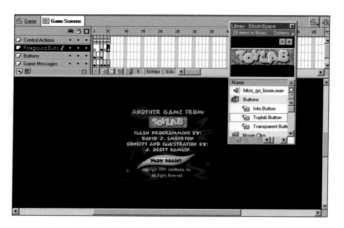

Create an instance of the Toylab Button symbol in the frame 5 keyframe of the Foreground Buttons layer.

5 Select the Toylab Button instance, open its Properties dialog box, and, on the Actions tab, assign the ActionScript.

In your own game, this URL would be a link to your Web site.

```
On (Release)
    Get URL ("http://www.toylab.com", window="_blank")
End On
```

6 Exit symbol-editing mode, return to the Game Screens layer of the Game scene, and drag an instance of Game Screens from your movie's Library onto the Stage.

7 Use the Transform Inspector to scale Game Screens to 120% of its original size, center it, and name the instance **gamescreens**.

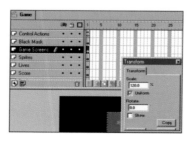

Instance Game Screens and scale it to 120%.

MODIFICATIONS

The design of this game is particularly interesting because the Missiles actually behave much as real ones might. They're self-propelled, and they explode when they hit something. This kind of behavior is commonly referred to as "object-oriented." Flash was originally designed as a linear animation tool, so the capability to create object-oriented systems with it is quite remarkable.

As mentioned earlier, you can make Bitzo In Space easier or harder just by adding or removing instances of the Moving Missile symbol. This scalability is also an attribute of object-oriented programming.

Last, this game is extremely easy to customize. Simply substitute new graphics where appropriate, taking careful notice of the sizes of the Bitzo and Missile sprites. The collision-detection code is tuned to the heights and widths of the original graphics—if you change the dimensions of the characters, you might need to alter this code accordingly.

APPENDICES

A Standalone Flash Projectors 292

B Flash Resources 300

C ActionScript 304

D A Look at the Executable for the
Flash 4 Magic CD 314

APPENDIX A

"The important thing

is this: to be able at

any moment to sacrifice

who we are for what

we could become."

—CHARLES DUBOIS

WORKING WITH STANDALONE FLASH PROJECTORS

One of the most exciting capabilities Flash

offers is turning your movies into standalone

projectors. The key advantage to this is that

the Flash movie doesn't need to be viewed

within a browser environment that has the

Flash player installed. In other words, the Flash

player is built into the standalone projector and

thus you can freely distribute the movie, know-

ing that your audience can view it.

Standalone Flash projectors aren't multiplatform. You will need to create Mac projectors for Mac users and Windows projectors for Windows users. Also, note that the standalone Flash projectors shouldn't be confused with the standalone Flash player. The standalone player is an executable application that comes with Flash and can be used to play Flash movies. Standalone Flash projectors have this Flash player built into them.

Standalone Flash projectors can be leveraged in any number of ways. Third-party applications can turn standalone Flash projectors into screensavers and much more. This appendix looks at several third-party applications to explore some of the advanced possibilities of standalone Flash projectors, such as

- Creating standalone applications with Flash
- Creating screensavers with Flash
- Setting up full-screen playback

CREATING STANDALONE PROJECTORS WITH FLASH

Flash 4 enables you to create standalone projectors for your Flash movies in both Macintosh and Windows format. These standalone Flash projectors can run without a browser and without the Flash plug-in. You can distribute projectors on the Web, as e-mail attachments—even on CDs—without worrying about whether the end user has the Macromedia Flash 4 plug-in.

Macromedia provides two ways to create a standalone projector with Flash 4: using the Publish command or using the Create Projector command.

The Publish Command

If you want to create both Macintosh and Windows projectors at the same time, you can use the Publish command within Macromedia Flash 4. To use the Publish command in Flash 4, follow these steps:

1   Save the Flash file.

2   Choose File>Publish Settings.

You might be tempted to select the Publish option instead of the Publish Settings option. However, the Publish option only exports .swf and .html files for the Flash file on which you are working.

3   Select the Windows Projector and Macintosh Projector options (see Figure 1).

Note: Flash gives the projectors default names according to what you've named the .fla file; however, you can uncheck the Use Default Names option if you want to give the files different names.

4   Click the Publish button in the Publish Settings dialog box.

Flash saves the projectors in the same directory in which the .fla is located, so you need to save your Flash file before you use the Publish Settings option.

Most of the external capabilities of Flash files will work in a standalone Flash file. For instance, you can refer to an external Flash file, you can have Flash communicate with an external server script (such as PHP), and you can use functions such as **Load Movie** with standalone Flash applications. However, external text files and

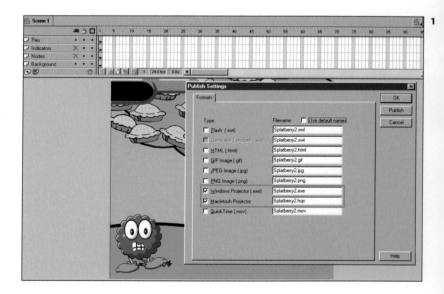

Load Movie operations will work only if any text file (or files) and any movies to be loaded in the projector are located in the same directory as the projector itself.

Flash does allow you to refer to specific URLs for text files and for loading movies; however, this means the viewer must have a live connection to the Internet for the player to work properly. Communication with JavaScript is essentially off limits for a standalone application because JavaScript requires a browser for processing.

One very nice aspect of Flash projectors is that you can use them to launch a browser if the user has a live connection to the Internet. This means you can include a button in your standalone movies that will link to your site. When the user clicks on the button, the standalone Flash application will open the user's default browser and load the URL.

All Flash projectors have a menu along the top (shown in Figure 2) unless you use the **FS Command (ShowMenu)** to remove it (which is discussed in the following section). Notable options in the menus are the capability to zoom in, zoom back out to 100%, play at full screen, and turn off the high-quality option (resulting in ugly aliased images). Controls such as Play, Rewind, Step Forward, and Step Backward are not available in the standalone projector.

2

The Create Player Feature

As mentioned earlier, Flash has another way to create a projector. You can create a projector from any .swf file by following these steps:

1 Open the file in the standalone player, which is located in the Macromedia\Flash 4\Players directory.

   If the standalone player is already registered on your computer, the .swf file should open automatically when you double-click it.

2 Choose File>Create Projector (see Figure 3).

   Of course, when you create a projector this way, you'll be creating the projector only for whatever platform you are on.

3

CREATING SCREENSAVERS FROM STANDALONE FLASH PROJECTORS

You can use several third-party applications, such as ScreenTime for Flash from MacSourcery, Screenweaver from GrooveWare, or the Living Screen Tool from Living Screen (see Appendix B for more information on these products), to turn Flash movies into screensavers. Each of these third-party screensaver utilities provides different capabilities, so we'll look at a few screensaver utilities to get an idea of some of the possibilities.

ScreenTime for Flash from MacSourcery

http://www.macsourcery.com

ScreenTime for Flash takes a Flash projector and turns it into a screensaver for either the Macintosh or the Windows platform. You need to purchase both the Macintosh and Windows versions of ScreenTime for Flash in order to create both Macintosh and Windows screensavers. ScreenTime for Flash generates an installation program that installs the Flash-based screensaver on a user's system.

To create a screensaver with ScreenTime, first you need to turn your Flash movie into a standalone projector. After you have a standalone projector, you can open it in ScreenTime for Flash and save the projector as a self-installing screensaver. The process can be as simple as Open and Save; however, ScreenTime for Flash also offers a few basic options to customize the screensaver (see Figure 4).

The Build a Demo option enables you to define how long the screensaver will work after it is installed. You can also specify a name for the screensaver, and you can specify what actions will shut down the screensaver.

With ScreenTime for Flash, you can create interactive screensavers. If you deselect the Quit on Mouse Movement option, for example, the screensavers will shut down only if the user presses a key on the keyboard. Therefore, the user can interact with the screensaver with a mouse, and you can turn interactive movies and games built with Flash into interactive movies with ScreenTime for Flash.

ScreenTime for Flash also enables you to create a custom credits screen for the screensaver. ScreenTime for Flash is available for both Macintosh and Windows.

4

Screenweaver 2 from GrooveWare

http://www.grooveware.com

Screenweaver 2, shown in Figure 5, turns a Flash standalone projector into a screensaver. (Screenweaver can also create standalone executables from just about any multimedia authoring system that enables you to export your project as an executable file, including Director, Astound, and PowerPoint.)

Screenweaver offers a large number of valuable advanced options. For example, Screenweaver supports the creation of Slideshow, .avi, and "transparent over the desktop Shockwave Flash" projectors (in other words, the screensaver can have transparent portions that show through to the desktop of the viewer's computer).

Screenweaver can create screensavers that expire after being installed for a certain period of time. In addition, Screenweaver has an unlock option that enables you to reactivate expired screensavers. You can also set up Screenweaver so that clients can reactivate the screensaver simply by entering their name and a valid serial number. A tool for creating these serial numbers is included with Screenweaver.

Screenweaver also has four options for turning off or waking up a screensaver: Left Mouseclick, Right Mouseclick, Mousemove, and Keystroke. You can turn off the

5

Mouseclick and Mousemove options to set the screensaver to be interactive via keystrokes. The Hangman game featured in this book, for example, could easily be used as a screensaver.

GrooveWare also offers an add-on to Screenweaver called FormDesigner, which enables users to completely design their own installer and settings dialog boxes for the screensavers. With FormDesigner, users can

- Generate organically-shaped forms based on a bitmap (shapes that show through to the desktop in predefined areas)
- Create and place text buttons, graphic buttons, and memo boxes
- Even add in animated .gifs and audio events

FS COMMAND PROJECTOR OPTIONS

More and more designers are opting to play their Flash movies full-screen on the Web. Also, if you are going to use your Flash movie as a screensaver, you will likely want to make it play back full-screen. Fortunately, Flash can handle full-screen displays without distorting the original image.

Because Flash movies are built with vector graphics rather than bitmap images, they are resolution independent. This means that you can zoom in on Flash graphics and they will maintain their high resolution. This also means that you can resize a Flash movie and it will still look great. You can make a Flash movie that's 320 pixels wide and 240 pixels high and then play it full-screen on a 1024 × 768 monitor and it will look just fine.

However, if your Flash movie isn't proportionate to the dimensions of the end user's screen, the movie might not look right at full screen. Therefore, it's advisable to create any Flash movies that you intend to use as screensavers at a size that is proportionate to standard monitor sizes, such as 640 × 480, 800 × 600, and 1024 × 768. Also note that if your Flash movie contains bitmap images, they might become undesirably distorted when the overall Flash movie is resized to full screen.

To force Flash movies to play back at full screen (without regard to the actual screen size of the user's monitor resolution), you need to use an **FS** command. Take the following steps to make a Flash movie play back at full screen:

1 Open a Flash movie and select a keyframe on frame 1 of the first scene (see Figure 6).

6

2 Choose Modify>Frame>Frame Properties>Actions, click on the + (plus) button, and choose FS Command from the drop-down menu (see Figure 7).

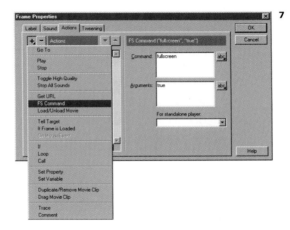
7

3 Type **fullscreen** in the Command box, type **true** in the Arguments box, and click OK (see Figure 8).

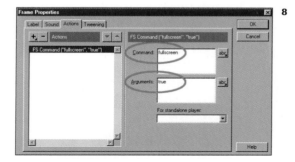

8

Now when you export your movie and play it in the standalone Flash player or create a projector, the Flash movie will play back at full screen. Flash also enables you to toggle on and off full-screen mode with a keyboard shortcut. The Windows toggle for full-screen mode is Ctrl+F, and the Macintosh toggle is Cmd+F.

Flash has several other FS commands worth knowing about—especially for creating screensavers.

- The **FS Command (allowscale)**, requiring either a **True** or a **False** argument. When **AllowScale** is set to **True**, the Flash movie (or screensaver) plays at 100% of the Projector's size (whether it's full screen or not). When you use **AllowScale** in combination with the **FS Command (fullscreen)** set to **True**, the Flash movie is scaled to fill the screen.

  When **AllowScale** is set to **False**, the movie is kept from scaling away from its original dimensions. If played back at a screen size larger than those dimensions using the **FS Command (fullscreen)**, the movie's background will border the movie.

- The **FS Command (quit)**, requiring no arguments. Basically, you use the **FS Command (quit)** when you want to add a button that the user can click to close the Flash movie or screensaver. You can use the **FS Command (quit)** to create interactive screensavers by creating your screensaver so that mouse movements and keyboard hits don't close it. Then you add the **FS Command (quit)** to the button so that users can exit the screensaver.

- The **FS Command (ShowMenu)**, requiring two arguments, **True** and **False**. As its name implies, **ShowMenu** can be used to remove the menu on standalone Flash projectors. The **FS Command (ShowMenu)** essentially turns off the right-click menu and the menu across the top of the projector; however, the title bar remains and a small empty bar (with no options) still appears when you right-click.

- The **FS Command (exec)**, requiring no arguments. The **FS Command (exec)** can be used to open any executable file, including .exe,.bat, and .com on Windows and AppleScript on the Mac.

MANIPULATING FLASH PROJECTORS WITH THIRD-PARTY UTILITIES

As noted, Flash projectors do have some limitations and potentially undesirable characteristics. For example, although you can use the **FS Command (ShowMenu)** to remove the menu on the Flash projector, you still have to live with the Flash logo and the Flash name on the title bar of the executable.

Fortunately, you can use third-party applications such as ProjectorLauncher and Jugglor (see Appendix B for more information on these products) to further manipulate Flash projectors. Take a quick look at ProjectorLauncher to see some of the possibilities.

ProjectorLauncher (currently available only on Windows98/NT) opens Flash projectors and enables you to make a variety of additions and edits. For example, you can include extra files with the executable, such an .html file that contains contact and product information or a .pdf file that contains printable instructions.

ProjectorLauncher also compresses the original Flash file up to 20% of the original size of the projector. For example, we used ProjectorLauncher to make edits on the Interactive Map Flash file featured in this book. The projector ProjectorLauncher created was 102Kb versus 559Kb, the size of the projector directly from Flash.

In addition, ProjectorLauncher enables you to define the size and position of the projector, as shown in Figure 9. You can also change the displayed icon of the projector (meaning you can use a custom icon) or you can remove the top menu bar in Flash projector altogether. Furthermore, you can remove the right-click menu—that is, nothing appears when you right-click versus the small bar with no options that appears when you use the **FS Command (ShowMenu)**.

With ProjectorLauncher, you can make a projector quit when the user presses the Escape key. You can also make the projector display a message when the user launches the projector to provide additional instructions or a warning.

Essentially, with programs such as ProjectorLauncher, you can make a Flash projector not *look* like a Flash projector, thus providing a more seamless and potentially more immersive and satisfying experience for your viewers. Being able to turn a Flash movie into a standalone application is very exciting. Look for more and more third-party utilities to leverage this powerful capability in new and valuable ways.

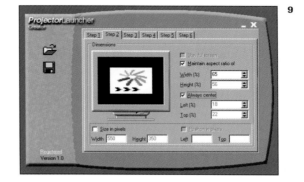

9

APPENDIX B

"I must create a system or

be enslaved by another

man's. I will not reason

and compare; My

business is to create."

—WILLIAM BLAKE

FLASH RESOURCES

Why would we include an appendix of Flash resources in this book? If you're a beginner, you probably need some basic tutorials. Even Flash veterans typically need to look up how to hook up Flash with PHP or perhaps a method for using JavaScript with Flash for a given dynamic requirement. When the Flash manual doesn't cut it, look into the resources in this appendix.

Another reason we included this appendix in the book is that Flash, like most Web technologies, is developing at a very rapid pace. New techniques are constantly being developed. When you're producing your latest masterpiece, it often helps to have a resource where you can ask questions or look up information about a specific task.

Finally, third-party development for Flash has taken off ever since Macromedia made Flash an open format. Many of the sites we include in this appendix have

- Links to other valuable resources that enable you to leverage Flash projectors in a variety of useful and fun ways
- Expanded input options for Flash

The resources in this appendix are only the beginning of an ever-expanding universe of third-party assets you can use with Flash.

Eyeland Studio

http://www.eyeland.com

Custom Flash game design and Flash game licensing.

Fig Leaf Software

http://www.figleaf.com

Fig Leaf Software offers training in Flash, Generator, Fireworks, and Dreamweaver.

Flash Central

http://www.flashcentral.com

Flash Central features several Flash galleries and links to numerous Flash resources, including Flash newsgroups, discussions, and lists.

FlashChallenge

http://flashchallenge.com

FlashChallenge features some of the best Flash sites on the Web. Sites are reviewed by staff members, and visitors vote for the best sites. FlashChallenge provides a much better filter for excellent Flash sites than Macromedia's Shocked Site of the Day.

FlashLite

http://www.flashlite.net/

FlashLite is home to a large number of excellent intermediate-to-advanced Flash 4 tutorials. Most tutorials come with free source files you can use to follow along with the tutorial. This site also features a classroom, games, a message board, and links to other Flash resources.

FlashFaq

http://www.flashfaq.net/home.asp

FlashFaq includes answers to frequently asked questions about Flash. You will also find tutorials, links, and free downloadable source files on the FlashFaq Web site.

FlashJester

http://www.flashjester.com/

FlashJester offers several excellent third-party tools for Flash, including Jugglor (a projector editor), JTools (the projector add-ons Jstart, Jweb, Jemail, and Jhelpor), and Creator (a utility that converts Flash files to screensavers).

FlashZone

http://www.flashzone.com/index2.html

FlashZone has the largest storehouse of Flash resources available on the Web. FlashZone offers a large number of excellent free downloadable source files (including source files for games and other complex Flash movies). FlashZone also provides a large number of well-written tutorials. In addition, the site's maintainers write regular informative columns, and the message boards are among the best available on the Web.

Living Screen

http://livingscreen.com

Living Screen sells several third-party tools for Flash, including an enhanced authoring environment and a screensaver utility.

ProjectorLauncher

http://www.mories.com/

ProjectorLauncher is a utility for Windows 9X/NT that you can use in combination with Flash standalone projectors. ProjectorLauncher enables you to do powerful things with Flash projectors, such as remove the menu bar and the right-click menu of a Flash projector—even more than the **FS Command (ShowMenu)**.

Sterling Ledet and Associates

http://www.ledet.com

At the Sterling Ledet and Associates site, you'll find hands-on training for Flash, along with training for other Macromedia tools such as Dreamweaver and Fireworks.

Macromania

http://www.users.bigpond.com/xtian/welcomenew.html

Macromania provides lots of free Flash files and tutorials. Most of the tutorials and files are for Flash 3, but they are usually relevant for Flash 4. Macromania is an especially good site for beginning Flash users.

Macromedia

http://www.macromedia.com

Macromedia's site contains solid galleries, tutorials, and tech notes; however, Macromedia's site is not nearly as informative as you might expect. The tech notes are the best resources, giving you information that you'll likely not find elsewhere. Nevertheless, Macromedia's site is hardly the definitive resource on its own technology.

MacSourcery

http://www.macsourcery.com

MacSourcery sells utilities (ScreenTime for Windows and Macintosh) that convert Flash projectors into screensavers. MacSourcery also sells royalty-free music you can use with Flash in a product called MusiCopia.

Moock Web Design

http://www.moock.org/webdesign/flash/index.html

Moock Web Design offers a large number of excellent advanced tutorials, including free downloadable source files.

NavWorks

http://navworks.i-us.com

NavWorks offers Flash tutorials and a few free demos. NavWorks also sells a product called Flash Foundry, which is a collection of Flash interfaces, props, tutorials, and audio clips.

Shockfusion

http://shockfusion.com

Shockfusion features live Flash-based chat and a Flash message board. Shockfusion also features a Flash-based radio and a developers' forum.

Screenweaver

http://screenweaver.com/swsite/

Screenweaver is a very robust screensaver program that can convert Flash files (among many other media types) into screensavers.

The Flash Guide

http://www.turtleshell.com/asm/tutorials/

The Flash Guide provides a large number of Flash tutorials (many with free downloadable source files) and links to Flash resources.

Virtual FX

http://www.virtual-fx.net/

Virtual FX offers numerous links to Flash resources as well as numerous high-quality Flash tutorials that come with free downloadable source files.

A P P E N D I X   C

"A picture

is a poem

without words."

—HORACE

ACTIONSCRIPT

The projects in this book use ActionScript to

enable advanced interactivity and programming

functions in Flash. For non-programmers—and

even seasoned scripters—working with and

understanding ActionScript can be a challenge.

Hence, for your convenience, we've included

this handy reference guide of actions, functions,

general ActionScript syntax, and tips we've

uncovered (the hard way).

ENTERING ACTIONSCRIPT: A GUIDE FOR BEGINNERS

Every project in this book requires entering ActionScript. Entering ActionScript in Flash is somewhat different from entering similar scripts, such as JavaScript or Lingo for Macromedia Director.

For example, here is a script written in JavaScript:

```
<SCRIPT LANGUAGE="javascript">
CurrentDate = new Date();
document.write ("The year is " = CurrentDate.getYear()+ ".")
</SCRIPT>
```

Here is a simple ActionScript script:

```
On (Release)
    Set Variable: "Feature" = "interface"
    Call ("/Library/:LoadView")
End On
```

The two types of script look quite similar, don't they? The difference is really a matter of convenience. To use the JavaScript, you type it letter for letter, line for line in a text editor or an HTML editor. However, you don't have to type Flash ActionScript letter by letter, line by line. In Flash, you enter ActionScript simply by selecting the Flash element (a button or keyframe) to which the script belongs, opening the Properties dialog box for that element, and assigning a series of actions on the Actions tab.

To open the Instance Properties dialog box for a button or keyframe, use one of these methods:

- Double-click the button or keyframe.

- Choose Modify>Instance.

- Right-click (PC) or Control+click (Mac) the button or keyframe and choose Properties from the pop-up menu that appears.

The preceding ActionScript is a script for a Button symbol. The **On (Release)** line indicates that the code will be executed when someone clicks and *releases* a button.

Now look at how you enter this code in Flash. If you aren't familiar with how to enter ActionScript, you might want to create a simple Button symbol and follow these steps:

1 Double-click the Button symbol to open its Instance Properties dialog box, and click the Actions tab (see Figure 1).

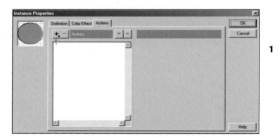

2 Click the "+" button and select Set Variable from the pop-up list (see Figure 2).

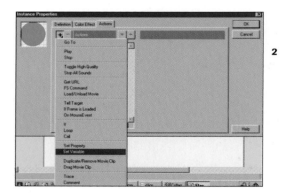

After you select Set Variable, Flash automatically writes some ActionScript in the Actions pane:

```
On (Release)
    Set Variable: "" = ""
End On
```

You can change the **Release** in **On (Release)** to any number of events.

3 Click the **On (Release)** and change the action, as shown in Figure 3.

3

The following incomplete line appears.

Set Variable: "" = ""

4 Click the line and type **Feature** in the Variable field and **interface** (with no quotation marks) in the Value field.

Flash completes the **Set Variable** line for you in the main field (see Figure 4).

4

5 To insert the **Call** line in the example of simple ActionScript, select the **Set Variable** line in the Actions pane, click on the "+" button, and select Call from the list of actions in the pop-up menu.

Flash provides much of the ActionScript for you (see Figure 5).

5

6 To complete the **Call** line, type **/Library/:LoadView** in the Frame field (see Figure 6).

6

As you can see from this example, you enter ActionScript by selecting statements and filling in their respective fields. Although this mode of entering ActionScript might prove tedious for experienced programmers, it does help minimize syntax errors and makes ActionScript a little more accessible for those new to scripting.

ACTIONS

As you might have guessed, ActionScript revolves around a set of actions that all perform unique tasks in Flash. You can assign actions only to a frame or a button, and they are written as ActionScript statements. In many cases, the name of an action and the wording of its corresponding ActionScript statement are quite different; Table 1 compares the two and lists a project in this book that uses the statement.

You can follow along by opening a blank Flash document, double-clicking the first keyframe in the timeline, and then selecting the Actions tab. For more detailed information about each action, refer to your Flash 4 documentation.

TABLE 1 ACTIONS IN ACTIONSCRIPT

Action Name	What it looks like	Project
Go To	Go to and Stop ("Try Again") or Go to and Play ("On")	Matching Game JukeBox
Play	Play	
Stop	Stop	
Toggle High Quality	Toggle High Quality	
Stop All Sounds	Stop All Sounds	
Get URL	Get URL ("http://shop. barnesandnoble.com/ =")	Book Finder
FS Command	FS Command ("allowscale", "false")	Dodge Game
Load Movie	Load Movie ("",) or Unload Movie ("") or Load Variables ("./text.txt", 0)	Poll
Tell Target	Begin Tell Target ("/Letter Buttons") Go to and Stop ("On") End Tell Target	Hangman

Action Name	What it looks like	Project
If Frame is Loaded	If Frame Is Loaded ("") ... End Frame Loaded	
On MouseEvent	On ("") ... End On	

If	If (password eq "Open")
	    Go to and Play ("Good")
	Else
	    Go to and Play ("Bad")
	End If
		Password

Loop	Loop While (SmileyCounter < 12)
	    Set Variable: "SmileyCounter"
	        = SmileyCounter + 1
	    Set Variable: "Smiley" &
	    SmileyCounter = False
	End Loop
		Memory Game

Call	Call ("/trig:cos")	Pong
Set Property	Set Property ("/slice"&temp, Rotation) = angle	Poll
Set Variable	Set Variable: "open" = False	Wack-a-Mole
Duplicate Movie Clip	Duplicate Movie Clip ("", "",) or Remove Movie Clip ("")	
Drag Movie Clip	Start Drag ("") or Start Drag ("", L=, T=, R=, B=) or Start Drag ("", lockcenter) or Start Drag ("", L=, T=, R=, B=, lockcenter) or Stop Drag	
Trace	Trace ("")	
Comment	Comment:	

Data Types

Whenever you are required to type in data when dealing with actions, you have to designate which data type you are using. Flash has three main data types: string literals, expressions, and numerals. You can change the data type of a field by selecting from a list of modifiers, described in the following sections.

String Literals

abc String literals are values taken "as is" and can consist of letters, numbers, and punctuation. This is the default data type, and you can recognize it because the values you type in will automatically have enclosing quotes when displayed to the left, in the Action pane. Here's an example:

Call ("DoCalculation")

in which **DoCalculation** is a string literal describing the label of a frame to be run by using the **Call** statement.

Expressions

≡ An expression is a value that usually requires further processing before it can be used. Expressions can consist of numerals, variables, operators, functions, and strings (strings must be encapsulated in double quotation marks, as in "the text"). Here is an example of an expression:

Set Variable: "TotalFruit" = Oranges + Apples

where **TotalFruit**, **Oranges** and **Apples** are all variables containing numeric values.

Numerals

123 This symbol specifies that a field consists of a numeral. A numeral consists of only numeric characters (1–9) and − (negative).

Operators

The term *operator* is a general programming term referring to symbols that perform calculations on data. An arithmetic operator such as the + sign, for example, adds two numbers, referred to as *operands*.

TABLE 2 Operators in Actionscript

Operator	Use
()	Used to set the precedence of evaluation. Inner parentheses are always evaluated first.
+	Arithmetic addition
−	Arithmetic subtraction
★	Arithmetic multiplication
/	Arithmetic division
=	Numeric equals (returns Boolean)★
<>	Numeric not equal (returns Boolean)
<	Numeric less than (returns Boolean)
>	Numeric greater than (returns Boolean)
<=	Numeric less than or equal to (returns Boolean)
>=	Numeric greater than or equal to (returns Boolean)
""	Used to denote a string inside an expression, such as "the text"
&	String concatenate (adds strings end to end)
eq	String equals (returns Boolean)
ne	String not equal (returns Boolean)
lt	String less than (returns Boolean)
gt	String greater than (returns Boolean)
le	String less than or equal to (returns Boolean)
ge	String greater than or equal to (returns Boolean)
not	Logical NOT (returns Boolean)
and	Logical AND (returns Boolean)
or	Logical OR (returns Boolean)

★ Note that Boolean simply means true or false. You can set any variable to be a Boolean value of **True** or **False**, and some functions also return Boolean results.

FUNCTIONS

For the sake of this table, assume that **FOO**, **INDEX**, and **COUNT** are all variables containing integers (whole numbers) and **BAR** is a variable containing a string (text). **FOO** is standard programming lingo and is generally representative of a number. **BAR** is representative of text.

TABLE 3 FUNCTIONS IN ACTIONSCRIPT

Function	Use
Eval	Used to get the value of an expression
True	Boolean true (1)
False	Boolean false (0)
Newline	Insert newline (carriage return)
GetTimer	The time in milliseconds since the .swf was opened
Int(FOO)	Converts **FOO** to an integer (chops a decimal point)
Random(FOO)	A random number from 0 to **FOO**–1
Substring(BAR, INDEX, COUNT)	Returns a substring of the string **BAR**, starting at **INDEX** and **COUNT** long (**INDEX** starts at 1)
Length(BAR)	Returns an integer that is the length of **BAR**
Chr(FOO)	Returns the character corresponding to the ASCII value **FOO**
Ord(BAR)	Returns the ASCII value for the single character **BAR**
Get Property(target, property)	Returns the current value of property for a given target

PROPERTIES

The following table shows all the properties of Movie Clip symbols you can obtain by using the **GetProperty** function.

TABLE 4 PROPERTIES IS ACTIONSCRIPT

Property	Value
_x	The X position of the center point of a Movie Clip (left to right)
_y	The Y position of the center point of a Movie Clip (top to bottom)
_width	The width of a Movie Clip
_height	The height of a Movie Clip
_rotation	The rotation of a Movie Clip (in degrees)
_target	The target path of a Movie Clip (includes FULL path)
_name	The name of an instance of a Movie Clip
_url	The full URL of the SWF that contains the Movie Clip
_xscale	The scale of the x axis (in %) of a Movie Clip
_yscale	The scale of the y axis (in %) of a Movie Clip
_currentframe	The current frame of a Movie Clip
_totalframes	The total number of frames in a Movie Clip
_framesloaded	The number of frames in a Movie Clip that are loaded
_alpha	The alpha (or transparency) of a Movie Clip (measured in %; 0 is fully transparent)
_visible	The visibility of a Movie Clip (True or False)
_droptarget	If a Movie Clip is dragged, its **_droptarget** value is equal to the path of the target directly beneath the mouse pointer. If the mouse is not over a Movie Clip symbol, **_droptarget** equals "**/**" the target path of the main Timeline.

DEALING WITH TIMELINES, LEVELS, AND TARGETS

Flash is built entirely around a system of Timelines, levels, and targets. When you begin a new Flash document, you have only one Timeline, which can be broken up into multiple scenes. When you create an instance of a Movie Clip symbol, Flash creates a second Timeline that operates independently of the first. In other words, if you use a **Stop** statement to halt the main Timeline, any Movie Clip instances on the Stage will continue to play, irrespective of one another.

Any time you create an instance of a Movie Clip symbol and then give it an instance name, you're creating a target. A target is essentially a named Timeline.

Target paths are used frequently in Flash and are essential information for **Tell Target**, **Set Property**, and **Set Variable** statements, as well as the **GetProperty** function. A target path can be simple or complex, depending on how far removed the Timeline you're targeting is from the one you're in currently.

For example, a full target path including level information might look like

_level0/movieclipA/movieclipA1

in which

- **_level0/** is the main Timeline of the currently loaded Flash Player movie.
- **movieclipA/** is the Timeline of a Movie Clip instance named movieclipA and exists on the current frame of the main Timeline.
- **movieclipA1/** is the Timeline of a Movie Clip instance named movieclipA1 that exists on the current frame of movieclipA's Timeline.

HINTS AND TIPS

The authors of this book learned ActionScript the hard way: by trial and error. We've put together a few pointers that we hope will keep you from bumping around in the dark:

- The properties of a Movie Clip are not updated *until* the .swf leaves the frame in which it is changed. Thus, to change loop of properties, you need to create looping Movie Clips with actions in them.
- Use the **Trace** statement to help you debug! When you choose Control>Test Movie, the **Trace** statement brings up a window to show the values of **Trace** statements.
- Flash has a consecutive action limit of 20,000. After that, Flash assumes it is stuck in an infinite loop and stops all further actions from being executed.
- When setting a variable or property that must be a whole number, be sure to wrap your expression in an Int() function first.
- To refer to variables outside of the current movie, you need to use standard **Tell Target** syntax, followed by a colon (:) and the name of the variable. When you need to refer to the variable **FOO** that is inside the Bar Movie Clip, for example, you use **/bar:foo**.
- Use unique names. No Timeline should contain more than one Movie Clip instance or keyframe with the same name or label.
- When entering long sequences of ActionScript statements, it's easy to forget to select the Expression modifier when entering arguments. When typing scripts from the printed page, always check to make sure your script matches that in the book. If you enter a string literal instead of an expression by mistake, your project will likely not work as expected.
- When sending commands to or reading properties of a target, you must be sure that the involved Movie Clip instance has an instance name. Without an instance name, the Movie Clip won't be a target and Flash will just ignore the command. If you find that your Flash Player movie isn't working, check your instance names and the references to the instance names to make sure that they match.

- Frame labels enable you to reference specific frames on a given Timeline. If you reference a frame label within ActionScript (using a **Call** statement, for example), make sure that the frame label you supply matches the actual frame label. For **Call** statements specifically, you must separate the target path and the frame label with a colon, like this:

    Call ("/movieclipA/:FrameXYZ")

  However, colons are not required for **Go To** statements.

- If you have text fields and don't include the font outlines, the text will actually render differently, depending on the platform. In most cases this isn't a major problem, but be sure to include font outlines wherever indicated, to maintain consistent operation of your finished projects.

- Each of the project files you work with in this book has a completed version available on the Flash 4 Magic CD. If you are having trouble getting a project to work, simply open the original full version in Flash and compare to see where you might be going wrong.

A P P E N D I X   D

"It is better to fail

in originality than

to succeed

in imitation."

—HERMAN MELVILLE

A Look at the Executable for the Flash 4 Magic CD

Appendix A looked at some of the additional things you can do with Flash standalone executables, such as creating screensavers. This appendix shows you how the interface for the Flash 4 Magic CD was created by using a Flash standalone executable and a third-party utility called Jugglor from FlashJester (www.flashjester.com), available only for the Windows platform.

A Primer on Executables

Before looking at how the CD interface was constructed, let's talk a little bit about executables in general. An *executable* is an independent program that, in general, doesn't require anything extra to run, as opposed to an .swf file from Flash, which requires the Flash plug-in or player to run or play.

Many executables are, in reality, multiple executables bundled into one. The main executable contains an interface with buttons that launch the other internal executables. For example, an executable for installing an application might contain an option for installing the main application, a separate freebie application, and an option for viewing PDF (Adobe Acrobat format) documentation. In this example, the main executable would contain the two executables for installing the application as well as the PDF file for the documentation. Therefore, you would have an executable with two executables and a PDF bundled within it.

Combining executables and related files into one executable is done for several reasons. Probably one of the most important is security. When you combine multiple files within a single executable, you are more likely to keep people from accessing files.

Another reason for combining executables into one is to provide a more seamless experience for the user. Combining multiple executables into a single executable makes it easier for them to all work together properly. If you have a button within your program that launches another executable, be sure that the other executable is located in the place the button calls. Otherwise, the button might try to launch an executable that's not there. Of course, dealing with a single file rather than multiple files is much easier, too.

Sometimes, however, including all your files and executables within one overall executable is not practical. In such a case, you can have an executable that opens some executables or other file formats—such as PDF, HTML (Hypertext Markup Language), and TXT (text) files—that are not part of the main executable or are external from it. In other words, you can have an executable with the capability to launch other executables or files that are built into it as well as other executables or files that aren't built into it.

The Flash 4 Magic CD Interface

The interface for the CD that accompanies this book uses the approach discussed in the preceding section. Having an executable contain or access other executables or external files is not unusual. What is unusual, however, is that the main executable on this book's CD was built with Macromedia Flash and FlashJester's Jugglor. This Flash executable is essentially the shell or interface used to access other content on the CD.

The process for generating this Flash interface and turning it into an executable that could access the contents of the CD was actually relatively simple. You can take a look at the basic procedure to see how easy it was.

When you want to launch or access an external file from your Flash movie, you use **FS Command ("exec")** which doesn't limit you to accessing executables. You can use **FS Command ("exec")** to launch just about any file that has a file extension, such as a .pdf file, a .txt file, a .doc file (Microsoft Word), or an .html file.

When you use **FS Command ("exec")**, you must enter the filename and its path, as shown in Figure 1. If you need to open anything other than an executable, **FS Command ("exec")** requires a special command. FlashJester's Jugglor has a built-in mini-application called JTools that generates this line for you (see Figure 2).

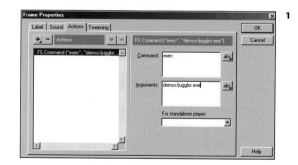

1

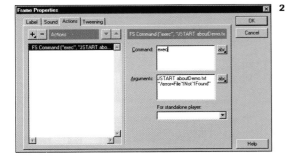

2

After the Flash file implements **FS Command ("exec")**, you export the Flash file as an executable. At this point, you can open the Flash file in FlashJester's Jugglor and use its Patch Movie option to find the external file so it will be bundled with the Flash executable (see Figure 3). The Patch Movie option ensures that the file you want to access from the Flash interface is contained within the overall executable.

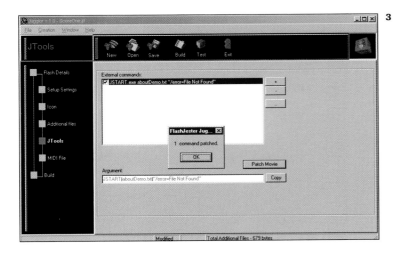

3

Here is the process: First, you set up the **FS Command ("exec")** with the proper argument (usually supplied to you by Jugglor's Jstart built-in mini-application). Next, you export the Flash file as an executable. Then you open it with FlashJester's Jugglor and use the Patch Movie option to bundle the files together in the overall executable.

FlashJester's Jugglor does provide some additional options. One option is that you can specify a particular application to open a file you want to launch with your Flash interface. For example, if you want to open a text file, you can specify that it will be opened by the Notepad utility in Windows. You do this with special arguments within the Jtools utility in Jugglor. The argument that would specify using the Notepad utility in Windows to open the text file would look like this:

WIN%notepad.exe

The **WIN%** portion of that line tells the executable to look for the Notepad utility in the Windows directory. The other options are

- **SYS%,** which tells the executable to look in the System directory
- **TMP%,** which tells the executable to look in the Temporary directory
- **LOCAL%**, which tells the executable to look in the path from which the executable file was run

In addition, FlashJester's Jugglor has several basic setup options worth noting. In particular, you can use Jugglor to disable or enable the following: sound, the right-click menu, mouse interaction, and keyboard action. You can also allow users to choose whether to disable each of these functions individually during setup. Jugglor has additional options, too, such as the Exit on ESC Key option, which means the executable will be closed if users press the Escape key on their keyboards. See Figure 4 for a list of the other options.

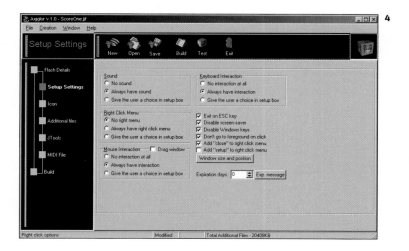 **4**

As you can see, using a Flash interface as the shell for a more powerful application is very easy. You can leverage other executables and file formats to create a shell for installing files, running screensavers, reading documentation, displaying product demos, and much more. The investment for doing this is minimal: all you need is a copy of Flash and a third-party utility such as FlashJester's Jugglor (www.flash-jester.com) or the ProjectorLauncher add-on (mories.com), which is capable of building an executable file similar to the one described in this appendix.

With Jugglor, you can specify the Window size and position (in other words, the size and position of the final executable, as in Figure 5) and set an expiration date. This handy third-party utility also enables you to replace the Flash executable icon with your own icon.

 **5**

INDEX

Symbols

& (ampersand) operator, 309

* (asterisk) operator, 309

" " (double quotes) operator, 309

= (equal sign) operator, 309

/ (forward slash) operator, 309

>= (greater than or equal to sign) operator, 309

> (greater than sign) operator, 309

<= (less than or equal to sign) operator, 309

< (less than sign) operator, 309

- (minus sign) operator, 309

<> (not equal sign) operator, 309

( ) (parentheses) operator, 309

+ (plus sign) operator, 309

24-Hour Internet Quote Clock, 156-158
    JavaScript, 159-160
    modifying, 161

A

actions
    Call, 307-308, 312
        Calculator, 89
        JukeBox, 80

Comment, 308

Drag Movie Clip, 308
    Dodge Game, 279
    Drag-and-Drop Interface, 68
    Map Explorer, 102-105
    Randomizer, 38, 46

Duplicate Movie Clip, 308
    Poll, 176

FS Command, 212, 308
    creating CD interface, 316-317
    Hangman, 266-269
    standalone Flash projectors, 295, 297-298

Get URL, 308

Go To, 308

If, 308
    Calculator, 87-88
    Password Keypad, 20

If Frame is Loaded, 308

list of, 308

Load Movie, 308
    Guestbook, 193
    JukeBox, 75
    Product Catalog, 137
    standalone Flash projectors, 295

Loop, 308
    Hangman, 268
    Memory Game, 230

    Poll, 176-177
    Wack-A-Molee, 240

On MouseEvent. *See* On MouseEvent action

Play, 308

Set Property, 308

Set Variable, 307-308
    Calculator, 87-89
    Lava Lamp, 32
    Poll, 177

Stop, 308

Stop All Sounds, 308

Tell Target. *See* Tell Target action

Toggle High Quality, 308

Trace, 308, 311

ActionScript, 305
    actions. *See* actions
    calculations, Shopping Cart, 145-147
    data types, 309
    functions. *See* functions
    guide to, 306-307
    hints and tips, 311-312
    operators, 309
    PHP scripting, Poll, 174-178
    properties. *See* properties

ActionScript Library, building, 40-42

algorithm-controlled movement, 253-257

_alpha property, 310
Alpha transparency, JukeBox, 74
and operator, 309
Answers field (Quiz), setting up, 199
audio files
    JukeBox, 75-78
    playing, Randomizer, 42-46
    Preloader, 7-8

B-C

blob animations, Lava Lamp, 28-29
Book Finder, 113
buttons
    adding
        Guestbook, 189
        Hangman , 272
        Map Explorer , 96-98
        Online Book Search , 119-120
    configuring (Poll), 170
    creating
        Product Catalog, 128-131
        Quiz, 201-208
        Online Book Search , 121
calculations in ActionScript
    Calculator, 84-89
    Shopping Cart, 145-147
Calculator, 83-90
    button layout, 85
    digital display, 86-89
Call action, 307-308, 312
    Calculator, 89
    JukeBox, 80
CD interface, creating, 316-318
Chr( ) function, 310
chrome (window frame), Drag-and-Drop Interface, 65
clicking, double-clicking (Drag-and-Drop Interface), 63-64
commands. *See also* actions
    Create Projector, 295
    Publish, 294-295

Comment action, 308
constructing Password Panel, 15-16
contents of window, Drag-and-Drop Interface, 65-66
Create Projector command, creating standalone Flash projectors, 295
_currentframe property, 310

D

data matching
    Memory Game, 227
    Quiz, 212-217
data types, 309
decision making, Memory Game, 230
digital display in real-time
    Calculator, 86-89
    Stopwatch, 52-53
Dodge Game, 276-281, 286-288
    modifying, 289
    mouse position tracking, 279
    object collision detection, 282-284
    score-keeping, 284
    text fields, 284-285
double-clicking, Drag-and-Drop Interface, 63-64
Drag Movie Clip action, 308
    Dodge Game, 279
    Drag-and-Drop Interface, 68
    Map Explorer, 102-105
    Randomizer, 38, 46
Drag-and-Drop Interface, 61-63, 68-69
    chrome (window frame), 65
    double-clicking, 63-64
    invisible buttons, 66-68
    window contents, 65-66
draggable interface elements
    Product Catalog, 147
    Shopping Cart, 145-146
_droptarget property, 146, 310
Duplicate Movie Clip action, 308
    Poll, 176

duplicating objects, Hangman, 272
dynamic data
    Guestbook, 182, 188, 193
    Hangman, 264-265

E-F

editing scroll bars, Product Catalog, 134
eq operator, 309
Eval function, 310
executables, 315-316
    creating CD interface, 317-318
exporting movies, 8-9
expressions, 309
    compared to string literals, 54
external text files (standalone Flash projectors), 295

False function, 310
Fig Leaf Software, 302
Flash Central, 302
Flash Guide, The, 303
Flash movies. *See* movies
FlashChallenge, 302
FlashFaq, 302
FlashJester, 302
FlashLite, 302
FlashZone, 302
frame labels, 312
_framesloaded property, 310
FS Command action, 308
    creating CD interface, 316-317
    Hangman, 266-269
    Quiz, 212
    standalone Flash projectors, 295, 297-298
fullscreen, playing Flash movies, 297-298
functions
    GetTimer, 55, 59, 310
    Int( ), 311
    list of, 310
    LoadView, 129
    Random, Lava Lamp, 32

G-H

ge operator, 309

Get Property( ) function, 310

Get URL action, 308

GetTimer function, 310
  Stopwatch, 55, 59

Go To action, 308

graphic symbols, Preloader, 7-8

GrooveWare (Screenweaver 2), 296-297

gt operator, 309

Guestbook, 181-193
  dynamic data, 182, 188, 193
  modifying, 193
  movies, loading, 185-186
  PHP scripting, 182-184
  text fields, 192

Hangman, 262-273
  duplicating objects, 272
  dynamic data, 264-265
  keyboard input, 266-269
  modifying, 273

_height property, 310

I-J

If action, 308
  Calculator, 87-88
  Password Keypad, 20

If Frame is Loaded action, 308

indicators, Quiz, 200

instances, replicating (Map Explorer), 106

Int( ) function, 310-311

interactive images, Map Explorer, 101-102

interfaces, creating
  for CD, 316-318
  Guestbook, 187

invisible buttons, Drag-and-Drop Interface, 66-68

JavaScript
  24-Hour Internet Quote Clock, 159-160
  compared to ActionScript, 306

Jugglor, 315

JTools, 302

JukeBox, 71-72, 81
  artwork for, 73-75
  audio files, 75-78
  random events, 78-80

K-L

keyboard input, Hangman, 266-269

keyframes, Password Panel, 18-20

Lava Lamp, 25-27, 32
  blob animations, 28-29
  power switches, 31-32
  random events, 30-31
  tweening, 29-30

le operator, 309

Length( ) function, 310

levels, 311
  Quiz, adding, 205-208

literals, string, 309
  compared to expressions, 54

Living Screen, 302

Load Movie action, 308
  Guestbook, 193
  JukeBox, 75
  Product Catalog, 137
  standalone Flash projectors, 295

loading movies
  Guestbook, 185-186
  Poll, 170

LoadView function, 129

Loop action, 308
  Hangman, 268
  Memory Game, 230
  Poll, 176-177
  Wack-A-Mole, 240

lt operator, 309

M-N

Macromania, 303

Macromedia, 303

MacSorcery, 303
  ScreenTime for Flash, 296

Map Explorer, 94-110
  modifying, 110
  scrolling and interactive images, 101-102
  zooming with a scroll bar, 102-105

Memory Game, 222-225
  data matching, 227
  decision making, 230
  modifying, 231
  random object placement, 228-229
  score-keeping, 226

minimizing windows with double-click event, Drag-and-Drop Interface, 63-64

Moock Web Design, 303

motion tweening, Lava Lamp, 29

mouse position tracking, Dodge Game, 279

movement, algorithm-controlled, 253-257

movies
  exporting, 8-9
  loading
    Guestbook, 185-186
    Poll, 170
  playing at fullscreen, 297-298
  testing, Poll, 177

_name property, 310

NavWorks, 303

ne operator, 309

Newline function, 310

not operator, 309

numbers, adding (Guestbook), 191

numerals, 309

O

object-collision detection, Dodge Game, 282–284

On MouseEvent action, 306, 308
    Dodge Game, 286
    Drag-and-Drop Interface, 69
    Guestbook, 190–191
    Lava Lamp, 32
    Map Explorer, 97
    Memory Game, 225, 228
    Online Book Search, 116
    Password Keypad, 16
    Pong, 248–249
    Product Catalog, 128
    Quiz, 202
    Randomizer, 38
    Shopping Cart, 146

Online Book Search, 114–123
    modifying, 123
    search engine with Flash, 123
    server-side scripting, 115–116

operators, list of, 309

or operator, 309

Ord( ) function, 310

P

Password Keypad, 13–23
    testing password match, 20–23

Password Panel
    constructing, 15–16
    keyframes, 18–20
    text fields, 17

photographs, adding (Map Explorer), 99–100

PHP scripting
    Guestbook, 182–184
    Poll, 168–169
        ActionScript, 174–178

Play action, 308

playback quality, Preloader, 5

playing audio files, Randomizer, 42–46

Poll, 164–178
    PHP scripting, 168–169
        ActionScripts, 174–178
    text files creating, 168–169

Pong, 246–249
    algorithm-controlled movement, 253–257
    modifying, 258
    trig with Flash, 250–252

power switches, Lava Lamp, 31–32

Preloader, 3–10
    audio files, 7–8
    graphic symbols, 7–8
    playback quality, 5
    progress bar, 5–6
    size reports, 8–9

Product Catalog, 125–140
    modifying, 140
    scroll bars, editing, 134
    scrolling text, 135–137
    zooming with a scroll bar, 132–133

progress bar, Preloader, 5–6

ProjectorLauncher, 303
    standalone Flash projectors, manipulating, 298–299

projectors. *See* standalone Flash projectors

properties
    list of, 310
    _target, Randomizer, 38

Publish command, creating standalone Flash projectors, 294–295

Q-R

Questions field, setting up (Quiz), 199

Quiz, 198–218
    data matching, 212–217
    indicators, 200
    modifying, 218

Quote Clock. *See* 24-Hour Internet Quote Clock

random events
    JukeBox, 78–80
    Lava Lamp, 30–31

random object placement, Memory Game, 228–229

random sequential events
    Randomizer, 42–46
    Wack-A-Mole, 239–241

Random( ) function, 310
    Lava Lamp, 32

Randomizer, 35–47
    ActionScript Library, building, 40–42
    playing audio files, 42–46
    sliders, 37–42

real-time digital display
    Calculator, 86–89
    Stopwatch, 52–53

referencing variables outside current movie, 311

Reset function, Stopwatch, 54

_rotation property, 310

S

score-keeping
    Dodge Game, 284
    Memory Game, 226

screensavers, creating from standalone Flash projectors, 295–297

ScreenTime for Flash, 296

Screenweaver, 296–297, 303

scripts. *See* ActionScript

scroll bars
    editing, Product Catalog, 134
    zooming with
        Map Explorer, 102–105
        Product Catalog, 132–133

scrolling and interactive images, Map Explorer, 101–102

scrolling objects, Shopping Cart, 147

scrolling text, Product Catalog, 135–137

search engine, Online Book Search, 123

server-side scripting, Online Book Search, 115–116

Set Property action, 308

Set Variable action, 307-308
    Calculator, 87-89
    Lava Lamp, 32
    Poll, 177
shape tweening, Lava Lamp, 29-30
Shockfusion, 303
Shopping Cart, 144-152
    calculations in ActionScript, 145-147
    draggable interface objects, 145-147
    modifying, 152
    scrolling objects, 147
size reports, Preloader, 8-9
sliders, Randomizer, 37-42
snapping sliders into place, Randomizer, 40-42
sound. *See* audio files
standalone executables. *See* executables
standalone Flash projectors, 293-294
    creating, 294-295
    manipulating with third-party utilities, 298-299
    screensavers, creating, 295-297
Start function, Stopwatch, 54-57
statements. *See* actions
Sterling Ledet and Associates, 303
Stop action, 308
Stop All Sounds action, 308
Stop function, Stopwatch, 54-57
Stopwatch, 49-59
    button activation, 58
    real-time digital display, 52-53
    Reset function, 54
    Start/Stop functions, 54-57
string literals, 309
    compared to expressions, 54
Substring( ) function, 310
symbol-editing mode, 37, 53, 188

T

target paths, 311
_target property, 310
    Randomizer, 38
targets, 311
Tell Target action, 308
    24-Hour Internet Quote Clock, 161
    Dodge Game, 281-284
    Guestbook, 190
    Hangman, 267
    JukeBox, 75, 77
    Lava Lamp, 31
    Map Explorer, 97
    Memory Game, 227
    Poll, 177
    Pong, 255
    Product Catalog, 146
    Quiz, 205-208
    Randomizer, 47
    Shopping Cart, 144
    Stopwatch, 58
    Wack-A-Mole, 235-238
testing
    movies, Poll, 177
    password match, 20-23
text fields
    Dodge Game, 284-285
    Guestbook, 192
    Password Panel, 17
    updating, Calculator, 86-89
text files, creating (Poll), 168-169
time-tracking
    Stopwatch, 49-59
    Wack-A-Mole, 235-238
Timelines, 311
Toggle High Quality action, 308
_totalframes property, 310
Trace action, 308, 311

transparency. *See* Alpha transparency
trig with Flash, Pong, 250-252
True function, 310
tweening, Lava Lamp, 29-30

U-V

updating text fields, Calculator, 86-89
_url property, 310

variables. *See also* Set Variable action
    referencing outside current movie, 311
Virtual FX, 303
_visible property, 310

W-Z

Wack-A-Mole, 233-234, 242
    modifying, 243
    random sequential events, 239-241
    time-tracking, 235-238
Web sites, 302-303
_width property, 310
windows, Drag-and-Drop Interface, 61-69
    chrome (window frame), 65
    double-clicking, 63-64
    invisible buttons, 66-68
    window contents, 65-66

_x property, 310
_xscale property, 310

_y property, 310
_yscale property, 310

zooming with a scroll bar
    Map Explorer, 102-105
    Product Catalog, 132-133

THE FLASH 4 MAGIC CD

The CD that accompanies this book contains valuable resources for anyone using Flash 4, not the least of which are

- **Project files,** the stripped down Flash files for use with the step-by-step projects
- **Finished files,** including the fully-functional ActionScript that you can inspect at your leisure
- **Flash-related third-party demos**, including Screenweaver from GrooveWare and Jugglor from FlashJester
- **FlashPack 1**, a $25 value from NavWorks that includes customizable Flash art, stock audio, and more

ACCESSING THE PROJECT FILES FROM THE CD

Each project in this book uses a pre-built Flash file that contains the artwork and/or audio you need to build the final utility or game. The Flash files have a .fla extension. Several of the projects also come with additional files, such as HTML, PHP, or text files.

All the files for a project are conveniently located in its respective Project Files directory. To access the project file for the Preloader project, for example, locate the following directory on the book's CD:

    Book Examples\Preloader\Project Files

To locate the project file for the Stopwatch project, locate the following directory:

    Book Examples\Stopwatch\Project Files

We recommend that you copy the project files to your hard drive, but that is not absolutely necessary if you do not intend to save the project files.

Note that if you are viewing files on the Macintosh platform, you may have to set the List Files Of Type option in the File>Open dialog box to All Files. Then you can see and select the files from within Macromedia Flash.

The finished files, including the completed ActionScript, are in the Finished Files directory for each project. The finished file for the Preloader project, for example, is located in

    Book Examples\Preloader\Finished Files

Colophon: Flash 4 Magic was layed out and produced with the help of Microsoft Word, Adobe Acrobat, Adobe Photoshop, Collage Complete, and QuarkXPress on a variety of systems, including a Macintosh G3. With the exception of the pages that were printed out for proofreading, all files—both text and images—were transferred via email or ftp and edited on-screen.

All the body text was set in the Bergamo family. All headings, figure captions, and cover text were set in the Imago family. The Symbol and Sean's Symbols typefaces were used throughout for special symbols and bullets.

Flash 4 Magic was printed on 60# Sterling Matte at R. R. Donnelley & Sons in Salem, Viriginia. Prepress consisted of PostScript computer-to-plate technology (filmless process). The cover was printed on 12-pt. Carolina, coated on one side.